Presbyterians in South Carolina, 1925-1985

Presbyterians in South Carolina, 1925–1985

Mid-Century Change in Historic Denominations

Nancy Snell Griffith
and
Charles E. Raynal

WIPF & STOCK · Eugene, Oregon

PRESBYTERIANS IN SOUTH CAROLINA, 1925-1985
Mid-Century Change in Historic Denominations

Copyright © 2016 Nancy Snell Griffith and Charles E. Raynal. All rights reserved. Except for brief quotations in critical publications or reviews, no part of this book may be reproduced in any manner without prior written permission from the publisher. Write: Permissions, Wipf and Stock Publishers, 199 W. 8th Ave., Suite 3, Eugene, OR 97401.

Wipf & Stock
An Imprint of Wipf and Stock Publishers
199 W. 8th Ave., Suite 3
Eugene, OR 97401

www.wipfandstock.com

PAPERBACK ISBN: 978-1-4982-3771-0
HARDCOVER ISBN: 978-1-4982-3773-4
EBOOK ISBN: 978-1-4982-3772-7

Manufactured in the U.S.A.

To the members of Presbyterian Churches in South Carolina.

Contents

List of Photographs | viii
List of Tables | xi
Acknowledgments | xiii
Abbreviations | xiv
Introduction | xv

1 Go Into All the World and Preach the Gospel: South Carolina and Foreign Missions | 1
2 Reaching Out to the Marginalized: Presbyterian Mission in the United States | 30
3 Church and Society: Worldly Amusements and Weightier Matters | 65
4 A Work of Real Spiritual Power: Women and the Presbyterian Church | 103
5 African American Ministries: Initiatives and Partnerships | 135
6 South Carolina Presbyterians and Higher Education | 167
7 Institutions of Care and Nurture | 209

Conclusion | 227
Bibliography | 237

Photographs

01 Arthur M. Martin (Courtesy of Presbyterian College) | xvi

02 Joseph B. Martin III (Courtesy of Neal Martin) | xvi

03 Graduates of the Nanking Theological Seminary, Japan (Courtesy of the Presbyterian Heritage Center, Montreat, North Carolina) | 4

04 T. Watson Street (Courtesy of Presbyterian College) | 10

05 C. Darby Fulton (Courtesy of Presbyterian College) | 13

06 Lewis Lancaster, Eliza Neville Lancaster, and Herbert A. Codington, MD (Courtesy of Herbert Codington) | 22

07 Herbert and Page Codington (Courtesy of Davidson College) | 25

08 Dr. Herbert A. Codington, MD, with Staff at Kwangju Hospital (Courtesy of Herbert Codington) | 26

09 Edward O. Guerrant (Courtesy of the Presbyterian Heritage Center, Montreat, North Carolina) | 32

10 Classroom at Boone Fork Institute (Courtesy of the Presbyterian Heritage Center, Montreat, North Carolina) | 34

11 Zoulean Anderson (Courtesy of the Presbyterian Heritage Center, Montreat, North Carolina) | 36

12 Goodwill Day School (Courtesy of Franklin D. Colclough) | 47

13 Lydia Mill Presbyterian Church, Laurens County, South Carolina | 56

14 J. Ferdinand Jacobs (Courtesy of Presbyterian College) | 57

15 Grace Covenant Church, Laurens, South Carolina | 62

16 Walter Lingle as a Student at Davidson College (Courtesy of Davidson College) | 67

PHOTOGRAPHS ix

17 J. Phillips Noble (Courtesy of J. Phillips Noble) | 81

18 Neil E. Truesdell (Courtesy of Presbyterian College) | 88

19 Governor John G. Richards (Courtesy of
    the University of South Carolina) | 90

20 John McSween (Courtesy of Presbyterian College) | 94

21 Mrs. Lillie B. Nelson, Goodwill Presbyterian Church
    (Courtesy of Franklin D. Colclough) | 104

22 Women's Training Conference in Montreat, 1955 (Courtesy of
    the Presbyterian Heritage Center, Montreat, North Carolina) | 111

23 Interdenominational Women's Conference, 1957
    (Courtesy of the University of South Carolina) | 112

24 Mission Haven, Columbia Theological Seminary
    (Courtesy of Columbia Theological Seminary) | 115

25 Attendees, Synodical Training School 1954
    (Courtesy of Presbyterian College) | 117

26 Mrs. W. Rex (Ann) Josey (Courtesy of Presbyterian College) | 118

27 Carol and Charles C. Heyward, St. James Presbyterian Church,
    Charleston, South Carolina (Courtesy of Charles C. Heyward) | 138

28 Mckinley Washington Jr. and his wife Beulah
    (Courtesy of McKinley Washington Jr.) | 139

29 Alex Batchelor (Courtesy of Presbyterian College) | 147

30 Charles Coles, first pastor of Nicholtown Presbyterian Church
    (Courtesy of Columbia Theological Seminary) | 150

31 Thomas J. James (Courtesy of Franklin D. Colclough) | 153

32 Joseph T. Stukes (Courtesy of Courtney R. Stukes) | 160

33 Robert E. Bligen (Courtesy of Franklin D. Colclough) | 161

34 Franklin D. Colclough, New Harmony Presbytery
    (Courtesy of Franklin D. Colclough) | 162

35 Columbia Theological Seminary, Columbia, South Carolina
    (Courtesy of Columbia Theological Seminary) | 168

36 J. McDowell Richards (Courtesy of
    Columbia Theological Seminary) | 170

37 Campbell Hall, Columbia Theological Seminary
    (Courtesy of Columbia Theological Seminary | 171

38 J. Davison Phillips (Courtesy of
    Columbia Theological Seminary) | 173

39 Neville Hall, Presbyterian College (Courtesy of
    Presbyterian College) | 175

40 Program of Deliverance Brochure (Courtesy of
    Presbyterian College) | 178

41 William Plumer Jacobs II (Courtesy of Presbyterian College) | 179

42 Religious Emphasis Week (Courtesy of Presbyterian College) | 182

43 Marc C. Weersing (Courtesy of Presbyterian College) | 186

44 Prebyterian College Goes Coed 1965 (Courtesy of
    Presbyterian College) | 189

45 Kenneth B. Orr (Courtesy of Presbyterian College) | 193

46 Chicora College (Courtesy of the University of
    South Carolina) | 194

47 William Plumer Jacobs (Courtesy of Presbyterian College) | 209

48 L. Ross Lynn (Courtesy of Presbyterian College) | 211

49 Home of Peace and Library, Thornwell Orphanage
    (Courtesy of Presbyterian College) | 212

50 Malcolm A. Macdonald on the right (Courtesy of
    Presbyterian College) | 214

51 W. McLeod Frampton (Courtesy of Presbyterian College) | 221

52 Charles Robert Tapp (Courtesy of Presbyterian Communities
    of South Carolina) | 223

53 Rendering of Presbyterian Home in Clinton (Courtesy of
    Presbyterian Home, Clinton, South Carolina) | 224

Tables

01 Presbyterian Parochial Schools, 1915 | 45

02 South Carolina Membership in Synod of
    the Atlantic Congregations | 137

03 PCUSA Schools Remaining in South Carolina in 1933 | 143

04 South Carolina Membership in Snedecor Memorial
    Synod Congregations | 145

05 South Carolina PCUS Statistics | 231

Acknowledgments

THERE ARE MANY INSTITUTIONS and people who contributed to this volume. Presbyterian College and Columbia Theological Seminary supported this book through their libraries and by contributing to its editing. We wish to thank all of the librarians, archivists, and individuals who have helped us along the way. This includes Sarah M. Leckie at Presbyterian College, Jan Blodgett at Davidson College, Chris Paton and Emily Corbin at Columbia Theological Seminary, Paula Skreslet at Union Presbyterian Seminary, and Ron Vinson at the Presbyterian Heritage Center in Montreat, North Carolina. Neal A. Martin and his family generously shared letters, papers, and photographs. Several other individuals also contributed photographs, including Herbert Codington; Franklin D. Colclough Sr.; James Crawford Jr.; Charles Heyward; Eva Johnson; J. Philips Noble; and Courtney R. Stukes. The Presbyterian Communities of South Carolina, supplied a photograph of Reverend Charles R. Tapp. Those providing interviews or answering questions included Franklin D. Colclough Sr., John B. Evans, Gordon Raynal, McKinley Washington Jr., Sidney West, and George Wilkes. John Griffith has been reading chapters for years. And last, but certainly not least, we want to thank our indefatigable editor, Rosemary Raynal, who persisted through many versions of this manuscript. Omissions and errors remaining are ours.

Abbreviations

ARP — Associate Reformed Presbyterian Church, 1822 to the present

PCA — Presbyterian Church in America, 1973 to the present

PCUS — Presbyterian Church in the United States, 1865-1983. "Southern Presbyterians."

PCUSA — Presbyterian Church in the United States of America, 1706-1958

UPCUSA — United Presbyterian Church in the United States of America, 1958 to1983

PC(USA) — Presbyterian Church (USA), 1983 to the present

Introduction

Background

This is the fourth volume of the *History of the Presbyterian Church in South Carolina*. The Synod of South Carolina asked George Howe to write the first volume in 1849. Howe, a graduate of Middlebury College and Andover Theological Seminary, was a professor at Columbia Theological Seminary in South Carolina from 1831 to 1883.

Volume I (1870) included accounts of the European origins of the colonial Presbyterian, Reformed, and Congregational churches in the coastal area from North Carolina to the northern part of Florida. In it Howe discussed the history of these and subsequent churches, with their early presbyteries and synods, through the end of the eighteenth century. In volume II, published in 1883, Howe extended the history to 1850, with the addition of various lists and records of churches and ministers through 1882.

The third volume, *The Presbyterian Church in South Carolina Since 1850*, was published in 1926. Work on this volume was begun by William Smith Bean, professor at Presbyterian College. He continued the narrative from 1850 to 1900. After his death in 1920, the Synod appointed a historical commission to finish his work. The completed volume was edited by Frank Dudley Jones and William Hayne Mills. At the time, Jones was a professor of philosophy and psychology at Presbyterian College, and Mills was a professor of rural sociology at Clemson College.

In addition to editing Bean's work, Jones and Mills completed the narrative from 1900 to 1925. The resulting history has separate chapters on the synod's institutions, major developments, and brief accounts of 274 congregations, nearly all of the active churches in the Synod of South Carolina in 1925.

In 1972 the Synod of South Carolina commissioned Arthur Morrison Martin to write the history of the Synod from 1925 to its anticipated merger in 1973 with the Synod of Georgia to become the Synod of the Southeast.

Arthur Morrison Martin (Courtesy of Presbyterian College)

That plan was eventually revised to include the 1983 reunion of the United Presbyterian Church in the USA (UPCUSA) and the Presbyterian Church in the United States (PCUS). Martin served as the Executive Secretary of the Synod of South Carolina from 1953 to 1973. When he died in 1982, the Synod of South Carolina asked his son Joseph B. Martin III to edit his father's notes and complete the history. When Joseph Martin fell ill, their draft of a portion of the history was turned over to Presbyterian College.

Joseph B. Martin III

As the century came to a close, the college asked Nancy Snell Griffith, college archivist, to complete the history. She asked Charles E. Raynal III, who was then the Director of Advanced Studies and Associate Professor of Theology at Columbia Theological Seminary, to join her in completing Martin's work. Raynal, who had been a pastor in several Presbyterian churches, is also the grandson of Frank Dudley Jones.

Volume Four: Presbyterians in South Carolina, 1925-1985: Mid-Century Change in Southern Denominations

There were two mainline branches of Presbyterianism in South Carolina during the middle of the twentieth century. One, sometimes referred to as the "southern" Presbyterian Church, was formed when southern Presbyterians left the PCUSA and established their own denomination in 1861. First called The Presbyterian Church in the Confederate States of America, it later became The Presbyterian Church in the United States (PCUS). In 1920 the PCUS had about 38,000 members, including about 350 black members, in South Carolina.

The other mainline denomination was the Presbyterian Church in the United States of America (PCUSA) and after 1958 it became the United Presbyterian Church in the United States of America (UPCUSA). Beginning in 1865, the PCUSA along with other northern denominations sent missionaries to the South to establish churches and parochial schools for the freed people. As a result of this evangelistic and educational ministry, by 1925 over 6,500 African Americans were members of northern Presbyterian (PCUSA) congregations in South Carolina.

The history of South Carolina Presbyterians between 1925 and 1985 covers a period of great development achieved through great difficulties. In the early years, the country was still dealing with the aftermath of World War I and the success of the women's suffrage movement. There was much discussion of the church's moral stance, particularly surrounding the passage and then the repeal of Prohibition. The bright hopes in the churches, with which the history written by Jones and Mills ended, were soon affected by the Great Depression which came early to South Carolina because of the boll weevil damage to the cotton crop, an economic disaster for the state. When World War II broke out, the necessities of wartime set the scene for a great period of church expansion between 1945 and 1960, accompanying the rapid growth of the state's economy and population. Later moral and cultural challenges resulted from the Civil Rights Movement, the war in Vietnam, and the mass protests that followed. The church increasingly began to comment on these issues and many others.

These cultural changes heightened the standing controversies between the social gospel and the individual gospel, between the liberals and the conservatives. Other issues such as church union, the role of women in the church, the church in the world, and the relative authority of governing bodies in the church structure took on an accumulated urgency far greater than the particular issues. The two wings of the church, tending under pressure toward their extremes, drew farther apart. As the Synod of South Carolina came to an end as a separate body on June 30, 1973—on the very next day, in fact—twelve of its congregations in Bethel Presbytery voted to withdraw from the Presbytery and from the Presbyterian Church in the United States, with others to follow in the years to come. The schism was the outgrowth of long-standing disagreements, some of which have characterized Presbyterianism in South Carolina for three hundred years.

In telling the story of South Carolina Presbyterians in the mid-twentieth century, this book relates religious life and practices to the broader social setting. The two Presbyterian denominations conformed to society but also provided leaders and embodied ideas that contributed to making their world different than it would have been without their influence. So in telling this story, we are looking for insights into how Presbyterians in South Carolina contributed to mid-twentieth century culture, connecting their religious life and practices to a larger social setting.

The official records of the Synod of South Carolina (PCUS) and the Synod of the Atlantic (PCUSA; UPCUSA, after 1958) naturally show preoccupation with the business of the churches and their pastoral work in worship, education, and mission. South Carolina Presbyterians in their regional governing bodies (synods, corresponding to one or more state lines, and presbyteries, covering one or more counties) deliberated separately, following the pattern of racial segregation in society, on the programs of their respective denominations until they came together in 1983. This story comes not only from their records but also from church newspapers and magazines, local histories, letters, memoirs, and interviews. It aims to contribute a final chapter to the histories of the Synod of South Carolina left by former generations and to add new material on the under-reported work of African American ministries in the state.

Our point of view recognizes with appreciation the men and women who worshiped together, engaged in mission locally and globally, built institutions of education and care, organized their life together, and offered their service to others. They also debated with each other about interpreting the Bible and the way Christian people should respond to culture and society, politics, and morals. Like other Christians, they both reacted to and shaped events within their congregations and outside of their churches. Their responses and their leadership show us unique aspects of the Presbyterian tradition while revealing much that they shared with a common Protestant religious culture in the South.

1

Go Into All the World and Preach the Gospel

South Carolina and Foreign Missions

BETWEEN 1925 AND 1985, the shape of foreign missions in the PCUS was ever changing. Although missionaries were sent out to evangelize, education and medical care were frequently tied to this goal. Increasingly, however, the desire to care for the sick and the poor and sometimes to effect social or political change became more prominent. This, along with increasing attempts to work with other denominations, caused tensions throughout the decades. Missionary work was also disrupted by several wars during this period and by the desire of the newly planted national churches to be self-governing. Descriptions of work on the denominational and synodical level, the responses of C. Darby Fulton, longtime head of the Board of World Missions, and the activities of South Carolina missionaries in the field serve to illuminate the developing tensions and the eventual changes in the missionary endeavor.

The Denominational Perspective

The Presbyterian Church has always viewed missions as a large part of its program, and work in foreign countries has often consumed much of the General Assembly's benevolence budget. Reverend Samuel Miller, speaking in 1835 before the Annual Meeting of the American Board of Commissioners for Foreign Missions, referred to the cause of missions "as the most precious cause in the world,"[1] and the purpose of this work was stated quite clearly in the report of the Southern Board of Foreign Missions in 1840: "In this world, there are *the elect* of God, who are the peculiar inheritance

---

1. Miller, "The Earth Filled with the Glory of the Lord," 304.

of Christ—and it is his command that his Gospel should be everywhere preached, as the grand instrumentality of gathering into his fold such as shall be saved, and of making manifest to principalities and powers—to his rational creatures in all parts of his wide dominion, his glorious grace."[2]

At its first General Assembly meeting in 1861, the newly organized Presbyterian Church in the United States (PCUS) heard a report from John Leighton Wilson concerning the importance of foreign missions and appointed an Executive Committee of Foreign Missions. Despite their recognition of "the missionary task as the unrivaled concern of the Christian Church," the turmoil caused by the Civil War forced the denomination to suspend all mission work except that to Native Americans.[3]

When hostilities ended however, the church quickly turned its focus to foreign missions. Only three years after the war ended, the fledgling PCUS sent Reverend Elias B. Inslee and his wife to China. During the next two decades, missionaries were sent to Brazil (1869), Mexico (1874), and Japan (1885). During the 1890s the denomination established missions in the Congo and Korea. By 1898 the "Church of Christ in Japan" had been established and was supervising boarding schools for both boys and girls and a women's Bible school.

In 1914, in order to provide trained lay workers for the various mission fields, the PCUS established a Training School for Lay Workers in Richmond, Virginia. By the fall of 1919 there were sixty-two students enrolled. That year sixteen graduates went into the foreign mission field. At this time, Presbyterian missions were run by a central "mission" in each country. Each mission included all of the missionaries who were serving in that particular country, and decisions regarding personnel, budget, policies, and relationships with the emerging local and national churches were made at a yearly weeklong meeting. The local mission presence was the mission "station," which encompassed all missionaries in a city or region. This group usually met once a month and served as the executive staff and board for any schools or hospitals in the station. Occasionally, the PCUS had more than one mission in a country. This was true in China, where there were two separate missions, and in Brazil, where there were three. The evangelistic work of the missionaries inevitably resulted in the organization of autonomous congregations which were eventually intended to band together into national churches.

---

2. "Report of the Executive Committee of the Southern Board of Foreign Missions," *Charlotte Observer*, December 19, 1840.

3. Fulton, "Centennial Address," 89.

The PCUS allotted a substantial amount of its resources for foreign missions. In 1922 half of the amount ($1.5 million) of the money given to all of the General Assembly's causes was allotted for foreign missions. This number, however, fails to show the true scope of mission giving. Along with the actual contributions through the General Assembly, individual churches and church groups were free to sponsor individual missionaries and to contribute to mission hospitals and schools on their own.

During these early years, women provided a significant amount of the funding for foreign missions. By 1875 Sunday school and women's missionary societies were providing one third of the entire amount given by the church to foreign missions.[4] In 1925 the amount given by these groups was $22,558. In 1925 the First Presbyterian Church in York was supporting two missionary couples, and their women's auxiliary had "clothed little Wilbur Hunnicut, of Brazil, from overcoat to gloves. They were also sending money and clothing to lepers in Korea and supporting a "Bible woman" in China.[5] These individual efforts by women's and young people's societies meant that the General Assembly's records on giving for missions never really reflected the true scope of the effort.

Between 1894 and 1924, denominational giving to foreign missions increased tenfold, from $143,000 to $1,390,000. The number of PCUS missionaries grew from 135 to 517; native workers increased from 140 to 3,600; organized churches, which had been 37, were now 275; and membership in those churches mushroomed from 2,700 to 50,000.[6] The church had missions including orphanages, schools, and hospitals, in China, Brazil, Mexico, Japan, Africa, and Korea. During this early period, the pattern was for Presbyterian missionaries to spend decades in the field, punctuated by occasional furloughs in the U.S. and increasingly interrupted by national and international crises. In many cases generations of the same family undertook the work.

There was also ecumenical work going on in several countries. The Nanking Seminary in China was run by the northern and southern Presbyterians, the northern and southern Methodists, and the northern Baptist and Christian missions.

---

4. Thompson, *Presbyterians in the South*, Vol. 3, 385.
5. Gist, *Presbyterian Women of South Carolina*, 105.
6. Thompson, *Presbyterians in the South*, Vol. 3, 136.

Early Graduates of the Nanking Seminary
(Courtesy of the Presbyterian Heritage Society, Montreat, N.C.)

The national Presbyterian church in Japan (the Nihon Kuristo Kyokai) was Presbyterian in governance, but resulted from the efforts not only of northern and southern Presbyterians, but of the Dutch Reformed and Evangelical and Reformed churches.[7]

During the latter part of the 1920s, the Depression began to affect mission funding and thus the placement of missionaries. Between 1929 and 1933, the number of Presbyterian missionaries working abroad dropped from 516 to 395. Starting around this time, some churchmen began to reconsider the focus of mission work and its tendency toward cultural bias. In 1930 the results of the Layman's Foreign Missions Inquiry were released. The Institute for Social and Religious Research, which grew out of the inquiry, began doing interviews at mission stations in India, Burma, China, and Japan. The findings were issued in a seven volume report called the Hocking Report and summarized in a one volume publication called *Rethinking Missions*.

According to the study, the rising tide of nationalism in the East reflected a rejection of western culture and institutions. Its main conclusion was that it was time for a change in the focus of foreign missions. Although the PCUS was not a participant in this process, its Standing Committee on Foreign Missions was quick to respond to these observations: "With utmost emphasis we repudiate that monumental folly miscalled 'Rethinking Missions.' Its true title should rather be: 'Rejecting Missions and Crucifying

---

7. Smith, *From Colonialism to World Community*, 17.

Our Lord Afresh.'" Nonetheless, the course of missions over the next several decades would slowly begin to conform to ideas in the Hocking Report, even in the more conservative PCUS.[8]

The 1934 Synod report on missions showed great promise: "More people professed faith in Christ than in any year since our work began some three-quarters of a century ago. Our devoted missionaries and their helpers and congregations followed up with great fervor the request of the General Assembly for special emphasis upon evangelism, and the harvest that they reaped is almost beyond conception."[9]

But conditions were changing around the world. According to the 1935 Synod report, "Our missionaries last year ministered to a world ill at ease. The conditions that we are somewhat familiar with now in our own land of unrest and shifting and change were accentuated in the lands of our missions. Industrial upheaval, economic depression, international realignment of friendship, the passing of ancient customs, the overthrow of governments and of religions, have been the common lot of most of the peoples."[10]

Still, there was progress. The mission to the Congo, begun in 1910, was anticipating the foundation of a new national church. In China, the hostility generated by the nationalist outbreak had dissipated, and the preceding year had been "the most fruitful in the seventy years of our work in the land."[11] According to Thompson, the church in Korea was growing, and the country itself was beginning to move into the modern age. The Presbyterian Church in Japan, a truly indigenous church which had its own leadership, was "the strongest Protestant group in the land, both in numbers and influence."[12] The only area of concern was in Mexico, where revolutionary conditions made it very difficult to conduct missionary efforts in some parts of the country. The nationalistic attitude so evident in Mexico would soon spread to all of the mission fields, as residents of these countries expressed "a determination to have absolute equality in all matters, whether great or small with all other nations, or individuals of other nations."[13]

Tension was increasing in the Far East. In 1937 the PCUS closed its 165 mission schools in Korea because the Japanese, who had occupied the country, were forcing the students to attend ceremonies at Shinto shrines. At the same time, the Japanese were bombing China. The early parts of this

8. Fitzmier and Balmer, "A Poultice for the Bite of the Cobra," 105–113.
9. Synod Minutes, 1934, 19.
10. Ibid., 1935, 36.
11. Annual Report, 1936, 10.
12. Thompson, *Presbyterians in the South*, Vol. 3, 427.
13. Ibid., 427.

war were fought in the part of the country where most of the PCUS missions were located, and the church lost property and was forced to evacuate a number of missionaries. By 1940 Japan had aligned itself with the Axis nations, and a year later, the Japanese and Americans were at war. The situation in Korea, where Christian pastors were being jailed and even tortured, was equally dire. By 1941, 124 missionaries had returned to the US, leaving only 69 in the field. Most of these were in China. Following the attack on Pearl Harbor, all but six of these returned; the remaining half dozen were not liberated until the war was almost over.

Within 18 months of the war's end in 1945, however, fifty-eight PCUS missionaries had returned to the Far East, most of them to China. Throughout the region, they found "property losses running into the millions—schools, hospitals, and churches standing with gaping windows and shattered walls; missionary homes had been divested of all furniture and disfigured by successive occupations."[14] To the surprise of many, even though the buildings were gone, the national churches had survived. There was a shortage of new missionaries. The Far Eastern Reoccupation Fund, expected to raise $1 million to support missionaries, was $500,000 short.

To remedy these needs, the PCUS launched a Program of Progress to fund mission work. Within two years, they had raised $2 million in addition to the regular benevolence budget. At the same time, giving to missions through regular benevolences increased, enabling the church to send out forty-eight new missionaries in 1949 and 1950.

The massive destruction of the war also caused a change in the focus of many missionaries. The homelessness, hunger, sickness, and death caused by the war affected them deeply. Missionaries began to see their role less as evangelism and more as action. There was also less emphasis on imposing American culture and more on establishing self-sufficient national churches. With the organization of the United Nations in 1945 and the World Council of Churches (WCC) in 1948, the idea of western superiority was further challenged, and countries insisted on being accepted as equals.[15] The recommendations of the Hocking report were finally being implemented.

With the Communist takeover of mainland China, the church's eighty-five years of missionary work there came to an end. By 1952 all of the missionaries had left the mainland. They left behind a dozen hospitals, a college, scores of schools, several theological seminaries, and numerous orphanages. The churches they founded were reaching 20,000 Chinese

---

14. Ibid., 429.
15. Smith, *From Colonialism to World Community,* 146

Christians.[16] Many of the missionaries displaced from the mainland settled on Taiwan and began new efforts among the aborigines on the eastern coast of the island, with university students, and at Changwa Christian Hospital.

The situation in Japan was dire. The seminary, schools, and many churches had been destroyed. There were also competing groups among Japan's Presbyterians. Many of the first PCUS missionaries to return to Japan were more conservative and as a result worked mostly with the Reformed Church of Japan. They were resistant to ecumenical work and refused to join the Japan Council of Churches. In addition, the PCUS was the only Protestant denomination in Japan to oppose the establishment of the Japan International Christian University (JICU). Instead, the PCUS opened its own men's college in 1950, a year before the JICU opened.

The same was happening in other countries. While there were the beginnings of some interdenominational efforts in Brazil and Ecuador, the PCUS remained largely resistant to this movement, with the old idea of the "sending" church and the "receiving" mission remaining the norm. The PCUS did participate in the World Council of Churches, however. In 1950 the General Assembly recommended "that we, as individual members of a participating church, labor and pray for the continuing effectiveness of the ecumenical movement"[17] and pledged $6,634 toward the cause. At the same time, giving to missions had dropped drastically. In 1951 PCUS contributions toward world missions had dropped from twelve cents of every dollar in 1920 to three cents in 1950.[18]

There was increasing discussion about whether converting people and planting churches should be the primary focus for mission efforts or whether the presence of Christians as doctors and educators was equally valuable. Some members of the church were beginning to see the importance of Christ's social teachings in regard to poverty, oppression, racism, and nationalism. The old patriarchal tradition of white supremacy was also disintegrating. Although these concerns were presented in a series of reports to the church's Congress on World Missions in 1951, the ultimate decision was that the missionary's purpose remained "to save men from a peril—from hell."[19]

Writing thirty years later, G. Thompson Brown had an interesting perspective on some of these issues which he framed in terms of whether the church desired to make disciples or converts:

16. Thompson, *Presbyterians in the South*, Vol 3, 430.
17. General Assembly, 1950, 89.
18. Sunquist and Becker, *A History of Presbyterian Missions*, 9.
19. Thompson, *Presbyterians in the South*, Vol. 3, 138–139.

> A convert is always an imitation made over in the image of the one who did the converting. A disciple is always an original—a learner of One in whose service is found perfect freedom . . . Today, at a time of rampant nationalism throughout the world, we need to listen to the call for "authenticity" from the churches in Africa, the insistence on the "Three Self Principles" (self-government, self-support, self-propagation) from the church in China, the cry for "self-reliance" from the churches of Latin America. At a time when Christianity is on the wane in parts of the West, we do not need replicas of our churches or mimics of our culture. We do need African, Asian, and Latin "originals" who will bring their own unique gifts into the kingdom of God.[20]

The Korean War erupted in the midst of this growing turmoil, forcing most missionaries to withdraw from the country, at least temporarily. When hostilities ended, the large number of Christians who had been living in the northern part of the country fled to the South, meaning that there were an estimated one million Christians in South Korea. Presbyterians predominated, resulting in the organization of the Korean Presbyterian Church through the combined efforts of the PCUS, PCUSA, and Presbyterians from Canada.

The rise of nationalism in Africa was beginning to cause problems for the church. There was the usual tension between the mission and the emerging national church. The resulting sense of paternalism resulted in many Africans feeling that they were not being treated as persons on an equal footing with the missionaries. The racial attitudes of PCUS missionaries, coming as they did from the South, were beginning to cause problems. Many of these same problems were beginning to crop up in other mission fields as well.

An ad interim report presented to the General Assembly in 1954 outlined these and other problems including the spread of Communism and "the inadequate identification of missionaries with the life and needs of the people served." The report stressed the need for missionaries to learn "how to fit themselves into the life and outreach of the indigenous church not as bosses and directors, but as counselors and servants."[21] This report was referred to the Board of World Missions, which in 1955 responded that it was aware of some of these issues but had no plans to change its policy in the immediate future.[22] The General Assembly did, however, change its policy

---

20. Brown, *Presbyterians in World Mission*, 8–9.
21. General Assembly, 1954.
22. Thompson, *Presbyterians in the South*, Vol. 3, 436.

concerning the JICU, and PCUS missionaries in Japan began to participate with both the JICU and the National Christian Council in Japan.

At the same time, Presbyterians in Brazil were making wide-reaching changes. In 1954, at a conference held in Campinas, they established the International Presbyterian Council. This body included twelve representatives from the national church and six each from the PCUS and the PCUSA. It would hereafter make all the decisions about Presbyterian work in Brazil, with the goal of gradually transferring all work in the country to the national church.[23]

Between 1955 and 1957, the PCUS conducted the "Forward with Christ" campaign aimed at raising funds to put 168 additional missionaries in the field. By 1957, $7.25 million had been raised.[24] Annual giving was also up. In 1958 the denomination set a new record in mission giving, $3,576,175.[25] When considered as a percentage of the church's entire benevolence budget, this amount seems impressive, but when inflation is taken into account, it was really a sharp decline from pre-war levels. There were almost five hundred missionaries in the field, the largest number of them in the Congo (165) and Brazil (130).[26]

Problems were emerging in Mexico and the Congo. In 1960, at a meeting of the General Assembly of the Presbyterian Church of Mexico, complaints arose from both ministers and elders about "what seemed to them a refusal by the aiding churches to recognize the Presbyterian Church in Mexico as a mature Christian body, a true church, in need of aid, but fully capable."[27] That same year, with little advance preparation, the Belgian government granted the Congo its independence. The result was tribal warfare, and all foreign missionaries were evacuated. Later in the year, some missionaries returned and met with leaders of the national church, who asked them to stay. Most did, remaining in the midst of continuing warfare.

C. Darby Fulton resigned as head of the Board of World Missions in 1961 and was replaced by T. Watson Street, a former professor at Austin Theological Seminary and a member of the Board.

---

23. Arnold, "From Sending Church to Partner Church," 183.
24. Dawson, "Counting the Cost," 46.
25. "World Missions Gifts Reach New High," *Southern Presbyterian*, 1.
26. Brown and Black, "Structures for a Changing Church," 62.
27. Thompson, *Presbyterians in the South*, Vol 3, 439.

Dr. T. Watson Street (Courtesy of Presbyterian College)

In 1962 Street convened a meeting in Montreat, North Carolina, attended by delegates from foreign missions and national churches, representatives of interdenominational missionary organizations, and seminary and college students. They were searching for ways to integrate mission work into the church. Their report called for "mutuality in international mission, the need to evangelize through actions as well as words, and the courage to experiment in response to changing times and social situations."[28] Delegates unanimously adopted the following statement: "That the structure of relationships of missionaries to a national church should be worked out by the national church in consultation with the Presbyterian Church in the United States."[29] These conclusions set the direction for mission activities during the 1960s.

In 1963 the Board ordered a study of present and proposed policies on personnel, finances, and church-mission relations. They decried the spread of materialism in American culture and called it "harmful to the church's witness."[30] Citing the many challenges facing missions, Dr. Street suggested that the church use more short-term workers including professors, doctors, pastors, students, and experts from other church boards. He affirmed that

28. Gill, "Historical Context for Mission," 18.
29. Brown and Black, 64.
30. "Church Faces World Mission," 1.

the church's concern was both evangelism and nurture—that both were legitimate forms of mission.

By 1964 there was increasing concern that the racial situation in the US would hurt the church's efforts in the mission field. Over two hundred current missionaries signed a petition decrying "various forms of racial segregation" in the church, saying that "our witness is affected adversely . . . by the existence of segregation in America which represents to the world, rightly or wrongly, a 'Christian' country . . . We feel it is a contradiction of the Gospel to allow it to continue in the church. The love of Christ is constraining us to do God's will in this regard within His Body, and to witness to the world that He calls all men to Christian fellowship as brothers in Christ."[31]

The denomination's membership in the World Council of Churches was beginning to pose a problem for some church members. The council's fourth assembly, held in Uppsala in 1968, took some positions on political and social reform which were troubling to southern Presbyterians. According to a 1966 editorial in the *Presbyterian Journal,* the "popular tide of 'mission'" was in danger of shifting almost totally toward "activism, inclusivism, and syncretism."[32]

In 1969 the General Assembly appointed an ad interim committee on the State of the Church to deal with some of the friction between the conservative and liberal factions in the denomination. The committee reported in 1970, citing several issues of concern. Among these were the church's stance on various social issues, the meaning of evangelism, and "disagreement over cooperation with non-Presbyterian societies" (presumably the WCC and the NCC). The denomination was slow to address these problems, which only caused an increase in dissension.

In 1970 Dwight Linton, a missionary to Korea, wrote an article criticizing the new direction of the Board of World Missions and asking for a separate board for "conservative" missions. The Board of World Missions declined to do this, maintaining that all of the different theological views on mission could be accommodated within the larger church. That same year, some of the denomination's more conservative members established the Executive Commission on Overseas Evangelism, intended to support "evangelical, conservative missionaries" and to pursue a mission philosophy "somewhat different from the PCUS Board of World Missions."[33] In 1973 they joined with the Continuing Presbyterian Church, which was in

---

31. General Assembly, 1964, 95.
32. "Students in Mission," *Presbyterian Journal,* March 2, 1966, 12.
33. Thompson, *Presbyterians in the South,* Vol. 3, 443.

its infancy and which would eventually become the Presbyterian Church in America.

In the midst of this controversy over the direction of the church's missionary efforts, the United Presbyterian Church of Mexico asked to sever relationships with both the UPCUSA and the PCUS. The organizations were separated for six years, from 1972 to 1978, with work being done cooperatively through the International Joint Mission Commission. Only with the organization of the border ministries along the US/Mexican border in 1984 was this relationship revitalized. In Brazil, the Presbyterian Church of Brazil (IBP) broke off its relationship with the PCUSA. Missionaries from the PCUS remained in the country, but their work was focused on transferring all mission work to the national church (IBP).

The controversy over the World Council of Churches continued. A resolution opposing the church's membership in the organization was brought before the General Assembly in 1973, but it failed. Opponents claimed that the WCC "sponsors and participates in activities which involve intermeddling in the internal affairs of emerging nations, including support of revolutionary activities . . . The 1973 Bangkok meeting of the World Council of Churches in its definition of salvation as liberation or revolution is clearly out of accord with Scriptures and the standards of the Presbyterian Church in the United States."[34]

That same year, the General Assembly appointed yet another ad interim committee, this one designed to study "the causes of unhappiness and division within our church" in the face of "imminent division." By the time this report was issued in 1974, the division had already begun, and the PCUS had lost a number of churches, a dozen of them in South Carolina, to the newly formed National Presbyterian Church (soon to become the Presbyterian Church in America, or PCA). The committee itself reported that the problems in the church were essentially the same as those reported in 1969, which had not been addressed. Among these were the various ecumenical relationships that the denomination maintained with organizations like the WCC and the NCC and "the redefinition of evangelism in terms of social action and the imbalance of social action as against evangelism."[35]

In 1975 the church reorganized its boards, creating a Division of National Mission and a Division of International Mission. T. Watson Street declined to head the new Division of International Mission and was replaced by longtime missionary and former East Asia Secretary G. Thompson Brown. During this time, demand for missionaries around the world

---

34. General Assembly, 1973, 122.
35. Ibid., 1974, 302-6.

seemed to be increasing. In 1977 the PCUS had requests for 175 additional missionaries to add to the fewer than three hundred who were currently serving.

In 1981 Clifton Kirkpatrick took over from G. Thompson Brown as the head of world missions. He was to spend much of his time coordinating work with the UPCUSA in anticipation of Presbyterian reunion. That year the PCUS raised $16.36 million for missions. While this seems impressive, when the Consumer Price Index is taken into account, it was actually a sharp decline in giving from 1944. By 1983 there were 226 PCUS missionaries in the field. Contributions began to increase somewhat, with most of the extra funds coming from designated gifts. The controversy over the World Council of Churches was to continue into the new denomination, however. In 1983 the General Assembly responded to a number of overtures by appointing a special committee to "study the causes of the questions, misunderstandings, and suspicions" that many members had toward the WCC and NCC.

C. Darby Fulton and the Changing Face of Missions

During much of this period, Charles Darby Fulton was the head of the Board of World Missions.

Dr. C. Darby Fulton (Courtesy of Presbyterian College)

His unease with the new direction of mission work reflected that of the denomination itself. His particular concern was that mission work was becoming more secular and less Christ centered, in other words, less evangelical. He had doubts about turning mission work over to the newly established national churches, and he feared that sending more short-term missionaries into the field would further dilute the church's evangelistic work.

C. Darby Fulton's father, Reverend Samuel P. Fulton, was a native of South Carolina and a longtime missionary to Japan. Darby Fulton was born in Kobe, Japan, in 1892, but he received almost his entire education in South Carolina. He received his early education at Thornwell Orphanage in Clinton and then went on to receive a BA from Presbyterian College. After receiving an MA from the University of South Carolina, he entered Columbia Theological Seminary to study for the ministry. Upon his graduation in 1915, he went to Princeton Theological Seminary where he received a Bachelor of Sacred Theology degree in 1916. He was ordained by Enoree Presbytery on June 25, 1915. In 1917 he married Nannie Paul Ravenel of Spartanburg, and the following year they departed for Japan where they served as missionaries from 1918 until 1925. Between 1925 and 1932 Fulton served as Field Secretary for the Board of World Missions, and from 1932 until 1961 he served as the Board's Executive Secretary. In the 1940s, Fulton became a frequent contributor to the *Southern Presbyterian Journal*, founded in 1942 by former missionary Dr. L. Nelson Bell in response to "a shift within the Presbyterian Church US away from acceptance of the complete integrity and authority of the Bible as the Word of God."[36] After Fulton retired as Executive Secretary, he taught at Columbia Theological Seminary until 1965. For all the years he served as Secretary and many of the years that followed, C. Darby Fulton sounded the alarm about the changes occurring in mission work.

In all of his writing, beginning in the 1930s, Fulton emphasized evangelism as the primary goal of the missionary. Although Jesus emphasized teaching and healing the sick in his ministry, Fulton felt that "the primary activity should be preaching, the conversion of souls."[37] He decried the secularism creeping into Christianity and the move away from emphasizing such basics as faith, repentance, and regeneration. Any effort that did not focus on personal redemption would, in the end, prove fruitless. After all, the manual of the Executive Committee of Foreign Missions clearly stated, "The great end of missionary life and service is the preaching of Christ and

---

36. Dendy, "How the Journal Began," 50-1.
37. Fulton, *Star in the East*, 50-1.

Him crucified to the non-evangelized peoples. All forms of missionary work must be subordinate to this end."[38]

Dr. Fulton became increasingly concerned about secularization following World War II. In his book *Now is the Time*, he noted that the overwhelming suffering around the world had caused the church to "think of our mission in terms of human pity, physical relief, social uplift, and philanthropy." While he recognized that Christians should be involved in relieving the widespread suffering, he saw a danger that by doing this the church would "lose sight of her spiritual and redemptive message." He also expressed concern that the church's medical and educational work might be separated from the overall goal of evangelism, noting that "it has even been said that there is a fundamental dishonesty involved in maintaining schools or hospitals with the purpose at the same time of winning students and patients to faith in Christ." He concluded, "Let the Church be the Church—not a political action committee, or an economic conference, or a foreign policy association. Let her emphasize again the great themes of sin and repentance and faith and salvation . . . This is her God-given commission. To exchange it for anything else is to sell her birthright for a mess of pottage."[39]

Fulton continued to stress this position well into the 1960s. In an article published in *Christianity Today* in 1966, he decried secular Christianity because it "dismisses the Gospel of faith and salvation as having little relevance to life and accepts instead 'another gospel' drawn from platforms of political, social, and intellectual liberalism," a gospel based on "man's physical and social needs." Through this process of secularization, "what God has done yields to what society must do; good news is replaced by good intentions; and evangelism disappears in favor of reform."[40]

In this same article, he bemoaned the lack of dissent when an executive for the Division of World Missions (DOM) of the National Council of Churches referred to the "amateurism and sentimentality" of most missions overseas, and recommended that they "take leadership toward a genuinely secular Christian faith . . . relevant and luminous with meaning in the scientific, world-affirming and world-understanding age in which we are set." Fulton reluctantly confessed his belief that "the evangelistic thrust of the 'old-line' denominations in overseas work is declining along with their proportionately diminishing place in North American missions as a whole."[41]

---

38. Ibid., 67.
39. Fulton, *The Time Is Now*, 27–30.
40. Fulton, "Evangelism the Heart of Missions," 11.
41. Ibid., 12.

Related to this question of evangelism was the rapid development of national churches. Fulton feared that the missionary work in each country was being turned over to the new national churches and that they were not the proper bodies to carry it out. Under this system, the national church would supervise all missionaries and handle all funds. Missionaries would only be sent when requested by the national church. In this way, "the board becomes, in effect, a subsidizing agency." [42]

In Fulton's opinion, these new churches were not able to focus enough of their energy on the missionary effort because they were dealing with many other organizational and programmatic issues. "A mission, on the other hand, is supremely concerned with evangelization, outreach, and extension . . . Their [missionaries's] interest is in winning new believers and establishing new churches."[43] In addition, the new national churches were still being subsidized by various mission boards, and Fulton felt that they could not really "develop a sense of their own missionary responsibility under such a system of subsidization. They tend to be confirmed as 'receiving churches,' whereas all churches should be 'sending churches' . . . Missions is primarily a matter . . . of the relation of the church to the believing world."[44]

Dr. Fulton also felt that the use of short-term missionaries damaged the evangelistic effort. Two hundred twenty-four (28 percent) of the new missionaries sent out in 1963 were expected to serve for five years or less. While he recognized the training, skills, and experience of these people who were experts in such fields as medicine, administration, technical vocations, agriculture, social service, Christian education, and church administration, he did not feel that they were the group "with the greatest promise in the field of evangelism." He felt that they were handicapped in their evangelistic efforts because they had no time to learn the language of the country or to understand the country's history, customs, and religious history.

Fulton was also concerned about the involvement of the PCUS with ecumenical organizations like the National Council of Churches. In 1943 he was part of a special committee appointed by the Executive Committee of Foreign Missions of the PCUS to study the constitution of the proposed North American Council of the Churches of Christ. In their report he and his fellow committee members, H. Kerr Taylor and J.P. McCallie, expressed many reservations about the proposed constitution. Article II of the constitution mentioned "the essential oneness of the cooperating churches in

42. Ibid., 10.
43. Ibid.
44. Ibid.

spirit and purpose." In the judgment of the committee, the various denominations had not yet reached essential oneness:

> The very existence of the denominations severally is evidence that they regard themselves as holding distinctive positions that they think are worth preserving. These particular positions are expressed not only in the creeds and polity of the various churches, but are reflected in the special emphases that appear in their respective program of activity, in missions, in education, in evangelism. Nor can they be dismissed as mere superficial differences in point of view. Often they lie deep in the faith and conviction of the church.[45]

The committee was also concerned that there was no statement of "our evangelical Christian position" in the proposed constitution. The inclusion of different denominations that did not agree on doctrine meant that doctrine was placed beyond consideration. Thus, rather than issuing declarations of faith, ecumenical organizations tended to concentrate on political, social, economic, and racial issues. The committee recommended that the General Assembly not join the council "because of the involvements that such membership would inevitably impose upon the whole Foreign Mission work of our church."[46] Fulton's later opposition to the establishment of the Japan International Christian University was based on concerns about control by other denominations, which would inevitably affect the university's theological stance.

By 1959 Dr. Fulton was increasingly being criticized for his lack of ecumenism. It seems, though, that he did not object so much to ecumenical cooperation as to the idea that the church would be bound by the pronouncements of ecumenical bodies like the National Council. In his defense, he cited many instances where the PCUS was cooperating with other denominations. Among these were the national Presbyterian churches in Brazil, Korea, Mexico, Portugal, and Taiwan and the Church of Christ in China, which was a collaboration between fourteen denominational missions. The PCUS was cooperating with the Methodists in Congo and cooperated with other denominations in seven of the nine theological colleges established in other countries. Other cooperative efforts included The Presbyterian Committee on Evangelical Cooperation, The United Andean Indian Mission, The United Mission in Iraq and the Amazon project in Brazil.[47]

45. Fulton, Taylor, and McCallie, "The North American Council of the Churches of Christ," 8–11.
46. Ibid., 11.
47. Fulton, "Contemporary Problems in Mission," 5.

In the end, Darby Fulton found himself increasingly aligned with the more conservative members of the PCUS. In 1966 he delivered an address at the opening of the Reformed Theological Seminary in Jackson, Mississippi. In 1969, at the first meeting of Presbyterian Churchmen United, he was one of six hundred pastors from the PCUS who signed a "declaration of commitment" avowing that "if the Presbyterian Church U.S. (Southern) changes its doctrine or polity by merger or otherwise, there will be a significant group to continue a denomination loyal to Reformed beliefs." Fulton said he signed the declaration in hopes that it would bring "new hope and comfort to many who earnestly desire a stronger evangelical emphasis during a time when theology is in a state of utter confusion."[48] Although Fulton did not in the end leave the PCUS to help organize what would eventually become the Presbyterian Church in America, he spoke at the first meeting of their General Assembly in 1973.

The Synod Of South Carolina And Foreign Missions

South Carolinians have always been staunch advocates of the church's mission efforts. In 1833 Reverend Thomas Smyth of Charleston encouraged the Synod of South Carolina and Georgia to establish the Southern Board of Foreign Missions. This independent board furnished both funds and missionaries for the mission field. Several of these early missionaries were from South Carolina, including George Washington Boggs who went to India in 1832, John B. Adger who went to Turkey in 1834, John Leighton Wilson who went to Africa that same year, and J. F. Lanneau who went to Jerusalem in 1836.

By 1925 there were a number of South Carolina missionaries who had been in the field for many years. Among them were Samuel P. Fulton, longtime head of the Kobe Theological Seminary in Japan; Reverend J.F. Price and his wife, Essie Wilson Price (China); Reverend and Mrs. William B. McIlwaine (Japan); Margaret Moore Douglas (Brazil); Reverend and Mrs. George W. Taylor (Brazil); Margaret Emelyn Craig (Cuba); Reverend and Mrs. W. G. Neville Jr. (Brazil); Reverend and Mrs. H. Maxcy Smith (China); Mr. and Mrs. R.E. McAlpine (Japan); and Dr. and Mrs. Lacy Little (China). Just beginning their work at this time were Dr. and Mrs. Mason Pressley Young (China); Hubert Thomas Bridgeman (China); Waddy H. Hudson (China); Reverend and Mrs. Henry L. Reaves (China); Florence Lois Young (China); Lina Elizabeth Bradley (China); and Reverend and Mrs. Luther

---

48. "Presbyterian Churchmen United," 125.

O. McCutchen (Korea). In 1924 the Synod of South Carolina had eighteen ordained missionaries working abroad: seven in China, four in Japan, three in Korea, two in Brazil, and one in Africa. There were numerous others, many of them women, who were not ordained.

In a number of South Carolina families, members of several generations joined the mission effort. Among these were Estelle McAlpine Hamilton, whose parents Robert E. and Anna Ballagh McAlpine were missionaries to Japan and China. Pauline Dubose Little, who served in China, was the wife of Lacy Little and the daughter of longtime missionary Palmer Dubose. C. Darby Fulton, son of longtime missionaries Samuel and Rachel Peck Fulton, would serve as a missionary to Japan and later as the head of the Board of World Missions. Eliza Neville, daughter of Presbyterian College President William G. Neville, had a brother, William Neville, who served as a missionary to Brazil. Eliza embarked on her own missionary career and married Lewis Lancaster. They served in China for many years, and their daughter Page married Dr. Herbert Codington. The Codingtons were to work in Korea and Bangladesh. Their stories, left behind in diaries and letters, illustrate the hardships experienced by missionaries and the changing face of missions and will be discussed at greater length in the following section.

Mission work permeated the work of the local churches. Children and young people were organized into missionary societies. These groups educated their members about mission work, raised funds, and sent supplies to mission hospitals. The Woman's Auxiliary participated annually in two large-scale mission projects, the White Cross project and the Birthday Offering. There were annual mission offerings taken up in churches each year, and missionaries on furlough spoke at many South Carolina churches.

South Carolina churches had always been generous contributors to the cause of world missions, but this began to change with the Depression, which started in South Carolina earlier than it did many parts of the country. By 1924 forty-four of the synod's congregations had been able to send nothing at all toward foreign missions, and by 1925 this number had increased to 166 congregations. Contributions were $108,000 in 1927 and $86,000 in 1928. Individual churches were asking for cost-saving measures. In 1931 the members of Harmony Presbytery asked the General Assembly to "fix the amount assigned to an individual or church for the support of a missionary on the actual salary paid for the missionary."[49]

By this time the Synod of South Carolina's gifts to foreign missions had fallen once again, to just $65,000. One presbytery, Harmony, had been able

---

49. General Assembly, 1931, 28.

to give only $770. The Synod in 1933 called these amounts "a new low-level for the Synod in a like period." Overall, between 1929 and 1933, the Synod of South Carolina's contributions to foreign missions fell by 60.1 percent. Foreign missions still received by far the largest amount of the synod's benevolence budget, however. Twenty percent of the budget in 1931 was going toward liquidating the debts of Chicora College; twenty percent of the remaining funds, however, were allocated for missions, almost double the amount going to any other cause.

Finally, following World War II, South Carolina churches began to increase their giving for missions. In 1946 giving was only $95,271. Four years later it had risen to $142,482. Like the denomination as a whole, however, South Carolina Presbyterians were becoming increasingly concerned about ecumenical work in the mission field and the church's membership in the WCC and the NCC. In 1956 a number of South Carolina presbyteries, including Harmony, Congaree, and Charleston, asked that the denomination end its membership in these groups because by belonging to them, the church gave "tacit approval of public pronouncements and resolutions that have been widely circulated, which do not express the convictions of the majority of the total membership and the leadership of both associations above referred to, openly envision the ultimate goal as organic union of all Protestant churches in one world church." The General Assembly refused these requests, but asked the Permanent Committee on Interchurch Relations to investigate the charges and further study the advantages and disadvantages of membership in the WCC.[50]

These concerns began to affect giving in South Carolina's congregations. In 1952 and 1953, the Synod of South Carolina received $44,746 less than it had budgeted for foreign missions. In 1960 the synod received only 70.47 percent of the amount it had budgeted, and in 1964 only 84.81 percent.

To raise awareness of foreign missions, missionaries on furlough visited churches across South Carolina. Some presbyteries organized youth rallies and retreats focused specifically on mission giving. However, giving to missions continued to drop, with contributions in 1965 totaling almost $18,000 less than the amount given in 1964. This was only 69.87 percent of the amount originally budgeted for the year. By 1968, although the WCC and the NCC were receiving only .08 and .11 percent of synod's budget, attempts were being made to separate these organizations out from general benevolence giving to the denomination. The WCC's fourth general assembly, held in Uppsala in 1968, further exacerbated this problem. It took some

---

50. General Assembly, 1956, 31–2, 52.

positions on political and social reform which troubled South Carolina Presbyterians. That year the Synod of South Carolina decided to let each individual presbytery decide whether to contribute toward the synod's part of the General Assembly's budget for both the World Council of Churches and the National Council of Churches.

South Carolina Presbyterians were also concerned about the politicization of the mission effort. In 1972 Enoree Presbytery submitted the following overture to the General Assembly's Standing Committee on World Missions: "Whereas the Board of World Missions has financially supported three African, Guerilla, revolutionary movements (in Mozambique, Angola, and Guinea) . . . and whereas Christ has called his Church to be an agent of peace and reconciliation between God and man and between man and man, and since it is traditional Christian ethics not to support in the name of Christ movements or groups engaged in assassination, murder, and political bloodshed," the presbytery asked the General Assembly to tell the Board of World Missions "to cease and desist from directly or indirectly supporting or contributing to foreign or domestic political, revolutionary movements, and if these funds allocated for the aforesaid groups have not been sent that the action of the Board of World Missions be rescinded." The assembly answered the overture in the negative.[51] By this time many of the more conservative PCUS churches in South Carolina were beginning to leave the denomination to join the newly established Presbyterian Church in America (PCA).

There was yet more concern about the denomination's membership in the World Council of Churches. In May 1976, nineteen representatives to the meeting of the Synod of the Southeast filed a petition concerning the selection of delegates to the WCC. They felt that the church's representatives to the council's meeting in Nairobi in 1975 were "pro-socialistic." They asked the General Assembly to choose "delegates who would, among other things, 'uphold the good name of the United States of America and defend it when it is being attacked.'" The original petition was given to the synod's committee on bills and overtures for further study. A decision was announced in 1977. The synod's Coordinating Council, having read the study and heard from several witnesses, felt that there was no proof that the denomination's representatives to the WCC were "pro-socialistic." They did not endorse the petition, but received it "with gratitude for the gracious and Christian spirit in which it was presented," and sent it to the General Assembly's Mission Board "as an expression of concern from some committed members of our Synod."[52]

51. Ibid., 1972, 132.
52. Synod Minutes, 1977, 83–4.

Throughout all this turmoil, the various institutions associated with the Synod of South Carolina remained closely associated with the missionary endeavor. From 1893 to 1903, Thornwell Orphanage had a Missionary Training School that produced approximately fifty graduates. Both Thornwell Orphanage and Presbyterian College offered free or discounted tuition to the children of ministers and foreign missionaries, thus preparing future servants for the church. Columbia Seminary's Mission Haven, supported largely by contributions from the church's women's organizations, provided short-term housing for missionaries who were on furlough, in transition, or studying at the seminary. In 1979 Presbyterian College established a Missionary-in-Residence program designed to bring a resident missionary or missionary couple to the college every year to acquaint students with opportunities in the mission field.

In The Field: The Lancasters And Codingtons

The Neville family of South Carolina had strong connections with world missions in the PCUS. Reverend William G. Neville, a native of Oconee County, South Carolina, served as president of Presbyterian College from 1904 until his untimely death in 1907. His son W. G. Neville Jr. became a missionary in Brazil. His daughter Eliza became a missionary to China, where she later married fellow missionary Lewis Lancaster. Their daughter Mary Littlepage (Page) Lancaster married Doctor Herbert Codington, and they too became missionaries. Another son Lewis Lancaster Jr. served as a missionary in Japan for twenty years before becoming the church's Director of Ecumenical Relations.

Reverend Lewis Lancaster, Eliza Neville Lancaster,
and Dr. Herbert A. Codington

Both Lewis and Eliza Lancaster and Herb and Page Codington kept a quantity of information about their work, information which is important in illuminating the joys, struggles, and heartbreaks of longtime missionaries in the field. Their work also reflects the changing focus of the church's missionary efforts over the years.

Eliza Neville started her missionary work when she arrived in China in 1917; she married Lewis Lancaster, a fellow missionary, in 1919. Like most missionaries of the time, the Lancaster's work was primarily evangelistic. Lewis started out doing country evangelistic work near Suchow (Suzhou), and Eliza ran the girls' school and later did mission work among the local women. According to Eliza, things were not always peaceful in the area: "There were many bandits in the country and sometimes in the city. Once sixty children in a school in our field were carried off by bandits and held for ransom."[53] In 1921 the Lancasters moved to Nanking (Nanjing), where Louis taught at the Nanking Seminary. By 1926 things were getting tense in Nanking, with rumors of coming unrest. Eliza and the children were evacuated to US and British gunboats, and in March 1927 the Communists invaded the city, "looting, burning and killing. Five foreigners were killed. Lewis was treated very roughly and almost killed. He saw our house looted and then later it was burned."[54] Lewis was ultimately saved by the family cook who hid him in his own home.

Meanwhile, the women and children who had taken shelter on the gunboats were taken downriver to Shanghai; the Lancasters had only two small trunks of belongings left to their names. Eliza and the children left for America in April, and since the Nanking Seminary was closed for eighteen months, Lewis soon followed. Eliza noted that since the Communists became active in China in 1921, she and her fellow missionaries were there during almost the whole time the Communists were taking over China.

By 1929 work in China had almost returned to normal, and the Lancasters, who had been living in Nashville, moved back to Suchow. According to Eliza, "neither Lewis nor I had any other thought than to go back to China when the way opened up."[55] Lewis resumed his evangelistic work, and Eliza concentrated on educating her own growing family and continuing her mission work among the women. Things were still not peaceful, with roving bandits and fighting among the warlords. The three missionary families in Suchow lived in a walled compound and were protected by a night watchman. In 1930 the women and children were once again evacuated, this time

---

53. Lancaster, "Memories of Life Together," 4.
54. Ibid., 5.
55. Ibid., 8.

to Pei Ta Ho in northwestern China. During the months they were gone, the Japanese began bombing the area. In 1933 the Lancasters were sent to Taichow (Taizhou), a much more primitive outpost where the lack of roads forced Lewis to abandon his pickup truck for a houseboat or wheelbarrow as he made his evangelistic rounds. They remained there for several years before returning to the US on furlough.

The family was prepared to return to China in August 1937 when they were told to delay their trip because of Japanese bombings in the area. Early in 1938, the other missionaries serving in China were evacuated, leaving behind them burned and pillaged mission stations. Later that year, when fighting moved to the west, the Lancasters were able to return to Japanese-occupied China, a period Eliza calls "those difficult years."

They returned to remote Taichow, which had been bombed by the Japanese and was overrun by rumors "which were many and frightful." With their children all safely studying elsewhere, Eliza was able to travel more with Lewis and even to spend an entire month in Tong Lu Chuang (Tong lu Chuan), a village with many Christians. There she and several other women went out to other villages during the day and then held night classes in Tong Lu Chuang in the evenings. But in 1940 they were evacuated again. Lewis remained in Shanghai to help with the evacuation and eventually escaped along the Burma Road after the US went to war with Japan in 1941.

The Lancasters returned to China in the spring of 1946, serving first in Shanghai and then in Chinkiang (Zhenjiang). Lewis was made Field Secretary in 1947, and they settled once again in Shanghai. According to Eliza, "Those years from 1946-49 were very hard. The Communists were gaining more and more... China had been at war from 1937 to 1945, and conditions got worse and worse until in May 1949, Shanghai fell to the Communists without fighting ... .Very soon we were restricted in our movements."[56] By 1950 Eliza and Lewis were back in the United States, ending over thirty years of dedicated service in a troubled country.

The previous year, Page Lancaster had married Dr. Herbert Codington, and they left immediately to start a medical mission in Korea.

---

56. Ibid., 21.

Herbert and Page Codington (Courtesy of Davidson College)

During the summer of 1950, while they were stationed in Mopko, they attended a mission meeting in Chunju. While there, they were warned that Korea was at war and that there might be local uprisings. They fled to Pusan (Busan) and then to Japan. By August, Herb, who had returned to Mopko, had once again been evacuated to Pusan. He planned to remain there "as long as he can be of service to the Koreans. Korea is where he belongs."[57] By October the five missionaries remaining in Pusan were able to go to Chunju, where Herb began treating badly wounded Communist soldiers. "Many Christians have come . . . in the past days telling stories of friends and loved ones who were killed or suffered under the Communist regime . . . Looking to the future, it seems that there will be much need for the missionaries and Christian leaders to seek to make known a spirit of Christian mercy to prevent brutal acts of revenge by the liberated South Koreans."[58]

By the following August, Herb was finally back in Mopko. He discovered that his language teacher's father, an elder in the church, had been killed and that Page's teacher, the wife of a pastor, had narrowly escaped execution. According to Herb, there were endless stories like this. The area was being inundated by refugees from the North, and between twenty and thirty UN camps had been established in their area. Communist guerillas were still raiding the camps at night, and Korean doctors refused to work there. "One feels the pressing need to pray for guidance in the work here as there are so many reasons for failure and wrong judgment, but most of

57. Letter from Page Codington, August 27, 1950.
58. Letter from Herb Codington, October 24, 1950.

all that the Lord will accomplish His work here and in the world in spite of man's failure . . ."[59]

That same year, the Codingtons moved to Kwangju (Gwangju) and Chulla-Namdo (Cholla Namdo), Korea, where Herbert Codington went to revitalize the Presbyterian mission's Graham Memorial Hospital. By 1956 the hospital had an average of 150 patients, and ground had been broken for a new building. The hospital had a full-time "Bible-woman" who visited the inpatients every day, as well as a part-time pastor. In a letter dated February 29, 1956, Page Codington expressed her hope for "every patient to meet and know the Great Physician through contacts with our Christian Staff... Seldom does a Christian institution find itself faced with a more urgent opportunity to meet the physical needs of so many in Christ's name and show the meaning of the Gospel . . ."[60]

Until 1958 the hospital focused its work almost entirely on treating tuberculosis. But by 1963, one third of the hospital's beds were being used for general medical use. The clinic saw 125 patients daily, and over 30,000 annually. This medical treatment was, however, combined with a healthy dose of Christianity: "Every person who comes to the clinic is challenged to become a follower of Jesus Christ. Preaching services are held each day in the clinic waiting room during the lunch hour. A more concentrated evangelistic program is carried out for the bed patients, who remain in the hospital for varying lengths of time. These patients, many of whom are facing major operations, are often eager to hear the message of new life in Christ."[61]

Dr. Herbert A. Codington with Staff at Kwangju Hospital

59. Ibid., August 8, 1951.
60. Letter from Page Codington, 1951.
61. Brochure about the Graham Memorial Hospital, 1963.

Dr. Won Kang was one of the doctors who helped to transform Graham Memorial from a tuberculosis hospital into a general hospital. He frequently went out with Dr. Codington's mobile clinic on the weekends. In a letter to Dr. Codington's son Rev. Herb Codington, he said that Dr. Codington's "dedication to service of the people still registers in my mind and minds of many in that district . . . Dr. Codington shared his love with the overall community with much sacrifice to himself for the cause of the Korean people." He spoke admiringly of "Dr. Codington's love of Korean people and greater cause of sharing God's love."[62]

In 1973 Herb and Page Codington visited the newly established country of Bangladesh, where they found people "enthusiastic to build a new country without a closed Islamic state." Protestant missionaries had already received thirty thousand converts, and the Catholic Church had converted over one hundred thousand. The Presbyterian Church decided to extend its mission in Bangladesh in 1974, and the Codingtons opened a clinic in the capital, Dacca (Dhaka), the following year. Although they were unable to disseminate any Christian literature or hold open services, they managed to communicate the Christian message through their individual treatment of patients.

Peter Willard, who went to Bangladesh in 1975, went into a church on his first Sunday there, looking for a place to stay. Dr. Codington introduced himself and invited Willard to stay with him and Page. According to Willard,

> People were continually coming into their tiny apartment for free medicines. Each time a beggar approached, Herb would give him money. He would sometimes tell him, "When you need more, come back" . . . In the hallway of his modest apartment he had a school for 40 beggar children . . . I never heard him say an unkind word. Instead of a new SUV, he drove around Dhaka on a motor scooter. Fifteen thousand of the poorest of the poor lived in the central park in the capital of Bangladesh, Dhaka. That did not look good to visiting foreign dignitaries. One day army trucks came and took the people ten miles north and dumped them on a hundred acre rice paddy called Tongi where Dr. Codington started his clinic . . . Herb Codington was no mere "do gooder" . . . Herb Codington was in Bangladesh because he believed God loved him enough to send his Son Jesus Christ to die on the cross in his place for his sins . . . His joy was now to obey Jesus Christ. Christ's last words, which commanded him to go into all the world. I don't think I have ever

---

62. Letter from Dr. Won Kang to Herbert Codington, September 2012.

observed a more servant like person than Herb ... I saw God in Herb Codington.[63]

Shortly thereafter, the regulations were relaxed, and the Codingtons were allowed to hold Christian worship services, provided there was not too much proselytizing and the message was ecumenical in nature. In a letter written in October 1976, Herb Codington suggested that "this real interest could be the result of all the Christian relief activity which has been going on in the camp of some twenty thousand over the past year, namely the Southern Baptist work projects of digging lakes for fish culture, new houses built by the Salvation Army, and the medical work at our clinic."[64]

There continued to be bumps in the road, however. In a letter written in September 1980, they reported that "at this time another ministry of the government has denied registration for our projects." These projects, located at Tongi and Alhadipur, were medical service and agricultural programs. The government had told them that they should be prepared to discontinue them entirely. Despite these occasional roadblocks, which were ameliorated somewhat by Dr. Codington's ability to procure medical help for some government officials, they continued their work.

In 1982 Dr. Codington described his work in the Tongi project. At the time it included two church groups and a widow's project which involved eighty women and combined sewing projects with daily Bible study. They were also providing prenatal, midwifery, and dental services. His goal was to provide "overall Christian influence in this large area ... which we believe will touch many lives there permanently for Christ."[65] By 1983 the Tongi Camp Church had seventy-five attendees, and a second congregation was growing in Tongi Town.

Dr. Codington officially retired around 1985, but continued to serve in Bangladesh until the late 1990s. Upon their return home, the Codingtons settled in Asheville, North Carolina, where they lived until their deaths in 2003.

Sixty Years Of Mission

Over the sixty years between 1925 and 1985, the face of world missions had changed radically. The depression resulted in decreased financial support, and the work was frequently interrupted by world and regional conflicts.

---

63. Email from Faith Willard to Herb Codington, October 29, 2008.
64. Letter from Dr. Herbert Codington, October, 1976.
65. Letter from Dr. Herbert Codington, October 29, 1982.

No longer was Christianity delivered to the people by all-powerful Western missions. More and more it became the purview of independent national churches. Mission work had moved from being primarily evangelical to addressing the needs of the whole person.

The self-critical neo-orthodoxy which swept the church in the 1950s began to erode Western ideas of superiority. The decline in colonialism, the formation of newly independent nations in the Third World, and the devastating war in Vietnam "undermined mainstream American protestants' pretensions to know or represent the essence of Christian discipleship." Indeed, protestants began to realize that they had for many years combined evangelism with imperialism. In addition, protestants realized that their missionary efforts had produced "a global Christian church, which contained diversities of discipleship that could leaven the spirituality of all Christians." Churches began to view mission work as "an integrated mission in partnership with domestic and overseas disciples."[66] Individual missionaries were no longer mere messengers from another culture, but began to work as partners with indigenous churches, and serve at their pleasure.

---

66. Coalter, Mulder, and Weeks, eds., "The Diversity of Discipleship," 165–91.

2

Reaching Out to the Marginalized

Presbyterian Missions in the United States

WHILE THE FUNDS INVESTED in home missions never approached those given to the foreign field, the PCUS was very active in mission work in the United States. What is usually referred to as "home missions" work in the Presbyterian Church actually had two components. The first, often referred to as local home missions, was the aid to new or weaker churches, providing evangelists or supply pastors to struggling, often rural, churches when they were unable to employ a full-time minister. The second task was to send forth laborers "to plant and gather the harvest of the Lord" in the "waste places" of the United States, "which are many and broad."[1] In general, although some synods and presbyteries supported similar efforts within their own bounds, this effort was referred to as Assembly's home missions. This wider effort existed in large part to support those synods and presbyteries, particularly those in the Appalachian Mountains, which had a larger population of unchurched and often uneducated people than less rural areas.

In the earliest days of home missions, the work was focused on following settlers as they opened up the frontier and helping them to build churches and hire ministers. Soon, however, new mission fields emerged, no longer based merely on geography but on need, opportunity, and the "vast areas of spiritual waste and destitution" across the country.[2] The immense number of illiterate, unchurched people in the United States was actually seen as a threat to the nation and its fledgling democracy. The hope was that a Christian America would eventually result in a Christian world, and, indeed, "determine the destiny of the human race."[3] Home mission efforts were also aimed at the growth of Presbyterianism in America. Indeed, by attempting to

---

1. "Report of the Executive Committee," *The Charlotte Observer*, December 19, 1840, 173.
2. McMillan, "Unfinished Tasks," 12.
3. Ibid., 26–32.

save America, the church was in fact saving itself. New areas of the country, including the rapidly developing Southeast, were ripe for growth.

Conditions in the rural areas of the Appalachian Mountains, especially the coal-mining regions, were harsh and ripe for mission work. When the textile industry arrived in South Carolina late in the nineteenth century, local churches found a vast new field of missionary endeavor. Many of the Presbyterian churches existing in former mill villages today are the result of mission work begun by local congregations. South Carolina Presbyterians contributed both a large number of missionaries and substantial financial resources to support work in both the Appalachian Mountains and the state's mill villages.

Immediately following the Civil War, Presbyterian Church (PCUSA) home missionaries began an extraordinary project aimed at educating the South's newly-freed slaves. Presbyterian schools in South Carolina were vital to this effort, and, along with institutions of higher learning like Biddle University (now Johnson C. Smith University) and Scotia College in North Carolina, furnished South Carolina with a large number of well educated African American teachers and pastors.

Work In The Appalachian Mountains

Mission work in the southern Appalachian Mountains began very early in America's history. These missions resembled foreign missions in that they were controlled by institutions far outside the region itself. Presbyterians viewed the well established churches in the region, which were primarily Methodist, Southern Baptist, Disciples, and Cumberland Presbyterians, as "sectarians loosed upon the region by the forces of the Great Revival . . . agents of error in need of rightful correction."[4]

Presbyterians, who valued order and self-control, were suspicious of the more emotional nature surrounding conversion and the self-abandonment exhibited by members of these churches in their revivals and camp meetings. They did not hold with the practices of some of the more evangelical churches in the region, especially that of baptism by immersion. They were also skeptical of the area's relatively uneducated preachers who, rather than working full-time, supported themselves largely in the same way their congregants did. All of these doubts caused less charismatic Protestant churches to view mountain people, who were actually quite religious in their own way, as ripe for conversion to "true" Christianity.[5]

4. MacCauley, *Appalachian Mountain Religion*, 346–7.
5. Ibid., 348.

This attitude, however, limited the influence of Presbyterians in the mountains. The PCUS's governing structure was highly centralized, and the denomination tended to import ministers from outside the region rather than developing and hiring native mountain pastors. They insisted on highly educated ministers, leading to a more intellectual slant that some locals found emotionally unappealing. As a result, even the earliest successful Presbyterian mission work took place mostly in larger valley towns or county seats.

One of the early influential Presbyterian missionaries in Appalachia was Dr. Edward O. Guerrant of Kentucky.

Edward O. Guerrant (Courtesy of the
Presbyterian Heritage Society, Montreat, N.C.)

He was a graduate of Jefferson Medical College in Philadelphia and Belleview Medical College in New York and had a Doctor of Divinity degree from Union Theological Seminary. In 1881, while he was serving a successful pastorate at Louisville's First Presbyterian Church, the Synod of Kentucky appointed him as evangelist to the eastern part of the state. He began holding tent revivals in rural mountain communities, often combining them with medical clinics. He established six Presbyterian churches in Breathitt County as well as three schools: Highland Institute in Guerrant, Witherspoon College in Buckhorn, and Stuart Robinson College in Blackey.

In addition to classroom and dormitory facilities, these schools typically included a church, a hospital, and an orphanage. His efforts, influenced by the progressive movement and offering both medical and social services, laid the basis for a more complete transformation of mountain life.[6]

By 1895 Presbyterian missionaries had also begun work among the mountain people in North Carolina. Reverend Edgar Tufts began visiting the Banner Elk area of North Carolina in 1895. In 1899 he opened an all-female high school and normal school, the Elizabeth McRae Institute for Girls, named for a summer school teacher from South Carolina who had later moved to eastern North Carolina. After generous support by Mrs. S. P. Lees, the name of the school was changed to the Lees-McRae Institute (now Lees-McRae College). In 1914 Tufts established the Grandfather Home for Children. In 1903 Reverend Joel Taylor Wade, who had previously served missions in North Carolina, Tennessee, and Georgia, founded the Nacoochee Institute in White County, Georgia. Two years later the Rabun Gap Industrial School was established to serve children in the lowland areas of nearby Rabun County.

In 1911 the work of these early missionaries was taken over by the church's Home Mission Board. That same year, the General Assembly appointed its first mountain superintendent. By this time it was clear that the path of Presbyterian missions would include a mixture of spiritual and educational outreach. In 1904 S. L. Morris, the denomination's Secretary of Home Missions, noted that unless the mountain people were first educated and then led to an organized church nearby, they would return to their former "unregenerate humanity."[7]

The schools, which taught the Bible and traditional academic subjects, also included instruction in more practical matters including industrial arts, agriculture, and domestic science. According to E. T. Thompson, "The attempt is made not to educate the young people away from the mountains, but to fit them for life in the mountains."[8] Like foreign missionaries, mountain workers were more than just teachers and pastors. They also worked in the community visiting homes, suggesting changes in sanitation and domestic science, and caring for the sick.

In 1915 the PCUS organized the Synod of Appalachia, thus establishing mountain work as a separate entity set apart from the usual synods which were drawn along state lines and setting it aside as missionary territory. Although mountain people were Americans and shared the Protestant

6. Akey, "Can We Be Saved?" 2.
7. MacCauley, "Appalachian Mountain Religion," 411.
8. Thompson, *Presbyterian Missions in the Southern States*, 236.

religious heritage, because of their "otherness," the church set them aside in a separate jurisdiction.

By 1922, there were about fifty mountain mission schools under the control of the PCUS. The Executive Committee of Home Missions controlled fifteen schools and thirty mission centers; these in turn reached forty-seven Sunday Schools and seventy-seven preaching points. In addition to those schools already mentioned, there were mission schools at Beechwood in Kentucky; Grundy and Blue Ridge in Virginia; Madison in West Virginia; Plumtree in North Carolina; and Mountaincrest and Caddo Valley in Arkansas. (The Plumtree School for Boys was formerly the boys department of Lees McRae Institute.) There were free medical clinics located at Lees-McRae in North Carolina and at the Highland School in Kentucky. There was also a newly-organized co-educational boarding school, the Boone Fork Institute, in Shulls Mills, North Carolina, organized by Reverend C. G. McKaraher.

Classroom at Boone Fork Institute (Courtesy of the Presbyterian Heritage Center, Montreat, N.C.)

Although none of this work took place in South Carolina, a number of early missionaries to the Appalachians were South Carolinians. Among them was Reverend Robert P. Smith. Smith was born in Spartanburg and graduated from Davidson College and Columbia Theological Seminary. He began his work as an evangelist in Enoree Presbytery and went on to be president of both the Reidville Female Seminary and Presbyterian College. In 1888 he left the college to become the general evangelist and superintendent of home mission work in Mecklenburg Presbytery (North Carolina). He was instrumental in organizing the new Asheville Presbytery in 1896 and later became its Superintendent of Home Missions. He spent thirty years organizing churches and preaching throughout the mountains. He also organized the Mountain Orphanage in Black Mountain.

By 1929 a number of other male missionaries from South Carolina had served in the mountains. C. S. Crowder of Little Mountain worked with Dr. Guerrant in Kentucky. Thomas Pennel of the same congregation served as a physician there. Reverend George Lucius Newton, who graduated from Thornwell, Presbyterian College, and Columbia Seminary, did domestic missionary work in Virginia, West Virginia, and Clinton, South Carolina. Reverend William Crosland Frierson of Anderson worked in Blackey, Kentucky, for a number of years and taught Bible at the Stuart Robinson School. In 1925 Reverend Clarendon Witherspoon Ervin of Indiantown started work in Glade Valley, North Carolina, and served as the principal of the high school there until his retirement in 1947. There were far more women working in the mountains than there were men, however.

At the same time that the PCUS was discussing whether women should be allowed to speak before mixed groups, Guerrant was relying heavily on their willingness to serve. By 1922 those employed by the Executive Committee of Home Missions were overwhelmingly women—73 women missionaries and teachers as opposed to sixteen ministers and nine laymen. The work was often arduous. Dr. Guerrant described one South Carolinian, a graduate of Converse College, who "lived alone in a remote cabin, slept in a bed she built herself, taught a school with twenty-four children, and walked more than a hundred miles a month making her rounds."[9]

By 1929 a large number of women from South Carolina had been engaged in mission work all across Appalachia. In Kentucky, Claudia Crowder of Little Mountain, Sarah Leona Blake of Greenwood, Nellie Holcombe of Thornwell Memorial Church, and Carrie Durant Reaves of Clarendon worked at Dr. Guerrant's mission. Leona Blake was working at the Highland School and later became a benefactor. Bessie Morrah of Mt. Carmel Church worked in the coal mining town of Corbin, Kentucky. The local Presbyterian pastor, Dr. William Boggs, was only able to go to Corbin once a month, "and this little lady was to try to hold the fort during his absence—build up a Sunday School, prayer meeting, Ladies' Aid Society, Young People's Christian Endeavor, Charity Association, see that children attended school, and Sabbath School, have community Christmas trees, and do personal evangelism."[10] This, among a population of nearly 10,000, called "for a lot of walking." By 1929 Miss Morrah was not surprisingly at home, recovering

9. Flynt, "Feeding the Hungry," 99.
10. Gist, *Presbyterian Women of South Carolina*, 751.

from a severe illness. Beginning around 1921, Mrs. J.L. Gray of Hodges worked at Roan Mountain in Tennessee with her husband, Reverend Joseph Lewis Gray, who was a native of Virginia. They also worked at Cove Creek in Carter County, Tennessee.

A number of South Carolina women also worked in Virginia and West Virginia. Zoulean Anderson of Florence did summer missionary work in the Virginia mountains from 1918 to 1921 and later served as the religious director at a West Virginia mining camp. There she organized a Sunday school, a Christian Endeavor society, a prayer meeting, and women's clubs.

Zoulean Anderson (Courtesy of the Presbyterian Heritage Center, Montreat, N.C.

After working with textile workers for several years, Alma McLaurin of McCall Presbyterian Church went to the Irish Creek Mission in the Virginia mountains where she worked for five years. The section was so isolated that she was not only a Christian worker but served as the area's doctor and nurse. Caroline Caldwell of Clinton went to West Virginia to do general evangelistic and social work at a mining camp there.

South Carolina women also worked closer to home. Hallie Covington of Marion worked at the Glade Valley School in North Carolina from 1912 to 1914 before becoming a foreign missionary. Cornelia McLaurin of Sumter spent one summer in the Virginia mountains and then began work at Glade Valley where she taught, gave music lessons, took care of the sick and dying, and generally "interest[ed] herself in all that interests her dear mountain people, and [was] rewarded by their warm glowing love."[11]

A number of South Carolinians worked at the Nacoochee Institute in Sautee, Georgia. Mae Blackwell of the Greenville Church near Due West started out teaching summers in a small mountain school, part of Nacoochee's extension work. She went on to work at both the Institute itself and at its newly established branch at nearby Tiger. She later worked at the Monroe Community House, part of the Institute. Virginia Neville of Clinton, daughter of former Presbyterian College president W. G. Neville and herself a graduate of the college, worked at the Nacoochee Institute after having served for several years as a missionary to China.

It is interesting to note the attitudes of the mountain people toward these women workers. A man in one of Robert P. Smith's congregations once told him, "We like to hear you fellows preach, and I am not saying anything agin ye, but if we can't git both, send us the women teachers. These women teach our children books and good manners during the week and on Sunday they teach all of us a lot of what is in the Bible. Tell your folks to send us the teachers, we can git along mighty well for a good while yet just with them doing the work."[12] During this period, the Synod of South Carolina was contributing sixteen percent of its budget to assembly's home missions. In 1919 this consisted of $49,138. The amount fluctuated over the years, amounting to $45,323 in 1920, $45,138 in 1921 and $39,805 in 1922. By 1926 attendance at the PCUS's mountain and mission schools had reached 3,107. Rabun Gap School was the best supported, receiving slightly more than $20,000 in 1926-27. Stuart Robinson and the Highland Institute were also fairly well supported, owing to regular annual donations by Mrs. Cameron Morrison of North Carolina and the C. E. Graham Foundation. C. E. Graham, who died in 1922, was a prominent resident of Greenville, South Carolina, where he owned several textile mills over the years. A Presbyterian, he was a generous donor to both home and foreign missions. Most others were receiving a mere fraction of this amount.

It was around this time, however, that the early effects of the coming economic depression became evident, and the PCUS began to experience a sharp decrease in contributions for all causes, including home missions. In 1926, for the first time, the Home Missions Committee faced a deficit and was unable to undertake any new projects. According to E. T. Thompson, "it was a fight to maintain the territory which had been won; a heart-rending

---

11. Ibid., 490.
12. Smith, *Experiences in Mountain Mission Work*, 47.

retreat." Between 1927 and 1930, denominational contributions to home missions were cut by $120,000, resulting in losses in both workers and mission outposts.[13]

As the economic depression worsened, this same decline in giving was evident in South Carolina. In 1928 the Synod of South Carolina budgeted $54,000 for assembly's home missions and received only $38,379. In 1929 contributions totaled only $35,770; by 1933 this was reduced to $15,673, a decrease of 56.1 percent.

A 1929 study of denominational schools in the Southern mountains done by the Russell Sage Foundation gives some interesting information about Presbyterian schools in the region. The PCUS was supporting a total of eighteen institutions, including one college and one orphanage. One of these schools was in Georgia, seven were in Kentucky, five were in North Carolina, two were in Tennessee (including King College), and three were in Virginia. Eight of these schools were totally under the sponsorship of the General Assembly. The others were supported directly by individual synods or presbyteries.

By this time, public schools in the mountains were improving, and there were more state and charitable agencies to deal with poverty and disease. Because of improved roads, the area was also becoming much less isolated. That year the PCUS decided not to compete with public schools, but to let the states take over where possible. In 1931 an ad interim committee reported to the General Assembly that there were too many mission schools, many in competition with public schools, and many others poorly located. The committee recommended that the church focus its attention on evangelism rather than education and that "no graded or high school would be continued unless it were needed for some special forms of training which was not provided by the state."[14]

This decision, coupled with the financial problems of the Depression, greatly reduced the number of Presbyterian schools in the mountains. In 1927 the General Assembly was supporting nine mountain schools and was cooperating with various synods and presbyteries in the operation of seventeen others. The assembly's 1931 decision and the sharp decrease in funding caused changes for many Presbyterian schools. That year Caddo Valley Academy ceded control to the local school board and became the Norman Public High School. Lees-McRae eliminated its high school department and became an accredited junior college. The Grundy Presbyterian School in Virginia and the Bachman Memorial School and Home became primarily orphanages, sending their residents to public schools for their education. By 1934 Thompson's "heart-rending retreat" had turned into almost a complete

13. Thompson, *Presbyterian Missions in the Southern United States*, 271.
14. Ibid., 237.

rout, with only Stuart Robinson, Highland Institute, and Brooks Memorial in Kentucky under the General Assembly's direct control.

South Carolinians continued, however, to be involved in the work. For instance Katherine O'Neall of First Presbyterian Church in Greenville worked as a Bible instructor at Lees-McRae College and a home mission worker in both Coburn, Virginia, and Ashe County, North Carolina. Reverend Joseph Smarr Robinson of Gaffney served as a home missionary in West Virginia and Kentucky from 1927 until 1947.

The economic situation stabilized somewhat during the latter part of the Depression and began to improve after World War II. By 1945 the Synod of South Carolina was giving $47,050 toward assembly's home missions. This increased to $65,923 the following year. After a steep drop to $49,799 in 1947, contributions remained around $60,000 for the two succeeding years.

Despite the improved economic situation, there continued to be attrition. During the war, Rabun Gap-Nacoochee closed its junior college because of reduced enrollment. It was, however, thriving otherwise and embarked on an ambitious building program. By 1955 only six schools were being supported by various church governing bodies. The General Assembly was in charge of only the Stuart Robinson School at Blackey, Kentucky, which had consolidated with the Highland Institute. Synods and presbyteries were in charge of Lees-McRae College at Banner Elk, North Carolina, Glade Valley High School in North Carolina, Rabun Gap-Nacoochee School in Georgia, and the School of the Ozarks in Point Lookout, Missouri. Stuart Robinson was to close in 1957. The School of the Ozarks became a four-year college in 1965.

Despite school closures, the PCUS attempted to continue its evangelistic efforts in the mountains. They were, however, greatly outnumbered by the Southern Baptists who claimed forty percent of the churches in 1957 and the Methodists who claimed about twenty percent. Another twenty percent were distributed among nine other denominations, with the PCUS having the most churches among them. By 1959 there were 577 mission posts in the mountains. The Southern Baptists still had the most, 121, and the Presbyterians were fourth, with 78. Many of the Presbyterian churches in the region, however, were weak and ultimately unsustainable. Only those in the larger towns and settled valleys were destined to succeed. In the meantime, other denominations, which had had no mission presence in the area in the 1930s, were beginning to put down roots. Among these were the Free Will Baptists, the Church of God, and the Assemblies of God.

Some Presbyterian institutions continued to change and prosper, however. Glade Valley School was still in existence in 1983. Shortly after reunion, the board of Lees-McRae College decided to seek status as a four-year college. This was granted by the Southern Association of Colleges and Schools in 1990. It continues to operate today, fulfilling its motto: "In the mountains, of the mountains, and for the mountains."

Rabun Gap-Nacoochee was another of these success stories. Over the years, it had grown from a mountain school to a Christian boarding school accepting students from a much larger area. Following the merger of the synods of South Carolina and Georgia, the school was under control of the resulting Synod of the Southeast and thus was directly supported by South Carolina Presbyterians. In 1974 the synod was expected to raise $26,000 to support the work there. Only a few years later, Rabun Gap-Nacoochee faced difficult challenges. There was a new consolidated high school in the area, and Rabun Gap lost both 160 public school students and the financial support the school board was providing them. The school became totally private and needed even more support from the synod to pay salaries and other operating expenses.

In 1978 the synod received a report from a task force appointed to consider the relationship between the Synod of the Southeast and Rabun Gap-Nacoochee. The task force concluded that since Rabun Gap was founded under the auspices of the Synod of Georgia, and since all of its trustees were elected by the newly formed Synod of the Southeast, that the synod should retain its relationship with the school but strive to increase its funding. An attempt was made to do this, with the proposed budgets for Rabun Gap to gradually increase from $35,000 in 1979 to $44,000 in 1983. Between 1975 and 1981, the synod's giving did actually increase by 44.7 percent (almost double the contribution given to Queens College), but at the same time, the school's budget and operating expenses had doubled. By 1984 Rabun Gap-Nacoochee was receiving more support from the synod than Queens or Thornwell.

According to Willis D. Weatherford, director of the Southern Appalachian Studies Project, and Earl D. C. Brewer, professor of religion and sociology at Emory University, the effect of all this mission work in the mountains was contradictory in nature. Religious groups did succeed in establishing valuable religious, medical, and educational programs. "Creative and forceful persons—preachers, teachers, doctors, nurses, others . . . devoted their entire lives to the welfare of mountain people." Financial support came in from across the country, and missionaries were able to render invaluable human services. This, however, is merely "the romantic, the biographical, the public relational, the idealistic aspect of foreign missions." There was a less appealing aspect in which mission work created "hundreds of struggling, substandard and subsidized churches." Rather than cooperation between denominations, the program created competition. Weatherford and Brewer concluded that "in the face of continued wide-spread human need, the tendency to subsidize substandard parishes on a competitive basis should give way to bolder strategies and designs cast in the ecumenical and co-operative framework."[15]

Freedmen's Schools

One important mission in South Carolina was not the responsibility of the PCUS but was nurtured by missionaries from the PCUSA. Shortly after the Civil War, the church began an educational mission for newly freed slaves that was to bear much fruit over the next century. This system consisted of both day and boarding schools on the elementary, secondary, and junior college levels and was affiliated with the church's Atlantic, Fairfield, and Mc-Clelland presbyteries, all of which were African American. The program was originally under the supervision of the Presbyterian Committee of Missions for Freedmen, which later became the Board of Missions for Freedmen. The New School Presbyterians established a committee in 1864 and the committee of Old School Presbyterians on June 21, 1865. This latter group soon had forty missionaries and teachers at work.

The Old and New School Presbyterians reunited in 1869, and their separate programs for freedmen were consolidated in 1870. Beginning in 1878, there was also a women's organization, the Department of Freedmen, which was often referred to simply as the Women's Committee. This separate women's group was abolished in 1923, and the women's work was conducted through the Unit of Schools and Hospitals which dealt primarily with boarding schools, and the Division of Work for Colored People, which worked with the day schools.

Although South Carolina established school districts in 1870, funding was very uneven, school terms were very short, and most of the schools were segregated. For the first fifty years after the Civil War, only one public school in South Carolina, the Howard School in Columbia which opened in 1867, offered an education for African American children in all grades. Booker T. Washington High School, opened in 1916, was the only public high school for African Americans in Columbia until 1948. In the rest of the state, very few blacks had access to any sort of high school education at all before World War I; thus, most black students in South Carolina were educated in private institutions, many of them operated by churches of different denominations.

The PCUSA stepped in very early to provide such institutions. Their work began in four states, North and South Carolina, Virginia, and Tennessee. The effort in South Carolina began in the late 1860s, largely led by the

---

15. Weatherford and Brewer, *Life and Religion in Southern Appalachia*, 83–4.

efforts of two freedmen, Ismael Moultrie and Paul Campbell. White Presbyterians, including Reverend Stephen A. Mattoon and Reverend Willard Richardson, were also influential. Inez Moore Parker writes of the scope of this educational mission in South Carolina: "In South Carolina, the major educational emphasis was placed on having numerous parochial schools, a few academies and institutes, and for a few years two junior colleges."[16] At its peak, the program was responsible for seventy-eight schools in the state. Indeed, South Carolina had by a large margin the greatest number of schools of any state.

In most cases, the earliest schools were associated with individual churches, which made them community centers and produced increased interest in both the church and the school. There were two types of schools operating in South Carolina: parochial schools, which were non-residential elementary and high schools, and boarding schools, which were academies and institutes, and sometimes went to the junior college level. The secondary schools aimed to prepare their graduates for college. Part of their mission was to teach Bible and the catechism and to prepare those called to ministry in the church for seminary at Lincoln University in Oxford, Pennsylvania, or Biddle University in Charlotte, North Carolina (after 1923, Johnson C. Smith University and Seminary), or Barber-Scotia College in Concord, North Carolina.

The earliest schools were usually run by a white minister and his wife and met in a room or two, often in the church basement. They were supported by the church but also charged tuition and were supported by donations of labor and money from the freedmen themselves. Gradually teaching responsibilities were turned over to African American ministers and teachers. Among the earliest schools in South Carolina were St. Mary's Grade School in Blackstock (1866), Brainerd Institute in Chester (1866), and Wallingford Academy in Charleston (1867). Goodwill Parochial School in Mayesville was also founded during Reconstruction. By 1872 its enrollment was over 350, making it one of the most active parochial schools in the state.

Several significant schools were founded during the last quarter of the nineteenth century. In 1881 Reverend J. P. Crawford of the Second Presbyterian Church, Cheraw, founded the Coulter School (later Coulter Memorial Academy). That same year, Reverend W. R. Coles founded the Immanuel Institute (later the Andrew Robertson Institute) in Aiken. In 1888 Reverend John Peter Foster organized the Salem Presbyterian Church and Industrial High School in Anderson. Kendall Institute, a secondary school in Sumter, was established in 1891 under the leadership of Reverend J. C. Watkins.

During this same period, Reverend Emory W. Williams and his wife Ella V. Chase founded the Ferguson Academy in Abbeville. This

---

16. Parker, *Rise and Decline of the Program of Education for Black Presbyterians*, 140.

coeducational academy focused on both the liberal arts and industrial education. Williams left the academy in 1891 and the Freedmen's Board took over the property. In 1901 it was renamed Harbison College. Fires in 1907 and 1910 resulted in its removal to Irmo in 1911.

When Reverend Williams left Ferguson Academy in 1891, he also left the PCUSA. He joined the Afro American Presbyterian Church and continued his educational efforts in Abbeville by establishing Ferguson-Williams College. In 1897 the General Assembly of the PCUS, in cooperation with the Synod of South Carolina, purchased the college for $3,000. At the time, the school was still being led by Reverend and Mrs. Williams, and there were 187 students enrolled. Ferguson-Williams, the only such school in the state supported by the PCUS, closed in 1920.

The curriculum of these institutions included religion, reading, writing, mathematics, history, poetry, public speaking, and music. Students were also taught Christian living, morality, and cleanliness. The schools were founded with a vision of basic social equality and the conviction that African American students were as capable as white students of learning not only reading, writing, and arithmetic, but also were ready and willing to receive a classical education. In this way the schools followed the educational philosophy of W. E. B. Dubois (born in 1868), who with Charleston native Francis Grimké (born in 1852), pastor of Fifteenth Street Presbyterian Church in Washington, D.C., was outspoken in the struggle for full equality for African Americans.

As time went on, there was some controversy about whether the education should be more focused on practical skills, and some schools added courses in industrial and domestic arts and agriculture. In *Race and Reunion: the Civil War in American Memory*, David W. Blight characterizes the differing visions of Booker T. Washington and W. E. B. Du Bois. Washington became best known after his address at the Atlanta Cotton States Exposition in 1895, in which he appealed to all citizens to look beyond racism, self-hatred, and segregation. He urged African Americans to overcome their loss of the vote and their second class citizenship by pursuing basic elementary and secondary education combined with training in agricultural and industrial arts, to work their way out of poverty.

Du Bois was not willing for education to accommodate a second class status for African Americans. He famously proclaimed in 1903, "The problem of the twentieth century is the problem of the color line." He was as firm as Booker T. Washington in his commitment to education, but his first commitment was to classical liberal arts. From it he drew upon the heritage of liberation and advocated political activism for African American freedom. The impact of both educators overlapped and shaped educational ideas.[17]

17. Blight, *Race and Reunion*, 362–4, 294.

Du Bois articulated the original foundation of the parochial schools, academies, and schools of higher learning established by the Presbyterian Church and other denominations in the South. They took as their first task teaching literacy and numeracy and developed it further in teaching the Bible and the classical heritage of learning in the West. The intention of this educational path was to enable African Americans to enter the mainstream of American society. Furthermore it would empower institutions like Johnson C. Smith University, Barber Scotia College, and many other church related institutions to develop African American leaders in the ministry and lay vocations.

When these original purposes were not sustained during the Jim Crow era, some of the schools began to adopt Booker T. Washington's program. Industrial and agricultural courses provided additional training at such South Carolina institutions as Larimer High School, Salem Industrial High School, Kendall Institute, and Harbison Agricultural and Industrial College. Strategies for surviving and thriving in a segregated South required varying educational and vocational plans. So the educational philosophy changed and became more diverse. However, the liberal arts tradition continued in the denominational schools and colleges, and Du Bois's influence was not lost on the African American communities in rural and small-town South Carolina, where it lived on to encourage the development of African American Presbyterian leadership in the civil rights era.

At the height of the program, the PCUSA was sponsoring seventy-eight schools in South Carolina. By 1878 upper level schools in South Carolina included Wallingford Academy (Charleston), Brainerd Institute (Chester), Fairfield Institute (Winnsboro), and Bluffton Institute (Bluffton). Between 1880 and 1890, the Committee either established or took over one or more schools each year. However, the economic recession of the 1890s curtailed the growth of the program and resulted in shorter school terms, smaller salaries for teachers, and the abandonment of some of the less prosperous schools. The effort was still an important one, however. In 1914 there were forty-eight Presbyterian schools in South Carolina.

Around 1915 the US Department of the Interior did a study of the various schools for African Americans in the US. They found that in 1910, there were almost 836,000 African Americans in South Carolina, accounting for 55.2 percent of the population. The illiteracy rate was high. Among those over ten years old, 38.7 percent were illiterate (as compared to 10.3 percent of whites). Almost $1.5 million dollars was being spent to educate 145,384 white students in the public schools. Only $305,084 was being spent for the 212,125 African American students. Teacher salaries per child aged six to fourteen were $10 per white student and $1.44 per African American student. The differences between schools for whites and those for African Americans were more pronounced in the counties where the black population was largest.

Given this situation, the private denominational schools in the state provided opportunities which filled in the gaps in public education. The Department of the Interior determined that the strongest Presbyterian Schools in South Carolina were the Andrew Robertson Institute in Aiken, Brainerd Institute in Chester, Coulter Memorial Academy in Cheraw, Harbison College in Irmo, the Goodwill Parochial School in Mayesville, and Kendall Institute in Sumter.[18]

Researchers visited thirteen other Presbyterian schools in the state, although they observed that since "it is apparent that it is practically impossible to give adequate supervision to such a large number of small schools, the Presbyterian work would be strengthened if the money now spent on the 43 small schools were concentrated on the stronger institutions. The department declined to visit twenty-nine of the schools in the state, deeming them "little more than Sunday schools . . . usually taught in the church by the local pastor."[19]

The thirteen schools visited were:

School	County	Enrolled	Attendance	Plant Value
Bethlehem	York		80	$500
Chesterfield	Chesterfield		85	$700
Emerson	Barnwell	190	90	$6700
Greenville	Greenville	74	35	
Harlean	Barnwell		97	$4900
Laurens	Laurens		10	$8300
Lebanon	Fairfield	205	45	$450
Nazareth	Fairfield	105	42	
Newberry	Newberry	40		
Norell	Oconee		49	
Presbyterian	Union	50		
Presbyterian	York		60	$800
Salem	Anderson	310	200	$1200

18. Department of the Interior, Bureau of Education, 1915, 471.
19. Ibid., 521.

Funding for the schools varied widely. Some were totally supported by the Board of Missions (sometimes aided by the public school system). Others used a combination of Board funds and/or public funds plus tuition and donations. For instance, in 1916 Salem Parochial in Anderson received $1,200, and almost $500 of this was from tuition and donations. Emerson Industrial had an income of $920, $780 from the Board and $140 from tuition. The school in Newberry was totally supported by the Board; the school in Carlisle had $225 in income in 1913, $150 from the county, $30 from the Board, and $45 from tuition and donations; Bethlehem Parochial in McConnellsville was funded by the Board and the county, with no mention of tuition.

By 1919 churches in the PCUSA were giving over $100,000 a year for the education of African Americans in the south, and women's and youth benevolent societies gave almost twice that amount. Thus the total amount given that year was almost $300,000. In addition, the African Americans who were benefiting from the schools contributed $115,409.40. The 1919 report of the Women's Committee praised these contributions: "Will you kindly notice how the Negro is helping himself? Have you seen any finer example of giving than this? Little money, high cost of living, sons away as soldiers, and all solicitors go to them as well as to us. This is a record of gifts of which they need not be ashamed."[20]

The yoking of schools and churches continued into the twentieth century. In 1919 eight of the twelve African American ministers in Atlantic Presbytery were also teachers or heads of schools. In Fairfield Presbytery this number was nineteen of twenty-nine, and in McClelland, nine of fifteen. Ministers's wives were also key contributors. Of ten schools in Atlantic Presbytery, six were run by husband-and-wife teams. In Fairfield, this number was fifteen of twenty-two, and in McClelland, four of ten.

During this period, there were six boarding schools in South Carolina. Harbison Agricultural College was a male boarding school. In 1919 the school owned property worth $90,000, employed ten teachers, and had an enrollment of 110. The five other boarding schools were coeducational. The Andrew Robertson Institute had a staff of five, an enrollment of 105, and property worth $8500. Brainerd Institute employed twelve teachers, had an enrollment of 206 students, and owned property worth $55,000. Coulter Memorial Academy had seven teachers and 319 students, and owned property worth $5,500. The Emerson Industrial Institute in Blackville owned property worth $10,000 and employed six teachers to educate

---

20. Thirty-Fifth Annual Report, 221.

198 students.[21] The Kendall Institute in Sumter also owned property worth $10,000 and had six teachers providing instruction for 252 students.

The remaining 36 schools in South Carolina were scattered across the state and were day schools. They varied widely in size. Five of them had less than fifty students, with Edisto the smallest at twenty-five. Six of the schools had enrollments of over two hundred, with Goodwill (Mayesville) the largest at 350.

Goodwill Day School

The same was true with property values. The Salem Industrial High School in Anderson owned property worth $9,000, while the school property in Winnsboro was only worth $500. The typical school term lasted for six to eight months, although the school in Ravenal met for only three months, and those in Ridge Springs and St. Charles for four.

It is clear from contemporary reports that some of the schools were woefully understaffed. Mrs. M. A. Robinson at Frazier Excelsior in Bamberg was responsible for 250 students. The school in Lancaster had one teacher for 137 students, and Lincoln in Due West had two teachers for 243 students. Yet with all their shortcomings, the effect of these schools was significant. By 1919 the schools in Atlantic Presbytery were educating 1,143 students, those in Fairfield 3,465, and those in McClelland 1,180.

---

21. Ibid., 24–37.

In addition to providing funds for such items as staff salaries and other operating expenses, the Board itself owned the property of many of the schools in South Carolina. All told, this property amounted to an investment of over $220,000 in the education of African Americans in South Carolina. The property was not what mattered, however. In their annual report, members of the Board of Missions for Freedmen declared, "We have labored with the distinct realization at all times that the chief aim of our work is not the building of schoolhouses and churches but the building of Christ-like characters among the people with whom we work."[22]

By 1925 the distinguished graduates of the Presbyterian schools in South Carolina included nationally known educator Mary McLeod Bethune, social worker Jane Harris Hunter (a graduate of Ferguson-Williams and the founder of the Phyllis Wheatley Association in Cleveland), Reverend George Waldo Long of Cheraw (a graduate of Brainerd Academy and the longtime head of Coulter Memorial Academy), Reverend Warren Julius Nelson of Mayesville (pastor of the Goodwill Church and head of the Goodwill School), and Arthur Henry George, who became a professor and later dean at Johnson C. Smith University. Dr. Daniel Jackson Sanders, the first African American president of Biddle University, attended Brainerd Institute before going on to Western Theological Seminary in 1871. Other South Carolina-educated presidents followed him, including Dr.Hardy Liston (Fairfield), J. W. Seabrook (Harbison) and Henry L. McCrory (Fairfield). Kelly Miller, a graduate of Howard University and Johns Hopkins University and the longtime dean at Howard was a product of Fairfield Institute.

By this time, the Depression was beginning to have a huge effect on South Carolina. Several factors in the state contributed to insufficient public education for African Americans. The economy of the coastal plain was primarily rural. By the early 1920s, the boll weevil had destroyed all the long-staple cotton and much of the crop in the upper part of the state, leaving large areas of the state in extreme poverty and causing South Carolina public education to lag far behind that of most other states.

Presbyterian schools also suffered, with schools closing across the South and the reduction of the school year from eight months to six. By 1925 twenty-one schools remained open in South Carolina. These were Wallingford Academy (Charleston), Larimer High School (Edisto), Goodwill (Mayesville), Ebenezer (Dalzell), St. Mary's Grade School (Blackstock), Immanuel Institute/Andrew Robertson Institute (Aiken), Brainerd Institute (Chester), Bethany Parochial (McConnellsville), Mattoon Parochial (Greenville), Lincoln High School (Due West), Emerson Industrial Institute (Blackville),

---

22. Ibid., 12.

Coulter Memorial Academy (Cheraw), Harbison College (Irmo), Grant Academy (Spartanburg), Kendall Institute (Sumter), Harden Academy (Allendale), St. James Parochial (James Island), Mary A. Steele Memorial (John's Island), Salem Industrial High School (Anderson), Irmo Parochial School (Irmo), and Frasier Excelsior School (Bamberg). St. Mary's, while it had been funded by the Board for many years, ceased to be supported by the church in 1922. It continued in operation, however, until 1956.

Two additional schools, Bethany in McConnellsville and Mattoon in Greenville, closed in 1929. While there were an increasing number of public schools for the state's African American students, there was still a desperate need for the parochial schools. In 1930 South Carolina was spending $53 on each white public school student and $5.20 on each African American, and white teachers were paid nearly twice as much as blacks.

The "Great Migration" of African Americans in search of work in the industrial cities of the North led to a major change in the population of South Carolina, which went from a majority of African Americans to a minority in 1930, the first census since 1810 in which white people outnumbered African Americans. Most African Americans who remained were punished by poverty, by racist attitudes, and by discriminatory laws that rendered public education unavailable for many and inferior for all African American children. At the same time, the educational system established by Presbyterians in South Carolina was overextended, with many small schools which were difficult to sustain. In 1931 the Board of National Missions of the PCUSA reported that three thousand students dropped out of the Presbyterian schools in the South because of lack of clothing and diminished financial assistance.

By 1932 two additional schools, the Immanuel Institute/Andrew Robertson Institute in Aiken and the Kendall Institute in Sumter, had closed. In 1933 the Board decided to close all schools in areas where public schools were available, as well as all boarding schools where most of the students were actually day students. This resulted in the closure of thirty-four of the Board's thirty-nine remaining South Carolina day schools and left only five day schools open in the state: St. James Parochial on James Island, Larimer High School on Edisto Island, Lincoln High School in Due West, St. Mary's Grade School in Blackstock (which remained open, but was no longer sponsored by the Board), and Grant Academy in Spartanburg. Only three boarding schools remained: Brainerd Institute, Coulter Academy, and Harbison Institute.

The attrition was to continue. Lincoln High School closed in 1936, Brainerd Institute in 1939, and Grant Academy in Spartanburg in 1940. Professor J. D. Martin Sr., who was in charge of Brainerd, fought long and hard to keep the institution open, citing the lack of other adequate educational facilities in the area, but the Board closed it because it would cost too much to renovate the plant. Coulter, however, seemed to be thriving. In 1933 it added junior college classes, and by 1943 it had a student body of 500. The junior college program, however, closed in 1947 and Coulter was turned over to the public school system in 1949.

These institutions continued to produce distinguished graduates. Bernice Stokes Robinson, who graduated from Coulter in 1932, went on to teach for forty-one years in Chesterfield County and later directed the Barbara Lawrence School in Cheraw. Reverend Samuel Mitchell Moore Jr. graduated from Brainerd Institute and became the longtime pastor of Bethlehem First United Presbyterian Church in McConnells. He also taught for many years at Old Torbit and Chester Junior High schools and was the charter president of the Chester NAACP. Elo Leon Henderson of Newberry County attended Harbison Institute and later Johnson C. Smith University and seminary. He served as Executive for the Synod of Catawba. Harold Boulware, a graduate of Harbison, was the lead attorney for the *Briggs v. Elliott* case in Clarendon County (1949), which the United States Supreme Court later bundled into *Brown v. Board of Education* (1954).

By the late 1940s, the winds of change were beginning to blow through the state. In 1948 it was estimated that 62 percent of adult African Americans in South Carolina were illiterate, a sign that the public schools may have been separate but far from equal. In December 1950, parents in Clarendon County filed suit over the issue of busing for black students. This suit was ultimately bundled with *Brown v. Board of Education*; the Supreme Court's decision in this case in 1954 forever struck down the concept of separate but equal. It took South Carolina almost two decades to adjust to this new reality. It was not until 1969 that the public schools were integrated on a token basis; full integration did not occur until 1971.

Presbyterian schools continued to close during the 1950s, with Edisto's Larimer closing in 1955, St. Mary's in Blackstock in 1956, and Harbison College in 1958. (Before it closed, Larimer became a community center for Edisto Island. During the ministry of Ural L. Brewer it joined the program of Citizenship Schools on the Sea Islands, initiated by Johns Island resident Esau Jenkins and led by Septima Clark and Bernice Robinson from Highlander Folk School in Tennessee.) The last Presbyterian school to remain open in the state was St. James Parochial, which closed in 1961. Thus ended a tradition of education that had lasted almost one hundred years.

These Presbyterian schools, along with those founded by other denominations, filled a huge gap in the public education system in South Carolina. They enabled thousands of African Americans to receive at least a basic education, and many of their graduates went on to college and graduate school, providing the state with a large pool of educated black leaders. Looking back over the remarkable development of denominational schools in South Carolina by missionaries from the North, we can see that in both their rise and decline, they reflected broad forces in the life of the United States from the ending of the Civil War and continuing into the period of Civil Rights.

Work in Mill Villages

Most of the Presbyterian Church's work in textile villages was already well established in 1925. Although there was an early cotton mill at Graniteville in 1846, the big boom in building didn't begin until the last two decades of the nineteenth century. In 1880 there were only fourteen mills in South Carolina, with slightly over 82,000 spindles. By 1900 there were 115 mills, with almost two million spindles. Most mill workers were farmers and their families from rural South Carolina and the southern Appalachians. The mill owners either built separate villages for them or built new, separate neighborhoods in existing towns. Homes were offered to the workers for a small sum, usually around $35 per month plus about $2 in utilities for an average house.

South Carolina's churches began to work with these new laborers almost immediately. All denominations recognized the mill villages as separate communities with unique populations. Since they were outsiders and only renting their homes, the workers had no real ties to the community and were often transient. In addition, townspeople often regarded the mill workers as inferiors because of their lack of education and the different way they dressed and worshipped. In turn, the mill workers themselves felt out of place in the established churches. So most of the mainline Protestant denominations established separate missions, Sunday schools, and eventually churches in the villages rather than welcoming the workers into their own congregations. Thus, while not being organized into separate presbyteries as the churches of the Appalachian Mountains were, mill churches were definitely considered separate, and their members were isolated from the mainstream, downtown churches. This echoed in a way the colonialism and cultural superiority that had characterized the church's early ventures into the foreign mission field.

Liston Pope, in his landmark study of Gastonia and its mills, notes that most of the organizers of the early cotton mills were leaders in their churches and were accustomed to some measure of control of the attitudes of their ministers and the church's decisions. In most cases the support of the churches was instrumental in establishing the mills themselves and in establishing outpost chapels and Sunday schools to insure that they would have an effective and obedient workforce. In some cases, local pastors were actually connected to the mills. Reverend William Plumer Jacobs was a founding director of the Clinton Cotton Mills. His intentions, however, were not what one might expect. He accepted this position with some high-minded purposes, among them to "have a word as to religious and school privileges for operatives" and to "have my say as to regulations in regard to moral character of the operatives." He admits that his intentions were somewhat subversive: "Those were not the things in the minds of those who elected me."[23]

According to Pope, the symbiotic relationship between mill owners and the religious institutions in their towns resulted in an unhealthy economic situation. Mill owners espoused idealism and Christian principles, but only when "some alteration offers economic advantage" would the owners accept it. Ministers saw new relevance in some of the changes suggested in the mills, and approved of them as benefitting the general welfare. "Those ministers who, being closer to the workers, see the more fundamental implications of the proposed change, are circumscribed by their own dependent relation to the mills and can voice no public criticism . . . Acquiescence of ministers . . . really helps the mills to make economic changes without opposition, as it abets the confusion of issues in the minds of those most affected."[24]

Pope notes, however, that this symbiotic relationship was one that changed over time. In the early days when the mills were established, the churches played a large role in shaping economic development, and the mill owners had much less power over them. In later years, however, economic factors came to have "more nearly shaped religious institutions than been shaped by them . . . Partially a source of industrial transformation sixty years ago, the religious institutions have become increasingly a product of that transformation and a guarantor of prevailing economic arrangements."[25]

The mill village church served as an arm of the welfare program that mill owners provided for their workers. Other aspects of the program included the provision of social workers, schools, and recreational programs. Such amenities served to ensure that workers were satisfied, would stay on the job, and would not push for unionization.[26] According to Liston Pope,

---

23. Jacobs, *Diary of William Plumer Jacobs*, 317–8.
24. Pope, *Millhands and Preachers*, 194–5.
25. Ibid., 331–2.
26. Wilhelm, "Cultural Modernization in Southern Cotton Mills," 16.

> The greatest contribution of the churches to the industrial revolution in the South undoubtedly lay in the labor discipline they provided through moral supervision of the workers ... Methods used in helping to convert an atomistic assemblage of rural individualists into a disciplined labor force, amenable to a high degree of social control, consisted of the inculcation of personal virtues (stability, honesty, sobriety, industry), provision of a center of community integration other than the mill itself, and emotional escape from the difficulties of life in a mill village. Both as disciplinarian and as safety valve, a village church became a valuable center for the constitution of a new industrial community."[27]

According to historian W. J. Cash, such welfare work reflected well on the mill owners and was a part of an older southern tradition, a paternalistic one "that it was the duty of the upper classes to look after the moral welfare of these people and get them safely into heaven at last – because that tradition had been introduced and firmly established in the mills by the founders of Progress ... it gloriously flattered [the mill owner's] vanity."[28] In a local example of this phenomenon, when the union church was dedicated at Clifton, South Carolina, the president of Wofford College compared the event to the dedication of the Temple in Jerusalem, and the Presbyterian minister who participated in the ceremonies noted that while the mill owners were responsible for providing buildings in which to conduct their business, they were not responsible for providing churches, from which he concluded that while "it is generally believed that corporations have no souls ... that is certainly false as to the Clifton Company."[29]

This concept was espoused in 1927 by South Carolina Methodist Reverend John W. Speake in the *Southern Textile Bulletin*:

> It is imperative that we think of Southern industry as a spiritual movement and of ourselves as instruments in a Divine plan. Southern industry is the largest single opportunity the world has ever had to build a democracy upon the ethics of Christianity ... Southern industry is to measure the power of Protestantism, unmolested ... Southern industry was pioneered by men possessing the statesmanship of the prophets of God ... I personally believe it was God's way for the development of a forsaken people.[30]

27. Pope, *Millhands and Preachers*, 29.
28. Cash, *The Mind of the South*, 210.
29. Carlton, *Mill and Town in South Carolina*, 104–5.
30. Pope, *Millhands and Preachers*, 24–5.

In 1907 August Kohn did an extensive study of life in South Carolina textile mill villages, including religious life. He found that in many mill communities, "the mill corporations made it an unwritten rule to subscribe to all church and other similar funds." He estimated that there were approximately two hundred churches of all denominations in the mill villages, and that "The corporations in all instances contributed to the building of the churches; in fact, in most cases, the building fund came entirely from the mill treasure."[31]

Often the early church buildings were union churches serving more than one denomination. Gradually, as the various denominations strengthened, they broke off to establish their own churches. Most churches established in the mill villages were Methodist or Baptist, although the Presbyterians did make attempts to reach this population. Several things hampered their efforts. Those workers who had attended church earlier in their lives had almost all attended Baptist or Methodist churches. The Presbyterian Church insisted that its ministers have both college and seminary degrees. Thus when the mill workers began to inundate upstate towns, there were fewer Presbyterian pastors trained and available to minister to them. Their high level of education also made it difficult for Presbyterian pastors to preach on a level that would appeal to the mill workers or to actually live among the people whom they served.

The first Presbyterian church in a South Carolina textile village was probably the one established at the Piedmont Mill village in Anderson County in 1880. For several years, services were held in a union church building built by the Piedmont Manufacturing Company and shared with the Baptists and Methodists. Each denomination eventually left to build its own church. The Presbyterians were the last to do so in 1904. According to the Jones and Mills history of the church in South Carolina, the Piedmont Manufacturing Company was "exceedingly helpful and liberal, having always manifested a deep interest in the churches of the town."[32]

Work in Pelzer was started in 1881 with the encouragement of Ellison Adger Smyth, a Presbyterian and head of the Pelzer Manufacturing Company. Other churches soon followed. The Rock Hill Presbyterian Church began working in the nearby mills as early as 1883 when they established White Memorial Chapel in Pineopolis to serve workers at the Rock Hill Cotton Factory. Reedy River Church in Conestee (Greenville County) was organized in 1887. That same year, the Young Men's Working Society of

---

31. Kahn, *The Cotton Mills of South Carolina*, 125, 149.

32. Jones and Mills, *History of The Presbyterian Church in South Carolina Since 1850*, 961.

First Presbyterian Church in Greenville started a mission Sunday school in an abandoned warehouse; by 1893 Third Church was established with forty members and its own building on Hampton Street. Churches were built at Clifton Mills in 1888 and at Spartan Mills in Spartanburg in 1890. In 1891 the Becca Presbyterian Church was organized in Roebuck by evangelist N. J. Holmes.

Until 1896 the establishment of new congregations was under the auspices of the synod's committee on home missions and remained the responsibility of local churches and presbyteries. That year, however, the synod hired Reverend N. J. Holmes to work as the synod evangelist, Reverend W. L. Boggs to work in Enoree Presbytery, and Reverend J. A. Wilson to work in Pee Dee Presbytery. In 1903 the synod made work in textile villages a part of its home mission emphasis. It was at this time that Reverend W. H. Mills began to work in the Horse Creek Valley in Aiken County. In 1905 the synod tried once again to begin work among the cotton mill workers. The effort was focused in the area around Spartanburg and was led by Reverend J. P. Stevenson. By 1908 the presbyteries were back in charge, but cooperating through synod's committee.

In his 1907 study of South Carolina's mill villages, Augustus Kohn noted that while there were still union churches in some communities, the Baptists and Methodists and the Presbyterians, where they had attracted enough members, had built their own churches. He found the mill workers to be "of a decidedly religious temperament . . . very constant in their religious duties." They were also generous in supporting their churches, and in his conversations with pastors, "they were unanimous in saying that in proportion to their means the operatives were very liberal towards their churches, and that they maintained their organizations with pride."[33] The Sunday school program was particularly strong, and the teachers, from the mill village itself, were surprisingly versed in the Bible.

At the time Kohn was writing, he listed the following Presbyterian churches in mill villages: Piedmont, Gluck Mills in Anderson, Graniteville, Conestee, and Chester.[34] There was also a church in Belton (Anderson County) which was built on the property of Belton Mills in 1904. The Saxon Mills Presbyterian Church in Spartanburg was organized in 1905. In addition, Dr. W. H. Mills was working in the Horse Creek Valley (Aiken County), where in four towns (Graniteville, Clearwater, Vaucluse, and Warrenville) with a population of 7,000, only one in eight of these belonged to any church, and only twenty-seven of them were Presbyterian. In 1907 a union church was organized in

33. Kohn, *The Cotton Mills of South Carolina*, 143–4.
34. Ibid., 148, 160, 169–71.

Ware Shoals (Greenwood County) under the leadership of Walter M. Smith, a stockholder in the Ware Shoals Company and an elder in the Presbyterian Church. By 1909 the Presbyterians there had organized the Memorial Presbyterian Church (now the First Presbyterian Church of Ware Shoals). The Monaghan Presbyterian Church in Greenville County was started as a Sunday school in 1909, and organized into a church that same year.

The situation in Clinton and nearby Lydia in Laurens County is illustrative of the difficulties, successes, and failures encountered by many churches attempting to establish Presbyterianism among this new constituency. In 1895 Mercer Silas Bailey, an elder in the Clinton Presbyterian Church (now First Presbyterian Church, Clinton), organized the Clinton Cotton Mills. By 1897 the Clinton Presbyterian Church had established a mission among the mill workers, and Thornwell Jacobs, a student at Princeton Theological Seminary and the son of the church's minister, was conducting services there. The church was organized in 1898.

In 1902 Mr. Bailey built an additional mill, the Lydia Cotton Mill, just outside Clinton. In 1904 Mr. J. W. Leak donated a lot for the construction of a chapel in the Lydia mill village.

Lydia Mill Presbyterian Church

At this same time, the session of the Clinton church hired Presbyterian College graduate and Columbia Seminary student William H. Boyd to supply both the Clinton and Lydia mill villages. In April 1905, the church appointed a committee to build a church at Lydia.

By 1906 the Sunday school at Lydia was thriving, but there was none being conducted at Clinton Mills. Neither church had a supply pastor. In 1907 the session of the Clinton church asked the resident Presbyterian ministers in Clinton to take over this work, but instead it was taken over by various church members who held a prayer meeting at Lydia twice a month and Sunday afternoon services each week at Clinton. By early 1908, Reverend Fred K. Smith was preaching every Sunday morning at Clinton Mills and holding two evening services at Clinton and one at Lydia each month. Another member of First Presbyterian was holding evening services at Lydia on the first Sunday of the month.

In the meantime, however, the Baptists were holding regular services in both locations, and by December, the session of First Presbyterian had decided to cooperate with the Baptists in a union Sunday school as long as half the teachers were Presbyterian. In early 1909 the church hired another of Reverend Jacobs's sons, J. Ferdinand Jacobs, as the evangelist at Clinton Mills, and in May of that year, Mrs. Julia Baker was hired as a deaconess to do missionary work there.

J. Ferdinand Jacobs (Courtesy of Presbyterian College)

She visited a large number of families in the village, and by September the average attendance at the Sunday school was sixty-eight. In 1910, J. B. Branch was appointed to preach twice a month at Lydia. During this time, a church building was built in the Clinton mill village, and the congregation was organized into the Second Presbyterian Church. J. F. Jacobs was called as the pastor, but the church building burned down in December of 1911, the members scattered, and it was removed from presbytery's rolls in 1914. Work at Lydia continued under Branch. He reported in October 1911 that he had "gone into many homes . . . and found the people cordial and responsive."[35]

Between 1912 and 1914, different students from Presbyterian College conducted the work at Lydia. Reverend A. H. Griffith of Reidville held a successful revival there in 1915, and sixty members were added to the church's rolls. In the meantime, First Church's Christian Endeavor Society rented a storeroom near the Clinton mill in an effort to resume the work there. The session decided not to organize separate churches at either Clinton or Lydia, but to keep them as mission outposts supplied by PC students during the year and supply pastors in the summer. The effort in Clinton itself eventually failed, and the work in the mill village was taken over by the Baptists, Methodists, and Pentecostals. First Presbyterian continued to support the chapel at Lydia until it was organized into an independent church in 1929.

M. S. Bailey's son C. M. Bailey, who supervised the mills in Lydia, made note of the 1929 events in his diary. On April 14, he reported that a protracted meeting was going on in Lydia with the purpose of eventually organizing a Presbyterian church there. On April 21, evangelist C. E. Sullivan preached at the school auditorium and succeeded in securing twenty-two members for the new church. On May 25, the church was organized with twenty-six charter members. Thomas Grafton, a graduate of Presbyterian College, was the pastor, and Dr. C. E. Sullivan was the president. Bailey's fervent wish was for "God's richest blessings [to] rest on this little church."[36] The church did succeed. In 1937 the trustees of the First Presbyterian Church transferred the lot and building to the officers of the Lydia Presbyterian Church. The church burned in 1950 but was rebuilt. In 1978 the Bailey Foundation donated money to renovate the building. The congregation still meets today under the leadership of Reverend Herb Codington. So of the two efforts in the Clinton area, both of which were nurtured by the mill owners and both of which had their growing pains, one succeeded and one did not.

---

35. Griffith, *All Beautiful the March of Days*, 29.
36. Moore, *The Baileys of Clinton*, 82.

In 1912 Thomas F. Parker summarized the work being done by the Presbyterian Church in the mill towns. Bethel Presbytery was contributing $1,900 annually to support three missions, one in Chester and two in Rock Hill. Each of these had a full-time pastor, and all three had Sunday schools. Charleston Presbytery was spending $600 on a mission in Graniteville. Enoree Presbytery was spending $718 on missions in Spartanburg, Laurens, and Greenville. As noted above, First Church, Clinton, had built a chapel at the Lydia Cotton Mills and was paying both a woman worker and a pastor who preached twice monthly.

Churches and presbyteries were not the only ones involved in this work. Thornwell Orphanage in Clinton was doing its part by providing room, board, and an education for forty-three mill children. Presbyterian College had one student who was the superintendent of a mill Sunday school, and three others were teaching in the school. Students were also responsible for the weekly prayer meeting there. Chicora College was also contributing, giving a free scholarship to a young woman from the mills each year.

More mill churches were organized in the next dozen years, including at Republic Mills in Great Falls (1912), Union-Buffalo Mills in Buffalo (1912), Rose Hill Church near Columbia's Palmetto Mill (1919), and Monarch Presbyterian Church in Union (1924). This church, sometimes also known as Monarch Mills, was renamed McCutchen Presbyterian Church in 1947. There had been a union Sunday school in the Watts Mill section of Laurens since 1905. In 1924 a group of Presbyterians under the leadership of Reverend C. T. Squires organized a separate Presbyterian Sunday school there. In 1927 this was organized into the Watts Mill Presbyterian Church. In 1926 the Dunean Presbyterian Church was organized in the Dunean Mill Village in Greenville. By 1929 the church had a new building.

In addition, there were several home missionaries from South Carolina working in the textile towns at this time. The Jones and Mills 1925 history of the Presbyterian Church in South Carolina notes that Minnie Wilson and Miss Hunter were working in the Horse Creek Valley in Aiken County, Claudia Fraser was working in Great Falls (Chester County), and Marie Gilbert was working at Ware Shoals.

According to Reverend G. M. Telford, author of a home mission study book for the Synod of South Carolina, there were seventy mill towns in Enoree Presbytery in 1927. He estimated that there were probably 140,000 workers and that only around 50,000 of these belonged to churches. At the time, there was home mission work in only twelve cotton mills. At Monarch Mills in Union, the synod's home mission committee had bought the Methodist church for $1,500 and given it outright to the Presbyterians.

Second Presbyterian Church in Spartanburg, whose pastor was the "stirring soul-winner" Reverend J. D. Henderson, had just completed a $40,000 building and had recently received one hundred new members. Monaghan Presbyterian Church under the leadership of the "vigorous" Reverend C. E. Piephoff was beginning to build a Sunday school addition and also boasted one hundred new members.[37]

In Piedmont Presbytery there were thirteen industrial communities, encompassing thirteen mills and approximately 30,000 people. Except for two communities, the Presbyterians had no churches or workers in the mill villages there. Some young women from the Assembly's training school were working during the summers conducting Bible schools, young people's organizations, and women's auxiliaries. The committee was helping to assist three distinct groups of churches, one of which was strictly textile. In the future they hoped to place pastors in mill communities, particularly those around Anderson where there were eight cotton mills with no Presbyterian presence. They also hoped to hire, in cooperation with the mill authorities and under the supervision of existing Presbyterian churches, community workers who could nurse the sick.

Telford reported that there were fourteen textile plants in South Carolina Presbytery, "with large communities of workers surrounding them."[38] Presbyterians were working in five of them: Whitmire, Ware Shoals, Laurens Mill, Watts Mill (Laurens), and Goldville (now Joanna).

During the 1930s, however, millworkers began to move increasingly toward more evangelical churches. According to Liston Pope, this phenomenon represented "a protest against the failure of religious institutions to come to grips with the needs of marginal groups, existing unnoticed on the fringes of cultural and social organization."[39] During this same period, the concept of the mill village itself was coming under fire, and Southern clergymen were among those questioning the effects of providing separate villages for workers. In 1929 the Congressional Committee on Manufactures issued a report on conditions in the textile mill villages. According to the report, the insularity of mill villages removed the operatives from participation in local politics. Village life had also proved "to be unfavorable to education, to religion, and to understanding and sympathy between the citizens of the mill village and those of the larger community."[40] The Committee recommended that the remaining mill villages be integrated into the larger community.

37. Telford, *Our Home Task*, 23.
38. Ibid., 37.
39. Pope, *Millhands and Preachers*, 140.
40. Jamieson, "Change in the Textile Mill Villages," 69.

As early as 1934, some textile companies began to sell the village homes to the workers. This movement apparently began in North Carolina, where the Elmore Corporation in Spindale sold the thirty homes in its mill village to mill employees. Other mills followed, and by 1941 twenty-five textile companies in Virginia, North Carolina, South Carolina, and Georgia had sold sixty villages, containing approximately 7,000 houses. There was a lull in sales during World War II, but between 1945 and 1948, 5,000 houses were sold in this same region. Although many ministers had spent years opposing the abolition of the villages, they soon "joined heartily in approval . . . and began to praise the joys and virtues of home ownership."[41]

By 1940 twenty-one of the 182 textile mills in South Carolina, or 11.5 percent of the total, had sold their villages. In most cases, if the mill owned churches in these villages, they were either given to the congregation or sold for a nominal price. By 1983 less than 5 percent of mill workers lived in company-owned houses.

George Perkel of the Textile Workers Union of America (TWUA), interviewed in 1986 for the Southern Oral History Project, noted that even though the village houses had been sold to the workers, the mill owners still exerted a large measure of control over the lives of their workers both at the mill and when they were not at work:

> Historically, textile employers in the South have been regarded as public benefactors, rather than as simply employers . . . regarded by the community leaders and by people generally as benefactors. And they set up these one-industry towns or company-dominated areas and part of the benefits that they received from that was almost complete control of local government . . . Many of them still retain the paternalistic idea of being responsible for their people . . . The mill management feels that he has a right to know not only what his worker does on the job but outside of work . . . They're still important in the church community, the education community, and through them they still retain a great deal of control over the lives of textile workers."[42]

This made it hard to organize unions in the area's textile mills, and in some cases, the churches added institutional support to the suppression of unions. When David Burgess, himself a Congregationalist minister, moved to South Carolina in 1947 to work on organizing the CIO (Congress of Industrial Organizations), he and his wife applied for membership in a Presbyterian Church in Rock Hill. According to Burgess, "it was a prestige

41. Pope, *Millhands and Preachers*, 192.
42. Oral History Interview with George Perkel, May 27, 1986.

church. Prominent textile owners were members. They thought I was a Communist... Pastor [Ken] Phifer was told by the members of the session that I ought not to be allowed to join that church because I was a communist and worked for the CIO. So he put his job on the line and said he would quit the church if my wife and I were not allowed to become members."[43]

Although a number of the early Presbyterian mill churches had closed by this time, some continued to grow and prosper. The church at Spartan Mills (now Second Presbyterian Church, Spartanburg) added an education building in 1941. In 1955 the church added a second education wing, and in 1980, a gymnasium now called the Gus Prill Christian Ministries Building was built. Watts Mill was also growing. In 1943 the Watts Mill Company canceled the debt on the church's property, deeded it a lot, and donated $8,000 to the congregation for the construction of a manse. The church's name was changed to Grace Covenant Presbyterian Church in 1945. In 1946 Grace Covenant had its largest membership, 131. The mill gave further money to the church in 1956 to cancel the debt on their recently constructed recreation building.

Grace Covenant Presbyterian Church, Laurens, S.C.

During the 1940s, the Aveleigh Presbyterian Church in Newberry began sponsoring a Sunday school mission in Whitmire. In 1948, following

---

43. Oral History Interview with David Burgess, September 25, 1974.

a gift of land from Mr. D. L. McCullough, this mission was organized into the McCullough Presbyterian Church with twenty members. The church added a new recreation hall in 1956 and a new kitchen in 1966. In 1946 Bethel Presbytery provided $1,000 to support a chapel at Winnsboro Mills in Fairfield County. In 1947 First Presbyterian Church in Greenwood started a mission Sunday school in the Matthews Mill village. The forty-eight member congregation met in the Community Hall until James C. Self, the owner of Greenwood Mills, donated the property and some funds for the first church building which was completed in 1954. At that time the church was named Second Presbyterian Church. By 1956 it had 138 members, and by 1966 membership stood at 150. It was renamed Fraser Presbyterian Church in 1974 in honor of its first pastor, Harry B. Fraser, who served from 1948 until 1958. In 1951 Harmony Presbytery provided $1,500 towards the church building at Lydia. The church's membership peaked at sixty in 1956.

Some PCUS churches, however, chose a more conservative type of Presbyterianism and left the denomination for the Presbyterian Church in America. Among these, with the dates they left the denomination, were Becca/Roebuck (1973), McCutchen Presbyterian Church in Union (1981), and Rose Hill Presbyterian Church in Columbia (1983).

Many of the early mill churches still existed in 1985, however, and were still members of the PCUSA (which was formed by a merger of the United Presbyterian Church and the PCUS). Among these were Piedmont Presbyterian Church; Second Presbyterian Church, Spartanburg; John Calvin Presbyterian Church (formerly Monaghan Presbyterian Church) in Greenville County; First Presbyterian Church, Ware Shoals; Grace Covenant Church in Watts Mill; Fraser Presbyterian Church in Greenwood; Dunean Presbyterian Church; McCullough Presbyterian Church; Third Presbyterian Church in Greenville; Lydia Presbyterian Church; and Pelzer Presbyterian Church. Some churches had seen a sharp decline in membership. Fraser had only 80 members in 1984 compared to a high of 150 in 1966. Grace Covenant's membership had also dropped to eighty. Lydia's membership, which had been as high as sixty during the 1950s, dipped to twenty-one in 1968. By 1984 it had rebounded slightly and stood at thirty. McCullough's membership had risen to fifty-three by 1968, but in 1982 there were only twenty-nine members. First Presbyterian Church of Ware Shoals, which had a membership of 309 in 1949, had only 133 members in 1984.

It is clear that the Presbyterian Church experienced mixed success in South Carolina's textile mill villages. In 1961 Ernest Trice Thompson described the difficulties that the Presbyterian Church had in the mill villages. He noted that the PCUS was "a middle-class church, lacking a vital relation to the community life around it, unaware, *complacently* unaware, of the religious needs and interests of large numbers of laboring people who are rapidly drifting away from any church . . . "[44] Reverend Arthur Martin echoed these sentiments in a sermon preached before the Synod of South Carolina in 1962. Although he was referring to more recent industrial development in the state, his comments are equally applicable to the situation earlier in the century:

> As industry has developed and rural workmen have moved into villages and cities to become industrial workmen, our Presbyterian Church has not been too quick or successful in following them . . . There is danger that our Presbyterian Church will be looked upon as a white collar or class church . . . The church needs more working men in its membership and also in its church courts . . . While we can thank God for the excellent Presbyterian churches we have now serving in industrial communities such as in Greenville and Union and Lancaster . . . we need more and stronger churches in industrial . . . areas, and we need ministers to man them." [While Presbyterians can] thank God for Holiness Churches which have moved into our industrial communities . . . this does not excuse us."[45]

Conclusion

Throughout the late nineteenth and early twentieth centuries, Presbyterians had been hard at work ministering to the less advantaged residents of the south. Home missionaries from the PCUS labored hard in the Appalachian Mountains and in the textile mills of the Carolinas. Others from the PCUSA engaged in a widespread effort to provide a quality education for the region's African Americans. These three efforts faltered, however, as the twentieth century advanced. Presbyterianism proved to be less attractive to mountain people and textile workers than the more evangelical faiths. In addition, the Depression decreased funding for such efforts. South Carolina's extensive system of parochial and boarding schools for African Americans fell prey to the Depression and to competition with new public schools for black students. The system, too large to support adequately, eventually ceded to public schools that were separate but clearly not equal. But this educational effort left an important legacy in the many leaders that were educated in its schools and colleges.

---

44. Thompson, *The Spirituality of the Church*, 39.
45. Arthur Martin Papers, "The Gates of Hell Shall Not Prevail," 2–3.

3

Church and Society

Worldly Amusements and Weightier Matters

THE SYNOD OF SOUTH Carolina's debates and statements about social issues between 1925 and 1985 reflect changes at the General Assembly level, including its ecumenical ties with other, churches as well as changes in the broader national and international setting. In the late nineteenth and early twentieth centuries, the denomination joined a common Protestant consensus for state laws enforcing Sunday as a civil holiday and opposing the manufacture and sale of beverage alcohol. In doing so it abandoned its previous commitment to avoiding political advocacy and spoke out on these issues. The synod's debates on issues such as temperance, observance of the Sabbath, dancing, divorce and remarriage, abortion, and homosexuality illustrate the pattern of change in its deliberations. They shed light on the priorities and struggles conscientious Presbyterians faced in considering historically important social and moral issues in the middle decades of the twentieth century.

The Synod of South Carolina brought forward diverse points of view for discussion and action. By gathering commissioners from across the state together in a governing representational body, the synod enabled local congregations to address broader outlooks than they would have otherwise readily considered. Sometimes the deliberations were hot and divisive, sometimes inconclusive, and sometimes productive. The way the Synod of South Carolina considered social ethics and political life changed continually and rapidly over the advancing years of the middle of the twentieth century.

A Changing Pattern in Considering Public Issues

During the earlier decades, the PCUS conformed to "the spirituality of the church," the teaching of James Henley Thornwell (born 1812, died 1862), professor at the Theological Seminary in Columbia and professor and President of South Carolina College. His philosophy restricted the scope of the church's governing bodies solely to the appeal of the gospel of Christ to individual conversion and salvation. This restriction was intended to maintain the church's "ministerial and declarative authority." It aimed to avoid deliberation or statements by church governing bodies on civil issues, leaving them to civil legislators.[1]

Slavery was the main public issue that Thornwell wanted banished from consideration. In the years after the Civil War, Thornwell's doctrine offered socially conservative members of the PCUS shelter from many of the stormy blasts of public debate. In the 1920s, the moral concerns expressed by the synod were largely confined to "worldly amusements," the dangers in the culture considered to be threats to personal salvation.

The strict separation between matters of personal salvation and public policy became less clear as the twentieth century progressed. The boundaries blurred especially in debates about Sabbath observance and Prohibition.[2] Initially these matters might appear to be matters of individual piety or morality. However, as they became enshrined in blue laws, closing business and public facilities on Sundays, and in the Prohibition Amendment to the US Constitution, many Christians became active in political advocacy. Southern Presbyterians joined the chorus, and Thornwell's strict exclusion of civil politics became impractical to follow in church debates.

At the turn of the last century, many US Christians, both conservative and liberal, felt that Sunday observance was a hallmark of Christian America. The PCUS was one of the founders of the American Sabbath Union, an interdenominational organization that was organized in 1888 and later became the Lord's Day Alliance. Ultimately, the General Assembly created a permanent committee on the Sabbath related to the International Sabbath Association in New York. In 1908 the Committee on the Sabbath reported bluntly, "If the Christian Sabbath goes, all is gone."[3] But by 1923, the Permanent Committee of the Sabbath and Family Religion had been abolished.

Furthermore the PCUS became one of the early members of the Federal Council of Churches of Christ in America (founded in 1908) to promote home and foreign missions. Some southern Presbyterians served in leadership roles for the council. Walter Lee Lingle served as chair of the Federal Council's executive Committee during the 1920s, and J. McDowell Richards, president of Columbia Seminary, served as vice president of the

1. Thornwell, "The Church a Spiritual Power, 490.
2. Coalter, Mulder, and Weeks, *Vital Signs*, 2–6.
3. Weeks, "The Scripture and Sabbath Observance," 269–70, 273–4, 282.

FCC during the early 1940s. Southern Presbyterians embraced ecumenical cooperation with other denominations.

According to Erskine Clarke, "From the first, the Council was a forceful advocate for the theological perspectives and social concerns of the social gospel. Among its purposes was to 'secure a larger combined influence for the churches of Christ in all matters affecting the moral and social condition of the people, so as to promote the application of the law of Christ in every relation of human life.'"[4]

Walter Lingle, President of Davidson College from 1929 to 1941, was one of the early proponents of the social gospel in the PCUS.

Walter Lee Lingle as a Student at Davidson College
(Courtesy of Davidson College)

First influenced by the theories of Walter Rauschenbusch (born in1861), Lingle embraced many social issues during his long career as pastor and educator. By couching his concerns in terms of Christ-like social service, he managed to widen the church's viewpoint without getting so far out ahead of it that he lost its respect. His popular course in sociology at Union Theological Seminary in Virginia and his editorship of the *Union*

---

4. Clarke, *Our Southern Zion*, 153.

Theological Review allowed him to lead many Presbyterians toward more interest in social issues.[5]

Lingle and other reformers in the PCUS walked a fine line between the doctrine of spirituality and social progress. They continued to emphasize the transformation of individual members as the fundamental hope for social change rather than urging the church to political action. However, in its public advocacy for Sunday blue laws and Prohibition and its collaboration with interdenominational efforts in foreign and home missions, the PCUS moved beyond Thornwell's strict doctrine.

In 1934 the PCUS, in answer to several overtures, one of them coming from Piedmont Presbytery in South Carolina, took note of its heightened concern for the application of the Christian message to the public order by establishing a Committee on Social and Moral Welfare. Over the years, the intent remained the same although the name of the committee was changed to the Committee on Christian Relations (1946), the Council on Church and Society (1966), and the Task Force on Social Concerns, created as part of the new Synod of the Southeast in 1973. The typical Presbyterian penchant for work by committees gave organizational form to its commitment to the consideration of public, social, and moral questions as part of its official work.

The 1934 General Assembly did not charge the newly formed committee with organizing a program or defining a future course, but only with reporting "a program of scope and attitude." Noting that the church's tradition had been separation of church and state and "our people are resolved to preserve that principle," the General Assembly also recognized that church members "are likewise determined upon guiding the churchman to a more effective citizenship."[6]

Church historian Ernest Trice Thompson viewed the committee's first report, submitted in 1935, as a milestone. It recognized the "responsibility of Christian men to apply the principles of Christian love and justice to all relationships." Thompson observed that previously the PCUS had focused its mission on evangelism and individual or family morality. Wider social problems like racism, economic inequality, industrial relations, and conditions in the South's numerous textile mills were virtually ignored.[7]

Thompson asserted that by this application of love and justice to social and political life, the southern Presbyterian denomination began to reclaim its Calvinist heritage of social ethics. However, he foresaw a new challenge

---

5. Flynt, "Feeding the Hungry," 106–13.
6. General Assembly, 1934, 33–4.
7. Thompson, *Spirituality*, 40–1.

that came with the expansion of social concerns. "The great problem here and in other areas has been, and will remain, to secure the acceptance of the social implications of the gospel, by the members of our church—acceptance that is resolutely translated into action."[8]

In 1936 the PCUS Committee on Social and Moral Welfare issued a wide-ranging report on a number of issues. They condemned gambling of all kinds, including trading on the stock market. They recommended the establishment of an alcohol education program, support of leaders who were in favor of world peace, and low prices for consumers. They asked for wage fairness, improved conditions for sharecroppers, and the abolition of child labor, lynching, and obscene movies.

There was lengthy discussion over what some considered alignment with partisan politics, and the report was amended to say that "the provinces of the church and the state are separate and one should not usurp functions of the other. These statements are merely given as an opinion of the committee and not to define the missions of the church." Committee chair Stuart R. Oglesby, pastor of Central Presbyterian Church in Atlanta (from 1930 to1958), made it clear that the recommendations were merely intended to "instruct our people within the church on social problems. We do not intend to go outside the church and tell the government what to do."[9]

A number of commissioners to the General Assembly, including R. F. Kirkpatrick of First Presbyterian Church, Anderson, protested the assembly's acceptance of the any part of the committee's report, declaring that "some of the matters concerning which this report deals are not only secular but they are of a highly controversial nature." They inquired, "Why should we leave our divinely given task to become embroiled like many of our sister churches in the bitter controversies now raging in the economic, political and social realms, and spend our energies upon the many human nostrums and panaceas, while we have ready at hand and as our exclusive right the one and only remedy which can effect a real and permanent cure for the ills of the individual, and, ultimately of human society?"[10]

By 1940, however, the committee's report reflected an increasing interest in society's problems. Saying "our church leadership has always sought to inculcate Christian principles for the solution of individual problems," it recognized that church members were also members of other groups and thus "shared in the sins of his society." It concluded that "religion has not infrequently been divorced from life, and . . . multitudes of church members

---

8. Ibid., 44.
9. General Assembly, 1936, 94.
10. Ibid., 1937, 59–60.

have felt that they were under no obligation to carry Christ with them into business or society.[11]

The Synod of South Carolina waited until 1939 to appoint its Committee on Social and Moral Welfare "in accordance with the set-up of the assembly." The first report of this committee to the synod in 1940 contains an eloquent defense of social action on the part of the church:

> The objective of the church in its broadest sense is the establishment of God's Holy Law in the hearts of individual men everywhere and in those institutions which express the corporate life of mankind . . . Certainly there is a testimony which the Church must bear to the social (including religious and political) institutions concerning their moral responsibilities and objectives. Nothing is further from the mind of our committee than to suggest that the Church adopt an attitude of sterile legalism or of precarious social actionism. Either course would be a betrayal of our mission. Our plea is for the Church to exercise its declarative functions by bearing testimony to the whole Counsel of God for all men and institutions of men everywhere.[12]

In subsequent years the synod, like the denomination, was less concerned about dancing, card playing, and observance of the Sabbath. Opposition to dancing and card playing, with some exceptions, had practically disappeared by the 1920s, while the denomination continued its concern about temperance and Sabbath observance. By the 1940s, while blue laws relaxed, customs of Sunday worship and Sabbath observance were beginning to compete for time with commerce, recreation, and the unrelenting requirements of the world crisis leading to World War II. Following the war, while allegiance to church going achieved its widest appeal in the history of the US, issues like school prayer, labor-management issues, poverty, race relations, and communism began to surface.

In 1945 the General Assembly made a statement on worldly amusements, rejecting the limitation of concern to Thornwell's "spirituality of the church" by broadening its sense of responsibility for social and moral concerns. The assembly declared that "principles and practices that mar Christian character and influence have their roots in the heart and may be, and often are, manifested as dangerously in business, politics, race relations, and in national selfishness and isolationism, as in amusements."[13] This last

---

11. Ibid., 1940, 127.
12. Synod of South Carolina, 1940, 36–9.
13. General Assembly, 1945, 143.

statement was an early indication of the direction the denomination would take in the last half of the twentieth century.

Following the lead of the denomination, that same year the Synod of South Carolina's Committee on Social and Moral Welfare presented a wide-ranging report on the moral problems of the day. Among these were the large number of war divorces, the use of Sunday as a weekend holiday, and the increase in sexual activity and venereal diseases. They recommended "church groups throw their whole influence in the agencies that are striving to find an adequate solution for the drink evil." They concluded, "The most effective way of handling all problems of vice is through enlightened public sentiment," and "all the teaching agencies of the church are urged to mold and shape public sentiment that will frown upon public evils and promote public virtues."[14]

In 1946 the General Assembly reorganized its Committee on Social and Moral Welfare into the Department of Christian Relations and increased both funding and staffing. The new department was intended to "produce suitable literature for informational and instructional purposes," to "speak to the churches" on social issues, and to "speak for the churches when commissioned to do so, or when the Assembly's [social] pronouncements are to be carried out." Among its stated goals were to "point out existing evils and unwholesome conditions which endanger the spiritual or moral welfare of individuals or groups or nations," and to suggest measures to ameliorate them. The committee was to recommend specific actions only when they promoted "the Christian welfare of our own or other nations, or of individuals or groups within these nations."[15]

That same year, the Synod of South Carolina heard from its study of the recreational programs of the church. Noting "the world is staging a brilliant offensive drive to educate our people to the theory that entertainment and recreation are the chief ends of human life," they recommended that the church organize a recreational program that would make "human life a bigger thing than can be staged on a playground."[16] They again denounced lascivious dancing and engaging in games and amusements on the Sabbath.

By 1948, the Synod of South Carolina had its own Committee on Christian Relations, which shared the aims of the General Assembly's committee. The committee once again reported at length on such moral issues as divorce, sexual delinquency, and gambling. Its reports brought

---

14. Synod of South Carolina, 1945, 33.
15. General Assembly, 1946, 167.
16. Synod of South Carolina, 1946, 39–42.

the expanding denominational commitment to public issues to pastors and members of Presbyterian congregations in South Carolina.

The committee also made a statement on economic life and the relationship between labor and management. The recent passage of the Taft-Hartley Act (1947), which regulated and restricted labor unions, was a matter of great concern to the textile industry in the state. Members were also concerned about recent decisions on religion in public schools. The Supreme Court ruled in *McCollum v. Board of Education* (1948) that public schools could not let students out of class or adjust class schedules for religious teaching during the school day even if they provided study halls or alternate classes for non-participants. The synod asked for a "redoubling of efforts to have the decision overruled."[17]

Local congregations sometimes let their social concerns be known at the General Assembly, the highest level of the PCUS. In 1949 Pee Dee Presbytery, in one of the most conservative regions of the synod, presented an overture to the General Assembly concerning euthanasia. Noting that "several hundred Protestant ministers and Jewish rabbis have gone on record publicly as approving the legalizing of the practice commonly known as euthanasia," and "at least two ministers of the Presbyterian Church in the United States have expressed themselves as in agreement with the purpose of such legislation," the presbytery asked the General Assembly to "hand down a deliverance regarding the practice of euthanasia." In answer the denomination's Committee on Christian Relations recommended "the Assembly advise that according to our understanding, we believe euthanasia is unscriptural and contrary to the law of God."[18]

The synod considered the relation of Christian faith to a variety of other moral issues in society. At their annual meetings, synod members participated in these discussions, sometimes with enthusiasm, sometimes with members objecting. The synod's openness encouraged representatives of local congregations to engage with other denominations in considering the social application of Christianity.

By the late 1950s and 1960s, there was increasing evidence of discord within the PCUS over its involvement in issues that some members regarded as purely secular. In his centennial address to the Synod of South Carolina in 1961, C. Darby Fulton, longtime head of world missions, warned:

> The same danger, so clearly seen by Thornwell, of the secularizing of Christianity by a gradual drifting into areas outside of the church's principal concern, calls us to renewed vigilance.

17. Ibid., 1948, 48.
18. General Assembly, 1949, 40.

The church herself can lose sight of her spiritual and redemptive message through absorption in the overwhelming political and economic issues of the day. This is crucial. It is not that we should talk less about peace, or relief, or 'the building of a new world.' This part of our message, the duty of man to man, is vital; but it is not enough . . . we are living on an 'unearned spiritual increment' that may exhaust itself in time unless it is replenished by a revival of vital faith in the cardinal doctrines of God, Christ, regeneration, and salvation. Hence the critical importance of holding to a central emphasis on the spiritual and redemptive message of Christ and Him crucified as the one hope in salvation of men.[19]

In the 1960s a variety of matters of public policy became controversial. In 1962, in *Engel v. Vitale*, the US Supreme Court had ruled that any officially sanctioned prayer in school was in violation of the First Amendment, even if the prayer was ecumenical and students were given the option of remaining silent or leaving the classroom. In response, Pee Dee presbytery urged the General Assembly "to join with other churches in asking the Supreme Court to refrain from such deliverances as may tend to establish our Nation before the world as a Godless Nation, and may tend to establish a Godless humanism as a national religion." The assembly's Standing Committee on Bills and Overtures declined to support the request, noting that the Supreme Court did not receive such protests.[20] In 1965 Harmony Presbytery addressed the topic of sexual relationships outside of marriage. Noting that even some ministers seemed to have no objection to such relationships, the presbytery affirmed that "the moral standards [had] not been abrogated, nor repealed, and . . . anyone who disobeys such does so at his peril and therefore dishonors God."[21]

Arthur Martin, Executive Secretary of the synod, while seeing the divisions in the denomination in its theological and social deliberations, was nonetheless hopeful. He voiced a moderate stance in his sermon "The Gates of Hell Shall Not Prevail Against Her," delivered during a worship service at the 1962 synod meeting: "[There] are problems before the church, theological, moral and social. Every problem challenges and threatens, and tempts us to fright and frustration. These trials threaten us with failure. We

---

19. Synod of South Carolina, 1961, 88.
20. General Assembly, 1963, 24.
21. Harmony Presbytery, May 18, 1965, 8.

may fail, local churches may fail, our Presbyterian Church may fail, but the Church of Christ cannot fail."[22]

South Carolina Presbyterians also worked on social issues through their support of the South Carolina Christian Action Council. This ecumenical organization, representing denominations statewide, provided information on public affairs and helped local congregations to educate their members on social and moral issues. Member churches included mainline denominations and independent churches representing both white and African American congregations. Over the years, the Council focused on such issues as gambling, the death penalty, race relations, the Vietnam War, poverty, communism, and anti-Semitism.

With the debate about social issues in the 1960s, the PCUS's cooperation with other denominations, widely appreciated during and immediately after World War II, became controversial. Objections to Presbyterian membership in the National Council of Churches (NCC) became a major issue in 1964. Arthur Martin wrote to the NCC that he had had "the dangerous honor" of trying to defend it against charges of communism at a recent synod meeting. He also noted, "We don't pay much for our part on the council (and that is begrudged bitterly by many in these parts)."[23]

In 1964 W. D. Workman, assistant editor of *The State*, wrote an editorial article about the NCC's involvement in the Mississippi Summer Project, organized by a coalition of Civil Rights groups to register African American voters. In the summer of 1964 over one thousand persons were arrested. Three or more Mississippi black people and four civil rights workers from other states were murdered during ten weeks marked by violence. Though the National Council of Churches did not organize the project, it offered, through its Commission on Religion and Race, to help train workers and provide ministers to accompany them as counselors and mediators. Workman objected to the liberal churches meddling in politics in this way.

Arthur Martin defended the NCC response. Citing information from the NCC, Martin noted that the civil rights workers involved in the project had been recruited by other organizations to work in Mississippi, and the NCC Commission on Religion and Race had merely offered volunteers to provide training for them. According to Martin, the workers would have gone to Mississippi even without NCC training. The NCC was in no way involved with "the policy, strategy or rationale of the project," although it

---

22. Arthur Martin Papers, "The Gates of Hell," June 1962.
23. Ibid., Martin to National Council of Churches, June 2, 1964.

did share in the project's intention to obtain full equality under law for all citizens of Mississippi and every other state in the nation[24]

On July 28 McQueen Quattlebaum wrote a spirited refutation of Arthur Martin's stance. He noted that the Synod of South Carolina had removed funding for the National Council of Churches because it did not agree with its policies. Numerous South Carolina presbyteries had futilely asked the denomination as a whole to withdraw from the NCC, but the General Assembly had declined to submit the request to its presbyteries for a vote. He concluded that he respected Arthur Martin's opinion, but he did not think he should be publishing such material in his role as executive secretary of the synod. He added that Congaree Presbytery, of which Martin was a member, had recently approved an overture stating that "no one has the authority to speak for any church organization unless that organization gives him the authority."[25]

In a personal letter sent to Quattlebaum on July 30, Martin reminded him that the General Assembly had included a non-budgeted item for the NCC and had also urged the church's representatives on the NCC to "use their influence to bring the council's actions more in line with our policies." He concluded that he had written to Workman as a private citizen; it was Workman who chose to identify him as the Executive Secretary of the Synod.

Martin's appeal for moderation and due process in ecumenical deliberations did not satisfy the objectors. A few days later, the low country churches of Harmony Presbytery gathered, and the vast majority of the commissioners voted to withhold all funds from the General Assembly's causes until the assembly withdrew from the NCC. Only one church, Shaw View, near the Sumter airfield, declined to approve because it objected to withholding funding to register complaint, not because it supported all the decisions of the NCC.[26]

Martin wrote about the pressures he felt in a letter to Reverend Dr. T. Watson Street, Executive Secretary of the Board of World Missions for the PCUS. Martin criticized Carl McIntire and J. Gordon Holdcroft of the Bible Presbyterian Church (organized in 1936) for using "continued blasts at Communism in the National Council of Churches, [and] unorthodox liberalism in our church[es]." The vocal conservatives, Martin said, wanted to encourage Presbyterian laymen to withhold funds from the agencies of the General Assembly, "and their next step would be to withdraw." Martin

---

24. Ibid., Martin to W. D. Workman, July 18, 1964.
25. Ibid., "Presbyterians and the Council," July 28, 1964.
26. Ibid., "31 Churches of Harmony Presbytery," July 1964.

continued, "Perhaps we should have two objectives in this time of crisis. One, to see if we can stop the National Council's headlong direct actions in the field of politics; and, two, watch the arch separatist as he dangerously endeavors to cut sheep out of the Southern Presbyterian fold . . . The coincidence of political and ecclesiastical objectives at this time does increase the danger."[27] Martin's prediction that churches would withhold funds as protest proved true, and the withdrawal of congregations from the PCUS came to pass in the decade following.

C. Darby Fulton, the former missionary to Japan and executive leader of the PCUS missionary effort, continued to voice a conservative position in the PCUS. Fulton believed that the NCC was so broad theologically that it was in fact shallow and lacked a strong basis in faith. Its message was primarily economic, political, and social, and similar to that of numerous secular organizations. Its activities often verged on lobbying. Even though the council did not technically speak for its member institutions, its pronouncements were often interpreted as "the voice of Protestantism."

In a letter written to Martin in October 1964, Fulton avowed,

> I have a deep sympathy for those in our Church who are dismayed over what they see as a rapid erosion of faith within our own denomination. At this point I share their concern . . . Our people have a real problem. Carl McIntire is not the solution. Because of the marked inroads of liberalism into the Council I feel that our membership in this organization is no longer an asset to our church . . . It has thrown the weight of its influence behind a sociological creed to the neglect of the Gospel of God's redeeming grace in Christ . . . We have no business lending our influence to an organization that has so far departed from the Church's primary trust.[28]

Fulton was a principled conservative, but he remained loyal to the PCUS. Others were planning to withhold their contributions and withdraw from the denomination, and congregations and presbyteries were joining the reaction.

In April 1968, Covenant Presbyterian Church in Columbia held a joint meeting of elders and deacons and informed the congregation that they had decided "to withhold all benevolent gifts of the congregation from the boards and agencies of the General Assembly and to divert these gifts to the causes of Synod, Presbytery, and the benevolent work of the local church." The officers explained,

27. Ibid., Martin to Reverend T. Watson Street, September 25, 1964.
28. Ibid., C. Darby Fulton to Reverend Arthur M. Martin, October 8, 1964.

> Your elders and deacons believe true stewardship demands a concern for the expenditure of the Lord's money . . . boards and agencies of the General Assembly have been using funds dedicated to God in ways which are, at best, questionable. Benevolent funds have been used to support strikes, to hire lobbyists in Washington, to use economic pressure on businesses, to promote socialism and selective pacifism, to aid controversial organizations outside the church, and in many other ways which are not agreeable to the mission of the church. An equalization process makes it impossible to designate effectively the benevolent gifts of a congregation. All General Assembly causes benefit equally from any contributions made, even those designated for specific purposes . . . Your officers took this action with heavy hearts, but with the assurance that it is their right according to the constitution of the Presbyterian Church and their duty to the consciences of themselves and of the large majority of Covenant Church.[29]

On September 11, 1968, the stewardship committee of Congaree Presbytery recommended that the budget for 1969 eliminate the General Assembly's causes and divide the funds between the synod and the presbytery. Conservative supporters organized by Reverend Hugh W. McClure III, pastor of First Presbyterian Church, Columbia, took responsibility. Others were opposed to the recommendation. Proposals for the presbytery to withhold funds from the PCUS offices were defeated on close votes. McClure then threatened to have First Presbyterian Church, Columbia, withhold its own annual gifts, about $60,000 to the General Assembly.

Arthur Martin wanted the synod to ply a moderate course through these storms. He wrote to Rev. Dr. Cecil H. Lang, who served at First Presbyterian Church, Columbia, from 1964 to 1972. Martin explained his position: "We have a time defending experimental board actions and protesting the extreme lefters. But we do love the church and will work and fight as needed to protect and promote her. By church, I mean, Presbyterian US, which to me is my visible church."[30]

For some, however, the middle was coming apart. W. D. Workman, then chief editor of *The State*, wrote an opinion piece called "Grapes and Thorns," taking aim at the NCC. This editorial prompted Martin to write to Dr. R. H. Edwin Espy, General Secretary of the NCC, still hoping for a middle path: "Public sentiment is critical and even bitter about the NCC and its 'meddling,' and editors like this one make a business of distorting

---

29. Ibid., Copy of an undated statement signed by Harry T. Schutte.
30. Ibid., Martin to Dr. Cecil H. Lang, September 20, 1968.

Council actions against it. We often wish the Council didn't take sides in open questions such as this one appears to be. It increases the difficulty of us who want to keep our churches in the Council."[31]

Denominational leaders were worried. In an undated letter to Dr. T. Watson Street, Executive Secretary of the Board of World Missions, Martin wrote that First Presbyterian Church, Columbia, would "probably seek some capital items to which they can give without 'fear of equalization' or 'integration.' We think the situation is right serious, but hope the tide locally will turn before long."

In May 1969, Arthur Martin noted that preachers who spoke out on social issues were often deemed communists: "In fact, so many preachers have spoken out . . . that it is getting to be the custom to say that 'the preachers have been brain-washed.' The question, of course, is who washes their brains." He believed that rather than the communists, the "Spirit of God in the Word of God" might be responsible, which "is what ought to happen to every minister of the Gospel as he studies his Bible and prayerfully prepares to preach its relevance to his day."[32]

The Martin family were active members of First Presbyterian Church, Columbia. On June 23, 1969, Arthur Martin's wife Mary sent her own personal contribution directly to Thomas B. Whaley, the treasurer of the church, designated for the Central Treasurer of Benevolences of the General Assembly. Along with her contribution she sent a statement of loyalty to the PCUS and all of its causes:

> I hope this will not cause you unnecessary trouble, but with the Minister and Session of the First Church seeking to choke the Assembly into submission by cutting off funds, we who love the Presbyterian Church and wish to support her worldwide work must be more careful than usual. The simple thing would be to make contributions through another church which supports the whole work of the Presbyterian Church, but I have known and still hope better things for the First Presbyterian Church of Columbia as a progressive leader in the Presbyterian Church, U.S.[33]

Meanwhile the PCUS, through its Council on Church and Society, continued to issue papers on a wide range of social issues including race relations, conscientious objectors, disarmament, economic justice, welfare reform, drug abuse, and prison reform. The Synod of South Carolina

---

31. Ibid., Martin to Dr. R. H. Edwin Espy, October 1, 1968.
32. Ibid., "Brainwashing," 2.
33. Ibid., Martin to Thomas B. Whaley, June 23, 1969.

appointed a similar committee in 1970. Its purpose was to pass on PCUS reports of special local interest, to "plan and promote programs designed to encourage Synod and her member courts in the social application of the Christian gospel," and to maintain contact with the South Carolina Christian Action Council.[34]

As a regional governing body, the Synod of South Carolina evidenced a greater commitment to denominational and ecumenical causes than many of its local congregations. As the synod was being taken into a new regional organization, the Synod of the Southeast, in 1973, South Carolina members requested that the new synod "give all due notice and encouragement to the Christian Action Council of South Carolina" and that "every endeavor be made to maintain the close relationship" of the council to the presbyteries of the state of South Carolina.

The Council identified six issues "to which the Church in South Carolina should give attention and leadership": race, public education, poverty, alcohol and drugs, government reform, and improvement of correctional and prisoner-rehabilitation programs. The regional body would continue to be an advocate for the application of the gospel to pressing matters of social compassion and equity.

In September 1973, the strains in the PCUS prompted General Assembly moderator Charles E.S. Kraemer to write in the *Presbyterian Survey*:

> There is considerable difference of interpretation in regard to the social implications of the gospel of Jesus Christ. Everyone believes that there must be social implications. Some would say that the fruits of the gospel in our relationships to our fellowmen should be manifest in personal and individual ways only. Others of us believe that it is not possible to be true to the whole gospel without getting into community and social and political areas. Those so commissioned come together, ask for the guidance of the Holy Spirit, discuss and argue and debate, and, by a democratic voting procedure, say, "This is what this court of our church interprets to be the will of God at this time." Those who believe they should object are permitted to object and to pray and work to influence the court to change, and no one is ever forced to go against what he or she conscientiously believes to be the Word of God.[35]

Dissident churches planned a December meeting to form a new denomination. In October, facing the withdrawal of 211 churches from the PCUS, J.

---

34. Synod of South Carolina, 1970, 51.
35. Kraemer, "A Pastoral Letter," *Presbyterian Survey*, October 1973, 3–4.

McDowell Richards, moderator of the Synod of the Southeast, sent a communication to the 639 churches in Georgia and South Carolina. He rejected the idea that liberals were leading the church to ruin and urged churches not to withdraw, but instead to "work through church courts to make the denomination 'pure and strong.'"[36]

Plans for the new denomination proceeded however, and resulted in the organization of what was to become the Presbyterian Church in America (PCA) on December 4, 1973 in Augusta, Georgia. The date was chosen to mark the 112th anniversary and place of the founding of the Presbyterian Church in the Confederate States of America in 1865, renamed Presbyterian Church in the United States. The strength of the leadership for organizing the PCA lay in Mississippi, Alabama, and South Carolina.

In 1974 the General Assembly reported continuing "unhappiness and division within our church" and "imminent division." The equalization of member contributions to fund the PCUS budget and the PCUS membership in the World Council of Churches and the National Council of Churches caused both unhappiness and division. Those leaving the denomination also had other grievances. For example, they cited the PCUS decision to approve divorce based on "non-biblical grounds," its 1970 approval of abortion for "socio-economic reasons," its funding of secular and sometimes controversial actions, and "numerous Assembly policy errors, such as approval of the new morality, civil disobedience, [and] social drinking." They were seeking a return to origins and traditions they wanted to maintain. The assembly expressed its fondest hope that "those who have not yet departed have confidence in our system, that persons of good spirit will seek to find a balance in the corporate life of the church so that they may remain in the PCUS with increasing satisfaction."[37]

The largest South Carolina group of departing congregations went to the PCA in the years between 1973 and 1979. A smaller group left shortly before and after 1983, when the Presbyterian Church (USA) brought together the two largest Presbyterian denominations (UPCUSA and PCUS). Between 1973 and 1985, fifty-one Presbyterian congregations joined the Presbyterian Church in America, and six left for the Associate Reformed Presbyterian Church (ARP).

The Synod of the Southeast, representing Presbyterians in South Carolina and Georgia, continued to make statements on social issues. Among its adopted goals and recommended objectives in 1978 was to encourage presbyteries and congregations to "cooperate with their local communities'

---

36. "Ignore Division Call," *Florence Times*, October 7, 1973, 7.
37. General Assembly, 1974, 302–6.

ministry in the area of human needs such as criminal justice, hunger, drug and alcohol abuse, child abuse, unwed mothers, one-parent families, and energy."[38] In 1979 the synod established a task force on social concerns designed to call attention to specific areas each year and to enable presbytery leaders to develop responses suited to their particular needs. The task force commented on a number of issues over the years including justice and compassion (1980), economic justice and the Christian faith (1982), and peacemaking and hunger action (1983).

Rev. J. Phillips Noble, pastor of First (Scots) Presbyterian Church, Charleston, represented the middle ground that held together.

Reverend J. Phillips Noble

In 1979 he discussed the reluctance to address social questions by the Synod of the Southeast:

> I realize that Presbyterians do many things individually as do local churches, but are there not some issues that the Presbyterian Church in Georgia and South Carolina as a collective body

38. Synod of the Southeast, 1978, 73.

needs to deal with? Are we so comfortable with our society that we have nothing to say or do? It is inconceivable to me that this is the case! I do not ask for controversy nor do I want it, but I want less an ease that doesn't deal with issues in our two states that affect human life. The Presbyterian Church has had and can have a strong influence in many areas. I personally would like to see this Synod find better ways to inspire and lead Presbyterians in grappling with important issues that affect human faith and life in our particular decade.[39]

The middle position espoused by Arthur Martin, J. Phillips Noble, and other more progressive pastors and members lasted through the divisions. Working at unity, sometimes in agreeing to disagree about the meaning and application of Christian faith, brought most members together in the 1983 joining of the PCUS and the UPCUSA to become the largest Presbyterian denomination in the United States.

Response of the Synod of South Carolina to Various Social Concerns

Temperance and Prohibition

South Carolina's Presbyterians were interested in temperance very early. "Solomon's Caution Against the Cup," a sermon delivered in 1730 by Josiah Smith, was probably the first temperance sermon preached by a Southern minister. During the early part of the nineteenth century, numerous temperance societies were established in South Carolina, many of them supported by Presbyterian pastors and lay people. But while southern Methodists and Baptists began to take a political stand on the issue, the PCUS confined itself to encouraging abstinence and describing the dangers of alcohol use and abuse. As early as 1909, other church courts like the Presbytery of North Alabama urged their people to support a prohibition amendment to the state constitution. This action echoed through the General Assembly for a number of years, as the 1910 General Assembly upheld the right of the presbytery to such an endorsement, and the 1914 General Assembly itself finally and officially endorsed the proposed prohibition amendment to the US Constitution.[40]

There were those who protested this move, feeling that this response was "a deliverance upon a political question and hence was a violation

---

39. Ibid., 1979, 34.
40. Coker, "The Sinnott Case of 1910," 254–8.

of the scriptural function of the Church of God and contrary to the historic position of our Church on the right of the Church to make political deliverances."[41] Among those who protested were Reverend S. C. Byrd, the president of Chicora College, Reverend G. M. Wilcox of Walhalla, Reverend Rollin T. Chafer of Fourth Church, Greenville, Reverend J. F. Matheson of Union, and Reverend F. D. Viehe of Bennettsville.

In 1915 South Carolina prohibited the public sale of alcohol statewide. Early prohibition did not eliminate the manufacture and sale of liquor in the state. According to historian Walter Edgar, bootlegging was rampant in the Carolinas at the time, with between 25,000 and 40,000 people involved in the illegal liquor trade.[42] In 1919 the states passed the Prohibition amendment to the US Constitution. During this period, the Synod of South Carolina made no official pronouncements on the subject.

This began to change in the 1930s. In May of that year, the South Carolina Democratic Party's Hampton County delegation asked the state Democratic Convention to endorse a state referendum on prohibition, declaring that "the noble experiment of the Eighteenth Amendment has been a complete failure, as Woodrow Wilson foresaw when he vetoed the prohibition law."[43] In the spring of 1933, following the election of Franklin D. Roosevelt and recognizing the impending repeal of Prohibition, the state legislature decided to permit the sale of 3.2 percent beer, which was considered non-intoxicating. This action promised to add more than $1 million in additional tax money to the state's treasury. The decision had a direct effect on at least one church institution. Based on the legalization, Thornwell Orphanage decided to refuse any state aid because the state derived part of its revenue from a tax on beer sales.[44]

In 1933 the Synod of South Carolina took up the issue but split over the traditional commitment to the old doctrine of the spirituality of the church and chose not to make their discussion of the alcohol laws a matter of official business. Instead, they took a recess so that those attending the meeting might hear "in their private capacity as Christian citizens" an address by Reverend C. E. Burts of the Southern Baptist Convention, representing those in South Carolina working to retain Prohibition. This bit of legerdemain by the synod was a nod to Thornwell's doctrine.

Reverend S. J. L. Crouch, Reverend G. W. Irby, and Reverend W. H. Mills protested this tactic, maintaining that it was impossible to separate the

41. General Assembly, 1914, 80b.
42. Edgar, *South Carolina in the Modern Age*, 37, 68.
43. "Seek Dry Law Referendum," *New York Times*, May 22, 1933, 3.
44. "Beer on Every Side," *New York Times*, April 9, 1933.

role of private citizen from the role of church representative for men in attendance at a church court. In addition, they felt that there were "questions upon which it becomes ... the duty of Church Courts to instruct the people as regards their political behavior." They went on to assert that "not only may a Church Court ... testify to the citizens individually and separately respecting their civil duties, but that Court may sometimes be required to testify to the nation itself."[45]

The commitment of South Carolina Presbyterians to Prohibition brought consideration of public policies clearly into the ordinary business of church government, and the voice of change in the protest would more and more guide the position of the Synod of South Carolina. In 1934, in advance of a non-binding liquor referendum included in the Democratic primary, the synod adopted a resolution on state laws governing the sale and distribution of alcohol. This resolution declared that the use of alcohol for beverage purposes poisoned the body, intoxicated the brain, dethroned reason, degraded morals, and jeopardized spiritual life, and asked church members to abstain from its use. More remarkably, the synod made a direct plea to the state government, asking the legislature to "refrain from partnership in this terrible business by clothing it with legality." The Synod no longer shunned political advocacy.[46]

Many Presbyterian ministers in South Carolina were staunch advocates of the temperance movement. One of these was Reverend Fred T. McGill of Greer, who used the church bulletin to expound on numerous issues, including the use of alcohol. He decried the deaths caused by drunken drivers on the highways and noted that, "S.C. legalizes liquor, encourages her people to buy it for the sale of taxes. How long, O Lord, how long?"[47]

Showing its determination to address the alcohol problem, albeit not in the political realm, in 1936 the synod appointed two members to meet with representatives from other denominations in a Council on Alcohol Education. In October of that year, these representatives recommended that the synod appoint two members to represent it on the Council, provided its functions be limited to alcohol education and not provide for any form of political activity. In subsequent years, reports from the Committee on Alcohol Education were given to the synod as supplements to reports of the Committee on Social and Moral Concerns. Thus, out of its reluctance to engage in politics, the synod managed to work through the ecumenical coalition for alcohol education.

45. Synod of South Carolina, 1933, 13–4.
46. Ibid., 1934, 10.
47. Blackwell, *A People and Their Faith*, 132.

During the 1940s, the synod concurred with the denomination's advocacy of personal abstinence from alcohol consumption. The PCUS was concerned about the damage to society caused by drinking (particularly for the military), the rise in alcohol-related accidents, and the prevalence of alcohol-related crime. The governing bodies encouraged citizen advocacy with state and local government for laws to curb liquor sales and consumption. The synod and presbyteries did not hesitate to criticize social customs, business practices, and state legislation. Widespread church opposition to alcohol consumption appears in frequent social pronouncements.

For instance, the synod heard a colorful report describing members of the liquor industry as "vultures abroad in our land," seeking to debauch young servicemen through alcohol. They decried the industry's "unbridled greed and the unprincipled preying on man's more sensuous nature in time of spiritual and moral tension and moral upheaval."[48] Enoree Presbytery endorsed public advocacy, urging members to contact their congressmen to "earnestly urge your active support to the amendment now under consideration in the Senate excluding alcoholic beverages from and around military posts."[49]

The critique of beverage alcohol called business interests to account and opposed the state's Alcoholic Beverage Control Act which provided licenses for the sale of alcohol. On hearing a report that the annual liquor bill for South Carolina had reached $46 million and that the liquor industry was one of the largest advertisers of the day, the synod urged action:

> Perhaps no nation at any time in the world has given such an example of the worship of profits as our nation has done at the command of the liquor industry. [Church members should strive] to speak out and act whenever and wherever the moral and social conditions demand words and deeds, to take more interest in the affairs of their government by seeking to enlist the good people to assume public obligation, to vote in all of the elections, and to bring to bear the ethics of the Christian religion ... upon community life.[50]

In 1945 the Committee on Alcohol Education submitted a report noting the "disturbing and disgusting" consequence of the Alcoholic Beverage Control Act, which would make the state "the official 'bar-keeper' within its borders and thus engaging directly in this foul work of making drunkards

---

48. Ibid., 1941, 49–52.
49. Enoree Presbytery, October 20, 1942, 14.
50. Synod of South Carolina, 1942, 46–9.

and sending her citizens to destruction."⁵¹ The synod's corporate action was more restrained. It asked the committee to concentrate on alcohol's influence on "the social and moral welfare of the state of South Carolina," including its effect on crime, mental health, and family life. They also asked them to "study the tremendous drain upon the finances of our state and the resulting increase in poverty." ⁵²

The committee submitted its report the following year. They concluded that 75 percent of all arrests in the state were a result of drinking by some of the parties, that increased use of alcohol resulted in an increase in insanity, and that alcohol was a cause of 90 percent of the divorces in the state. They noted that South Carolinians spent $60 million annually on alcohol, with $40 million of this going to out-of-state distillers and wholesalers, and quoted a judge who declared that bootlegging had increased 100 percent since the repeal of Prohibition. Noting that many of the state's legislators had been "blinded by the revenue so that they could not see the evils of the liquor traffic," the committee recommended that there should be local option elections where citizens could decide about the sale of alcohol in their communities. Committee members requested that ministers, elders, members of the Woman's Auxiliary, and religious educators discuss these issues in their local churches.⁵³

Subsequent reports recommended abstinence on the part of church members, urged the government to enact and enforce controls on the manufacture, sale, and use of alcoholic beverages, and decried the use of alcohol revenues for the purposes of education, maintaining that "it is wrong to let [our children] grow up with the impression that their education is in any measure dependent upon the volume of whiskey and beer that may be bought and drunk by their elders."⁵⁴ They commended the work of the South Carolina Federated Forces for Temperance and Law Enforcement and Alcoholics Anonymous and urged church members to give them their moral and financial support.

In 1949 the committee's report dealt with the liquor industry's advertising campaigns, particularly a campaign launched by the beer industry entitled "Home Life in America" which encouraged daily beer drinking in the home. "It will be an evil day for America when the home life of our people becomes befouled with the stench of alcoholic beverages in whatever

---

51. Ibid., 1949, 33.
52. Ibid., 1945, 48–9.
53. Ibid., 1946, 52–6.
54. Ibid., 1948, 50–1.

form."[55] They also expressed concern about social drinking by church officers and members. These sentiments continued into the 1950s. In 1966 the synod cautioned against more liberal liquor laws and urged that greater revenue go toward enforcement. The joint pressure of the churches in the state led to the defeat of a proposal for more permissive laws. However church advocacy for liquor legislation diminished during this time.

In the 1970s the PCUS moved away from strong advocacy for voluntary abstinence and expressed its concern for alcoholics in therapeutic terms, "their health and wholeness of life and with the health and wholeness of society."[56] The denomination affirmed the focus on education and rehabilitation, and on the creation of a society which did not encourage excessive drinking. Thus, in a little over sixty years, the emphasis of the PCUS had changed from advocating total abstinence and prohibition laws to educating its members about alcohol use and aiding in rehabilitation of alcohol abusers.

The early cooperative efforts of South Carolina denominations first in advocacy for prohibition and later against its repeal became the beginning of a very significant ecumenical organization, the South Carolina Christian Action Council. The Council grew out of the interdenominational South Carolina Federated Forces for Temperance and Law Enforcement, organized in 1931 to foster "the elevation of the moral order, the promotion of temperance, and those projects that look to the curing of injustice and evil." Representatives at this first meeting declared that "the time has come for our several denominations . . . to join hands in the common fight to preserve a Christian standard of morals, righteous laws, law observance, temperance, patriotism, and righteousness."[57]

This group included several prominent Presbyterians over the years, among them Reverend J. M. Wells, Governor John G. Richards, Reverend C. T. Squires, and Reverend Sam Phillips. Reverend Neil Truesdell, the pastor of Aveleigh Presbyterian Church in Newberry, served on the 1950 committee that recommended the name change to the Christian Action Council and the adoption of a constitution which allowed for a focus on issues other than temperance.

---

55. Ibid., 1947, 39; 1949, 68–9.
56. General Assembly, 1970, 123–4.
57. "Churchmen Join in Morals Move," *Clinton Chronicle*, September 8, 1931, 3.

Reverend Neil E. Truesdell (Courtesy of Presbyterian College)

Truesdell served as the Council's president from 1960 to 1964. It was his statement in support of Harvey Gantt's admission to Clemson that galvanized other churches to take up the cause. Dr. Joseph T. Stukes, a ruling elder and college professor of history, chaired the planning committee for the first Inter-Collegiate Seminar in Legislation and Government and served as the council's president from1969 to 1972. Other Presbyterians who were prominent in the council's work were Arthur Martin, William Boyd, Scott Barnes Jr., Palmer Patterson, and William Arthur. The council gradually developed from a one-issue organization to "a broad-based social concerns agency, ecumenical in nature and purposes . . . functioning as an information-educational advocate for the churches' involvement in ecumenism and public affairs."[58]

Observing the Sabbath

At the beginning of the twentieth century, most Protestant denominations considered observance of the Christian Sabbath essential for the spiritual

58. Synod of South Carolina, 1983, 75.

health of the United States. The PCUS had formed a Permanent Committee on the Sabbath in 1878. Preachers urged their flocks to say no to Sunday railroad and trolley travel, Sunday newspapers, and attendance at concerts and sporting events on Sunday. As in the case of beverage alcohol, Presbyterians were comfortable with a counter-cultural edge in urging Sabbath observance.

Many of the church's Sabbath concerns were more or less openly political. In 1893 the General Assembly objected that the Columbian Exhibition in Chicago was open every day of the week. World War I and the popularity of Sunday sports and other recreational activities only increased concern. The General Assembly of the PCUS congratulated Woodrow Wilson for "stemming the tide of Sabbath desecration in the armed forces." The assembly called on church members to "work with political leaders to insure Sabbath laws, necessary for both national survival and Christian freedom."[59]

After the war, in the midst of the Roaring Twenties, it became increasingly hard to maintain traditional values. By 1923 the General Assembly had disbanded its Permanent Committee on the Sabbath and Family Religion, choosing to address the issue through its Committee on Publication and denominational involvement in the Lord's Day Alliance.

Sabbath observance was an important issue in South Carolina. During this period, seven out of ten South Carolinians belonged to a church, the second highest percentage in the United States after Utah. This made the churches a powerful force in addressing Sunday openings and the pursuit of sporting events and leisure activities like golf on Sundays. In order to curb these practices, the South Carolina legislature re-enacted the state's centuries-old blue laws in 1922. Among the activities prohibited were public sports (such as football, baseball, and horse racing), plays and movies, and outdoor pursuits such as hunting and fishing. The laws prohibited merchants from selling gasoline, soft drinks, cigars, cigarettes, and ice cream on Sundays.

When Governor John G. Richards, a Presbyterian elder, was inaugurated in 1927, he came into office declaring that he would make South Carolina a "leader in righteousness" before the world.

---

59. Weeks, "Faith and Political Action," 111.

Governor John G. Richards (Courtesy of the
University of South Carolina)

He served as governor until 1931 and was fairly successful in stamping out such forms of gambling as lotteries, games of chance, and slot machines. However, his crusade to enforce the blue laws caused a statewide furor.[60] Beginning in early 1927, Richards stepped up enforcement statewide. Drug stores, cigar stands, refreshment stands, and filling stations were closed, and newspaper boys could not sell their papers on the streets. Restaurants were open to serve food but could not sell tobacco. Officials swore out warrants for offenders in Greenville and Aiken. In an interesting twist, since the blue laws actually prohibited Sunday arrests except in cases of treason, felony, or breach of peace, police could not actually arrest the wrongdoers. Local courts were brought into the fracas and promptly threw out the cases.[61]

By the end of March, he had suspended his campaign, but he renewed his efforts in 1928, ordering the sheriff of Charleston County to arrest those participating in automobile and boat races and free movies on the Sabbath. That year the legislature further relaxed the Sunday laws, and Governor

---

60. Edgar, *South Carolina in the Modern Age*, 66.

61. "Clamp Lid on Entire State," *Clinton Chronicle*, February 24, 1927, 1; "Blue Laws are Revived," *New York Times*, February 21, 1927, 19.

Richards called it "a direct attack upon the fundamentals of our Christian civilization."[62]

After 1931 the denomination's emphasis on Sabbath observance began to wane. Although the General Assembly's Permanent Committee on the Sabbath in 1948 voiced concern that "the neglect and profanation of the Day has continued and increased to an alarming and distressing degree," by 1950 the committee itself disappeared.[63] A report from a temporary committee in 1958 recommended reinterpreting the idea of Sabbath observance, viewing it as a family day and a time of rest and recreation. Leisure activities such as physical exercise, reading books, and listening to music, all typical weekend activities, were recommended.

Concern lingered on the local level, however. In 1959 Reverend W. McLeod Frampton, pastor of First Church in Orangeburg, offered a resolution to the Synod of South Carolina noting a "growing tendency to secularize the Lord's Day," and asking for "a study of certain practices, programs, and activities which are being scheduled on Sunday," and "to contact officers of our sister denominations requesting their cooperation and support of a united effort in correcting practices which violate the Christian concept of the Day."[64]

After a year's study, the report of the Committee on Secular Practices on the Lord's Day recognized the Sabbath as a time of the most intimate union of the Christian with the Lord. Noting attempts in the courts to overturn blue laws and the increasing number of business, entertainment, and recreational programs scheduled on Sunday, it recommended starting a program of active cooperation with other denominations for the sacred observance of the Lord's Day.

The committee expressed a concern about secular society, asking pastors and elders to discourage church members "from participating in business, commercial entertainment, or recreation on the Lord's Day, and asking that members recognize the spiritual nature of the Day and abstain from participating in buying goods or attending commercial entertainments or recreations on the Lord's Day."[65] Members of Charleston Presbytery addressed this issue at a meeting in May of 1961. Noting that television, magazines, and movies were powerful influences, they urged church members to "speak to the ills of our society . . . refrain from un-Christian activities . . .

---

62. Cann, "John G. Richards and the Moral Majority," 21.
63. General Assembly, 1958, 181.
64. Synod of South Carolina, 1959, 56–60.
65. Ibid., 1960, 56–9.

[and] promote Christian ideals in business life, social life, community life, as well as in the home."[66]

The concern about Sunday observance diminished after the 1960s. The General Assembly of the PCUS began to conduct its church business on Sundays, although it did provide for delegates to attend church services, delaying the start of the session until three o'clock in the afternoon. In 1969 members of the Lord's Day Alliance questioned their decision.

In response, the General Assembly defended Sunday church business: "We feel a full understanding has been reached that our General Assembly recognizes the Lord's Day as not one to be marked only by prohibitions, but is a day dedicated to the worship and service of the Lord. Since the General Assembly is gathered for these very purposes, we have affirmed to the Alliance that no distinction can be made as to what part of the General Assembly's docket is appropriate for Sunday."[67]

A similar instance arose in the Synod of the Southeast as late as 1973. Harmony Presbytery protested a synod meeting scheduled for Sunday, July 1, citing the inconvenience of such a meeting for ministers and ruling elders and its disobedience to the Fourth Commandment as well as the Confession of Faith and the Larger and Shorter Catechisms." This protest was fruitless; the synod held the meeting as scheduled.

Dancing

The PCUS had long-standing questions about dancing. The church's early concern about dancing, one of the threatening "worldly amusements," continued into the twentieth century. In 1927 members of the Presbytery of South Carolina raised concerns about dancing and other social activities on the Presbyterian College campus. While dancing was prohibited on the campus itself, dances were held off campus at Copeland Hall in downtown Clinton. The Board of Trustees of the college assured the presbytery that they disapproved of "dancing on the Campus; of young ladies visiting the fraternity halls unchaperoned; and of the commercialization of the social activities of the students," and promised to refer their disapproval to the President and faculty of the college "with the request that they take such steps as may seem desirable to give this policy effectiveness in the campus life."[68]

---

66. Charleston Presbytery, May 16, 1961, 6.
67. General Assembly, 1970, 202.
68. Presbytery of South Carolina, Fall 1927, 72.

In 1932 six Clinton pastors, including D. J. Woods of First Presbyterian and L. Ross Lynn and Samuel P. Bowles of the Thornwell Memorial Church, asked the synod to overrule an action of the Board of Trustees of the college permitting four dances per year on the campus. The local ministers regarded the board's action as "detrimental to the best moral interest of our town and to the work of our churches."

A committee studying the request concluded "while recognizing the perplexing situation confronting the Board and Faculty with reference to this all too prevalent form of worldly amusement . . . promiscuous dancing with its glaring physical contacts tends to lower the spiritual tone of those engaging therein, and not seldom leads to the gravest consequences." The synod responded that "modern social dancing is an amusement that wars against growth of Christian character." It asked that the synod's educational institutions forbid dancing on campus and advised that housing "participants of the opposite sex" in campus dormitories on the occasions of dances held off campus was "an unwise procedure."[69]

In 1934 the student body at PC asked the synod to cease intervening in social activities on campus, thus providing an opportunity for review of the 1932 decision. A special committee consisting of Reverend John W. Davis, Reverend F. Ray Riddle, and Elder Henry E. Davis considered the petition but reaffirmed the previous position, observing that the matter of dancing presented a question of Christian principle and not merely a detail of social activity.

The synod's response caused repercussions on the campus. A college trustee who was a lay delegate to the synod spoke strongly against the student petition. When the college newspaper, *The Blue Stocking*, was critical of his stance, the trustee demanded a public apology and disciplinary action. President John McSween, himself a Presbyterian minister, was unable to extract the apology and refused the disciplinary action on the basis of free speech. The board member subsequently resigned and withdrew his support of the college.

---

69. Synod of South Carolina, 1932, 28–9.

Reverend John McSween (Courtesy of Presbyterian College)

President McSween, in his subsequent report to the Board of Trustees, said,

> The debates in the Synod of South Carolina on the matter of dancing here at the college have not helped our cause. It has seemed to me that much unnecessary heat has been released in these debates and many statements made in the heat of the debate which were unnecessary, unfounded and harmful not only to the college but to the whole matter of the relationship of the Church to her young people . . . It is my conviction that this board is better qualified to direct the details of the social life of our students than a body like the Synod.[70]

At a meeting of Enoree Presbytery in 1944, members asked the denomination to make a statement on recreation in the churches, for the reason that "former deliverances of the General Assembly on the subject of dancing are obsolete and do not apply to present day conditions, and . . . congregations of our denomination are promoting round dancing, often accompanied, according to reliable reports, by practices, which, together with

70. South Carolina Presbytery, 1934, 62.

the dancing, bring reproach and condemnation upon the Church and great grief to many of our members."[71]

Their request, however, was never delivered to the offices of the PCUS. In 1945 the synod's Committee on Judicial Business refused to hear a communication from Reverend John C. Blackburn on dancing at the First Presbyterian Church in Columbia. The committee noted in their decision that no member of the church and "no group of the citizens of the community appearing personally or otherwise," had joined in Reverend Blackburn's complaint, and that he had no evidence to support his claim of "lasciviousness, uncleanness and fornication in connection with the dances."[72]

After World War II, protests against dancing disappeared. In 1945 *The Presbyterian Outlook* polled two hundred ministers and their wives on the subject of dancing and found that one third of ministers and one half of their wives had danced before marriage, that nine out of ten children of ministers danced, and that more than 75 percent of the church's youth danced.[73]

That same year, the General Assembly decided that it was impossible to use scripture to condemn dancing per se, and that "lascivious" dancing was already almost universally condemned. Activities like dancing, going to the theater, and playing cards were not evil in themselves but were sometimes perverted by evil motives. The assembly advised, "It would be better for the Church to warn against over-indulgence in, and abuse of these and other amusements, and to encourage positively all wholesome recreation and fun . . . If a Christian finds that his amusements . . . are taking him away from Christ, it is his duty to give up, or to bring them into conformity with the Christian ideal."[74]

Divorce and Remarriage

During the 1920s, the PCUS began to be very concerned by the rising divorce rate. At the time, the denomination recognized only two legitimate grounds for divorce, infidelity, and willful and prolonged desertion, and allowed remarriage after divorce only to an innocent party in the case of infidelity.

In 1929 the denomination's General Assembly heard from a temporary committee studying divorce. The committee recommended that willful desertion be removed as legitimate grounds for divorce and reaffirmed that

---

71. Enoree Presbytery, April 11, 1944, 11.
72. Synod of South Carolina, 1945, 53-4.
73. Thompson, *Presbyterians in the South*, Vol. 3, 515.
74. General Assembly, 1945, 152.

the innocent party in case of infidelity was permitted to remarry, but not in haste. In the event of remarriage, "both persons should recognize the sacredness of the marriage vows before God, as apart from a civil contract." Appended was a lengthy minority report. Those who disagreed with the majority felt that "refusing to recognize divorce except for adultery, the Church actually encourages immorality, illegitimacy and concubinage ... [and] in our judgment, brutality, willful and prolonged desertion, sex perversion, and perhaps some other causes constitute what may be termed 'moral equivalent [of infidelity]' ... However desirable it might be to have a uniform rule, the matter of the remarriage of divorced persons must be left to the judgment and conscience of the individual minister."[75]

For the next decade, the denomination continued to consider its stance on divorce and remarriage and continued to affirm that the limited grounds for divorce were adultery and willful desertion. These grounds remained the acceptable standard. It further defined "willful desertion" as not "mere separation, through agreement or otherwise," but "*malicious* desertion." In the case of desertion, only the innocent party would be eligible for remarriage in the church. In 1938 its advisory committee recommended that each presbytery appoint a Permanent Advisory Committee on Divorce and Remarriage to decide case by case whether a proposed remarriage would be acceptable to the Church.[76]

Since South Carolina was the only state in the union where divorce was illegal on any grounds, this discussion at first seemed irrelevant to the state's Presbyterians. However, divorces were easily and cheaply available in neighboring states. In Augusta, Georgia, divorces outnumbered marriages by a factor of three to one, largely because many South Carolina couples crossed the border to have their marriages dissolved. According to an article published in *The New York Times*, there were 157 marriages performed and 504 divorces granted in Augusta in 1936.[77] South Carolina citizens were debating the issue. In 1937 the state legislature defeated a proposed constitutional amendment that would have permitted divorce, but the amendment eventually passed in 1949, legalizing divorce in cases of adultery, desertion, physical cruelty, and habitual drunkenness.

In 1948 South Carolina Presbyterians expanded their concern to the impact of divorce on family life. In anticipation of the 1949 vote, the Synod of South Carolina's Committee on Christian Relations delivered an

75. Ibid., 1979, 142–7.

76. Ibid., 1938, 114.

77. "Would Make Georgia New 'Reno' of the Nation," *New York Times*, January 18, 1937, 19.

extensive report on strengthening the Christian family. While urging that only the innocent party in any divorce be permitted to remarry, the committee recommended that voters "exercise their best Christian judgment in the upcoming vote . . . [and] refrain from a Pharisaical legalism in regard to divorce as in all matters. While trying to safeguard the institution of the home we must avoid doing violence to individual personality and bear in mind that the function of the church is redemptive."[78]

In 1950 the committee urged local congregations to order copies of the General Assembly's report on divorce and remarriage. Presbyteries in the local regions of South Carolina appointed study committees on the family. Bethel Presbytery had already created a committee on Christian Home and Community which dealt with divorce in addition to other moral concerns. In 1950 Pee Dee Presbytery established a Committee on the Remarriage of Divorced Persons to advise ministers. Congaree Presbytery's advisory committee, formed in 1942 and intended "to counsel with Ministers seeking advice on problems of remarrying divorced persons and to counsel with others who seek advice on remarriage of divorced persons," became the Committee on Remarriage of Divorced Persons in 1951.[79] In 1953 the Presbytery of South Carolina organized a similar committee. These committees endured into the 1960s, advising congregations and pastors how to offer appropriate pastoral care in the case of divorce.

It was more than a decade after South Carolina law permitted divorce that the General Assembly made a definitive pronouncement, loosening the grounds for divorce. Couples should consider divorce only as a last resort, appropriate "where a continuation of the legal union would endanger the physical, moral or spiritual wellbeing of one or both of the partners or that of their children."[80]

In the case of an application for remarriage, "the minister's chief concern shall be the applicant's present fitness of heart and life for the intended marriage." If the applicant for remarriage had been at fault in the previous relationship, "the mere fact of previous guilt (however grievous) should not be held as a rigid and final disqualification for remarriage under the auspices and with the sanction of the Church." In all cases, the minister was to be mindful of "what this person by God's grace has now become and what, with God's help, he (or she) honestly intends and hopes to do in the future."[81]

78. Synod of South Carolina, 1948, 46.
79. Congaree Presbytery, January 9, 1951, 21.
80. General Assembly, 1959, 70–1.
81. Ibid.

Not all South Carolina churches agreed, however. Enoree Presbytery asked the General Assembly to reconsider its actions. In its report to the presbytery in April 1959, committee members noted that there was a further need "for revision and clarification of the Church's position with respect to marriage, divorce, separation, annulment, and remarriage," and asked for careful biblical study of the "Scriptural proof texts alleged to support positions," as well as further clarification of the role of the minister in counseling couples.[82]

The issue of divorce of clergy surfaced in the 1970s. In 1974 the Commission on the Minister and his Work of the Presbytery of South Carolina reported with regret that one of its ministers was in the process of being divorced. Noting that the General Assembly had ruled in 1941 that each presbytery could decide whether a divorced minister could serve, the presbytery went on record as sharing "the grief of the breakup of this family," reaffirming the Bible's admonition that marriage should be "till death do ye part," but at the same time allowing the minister to continue his work.[83]

Abortion

In the early 1970s, the PCUS was torn by the abortion debate in society at large and among its members. The General Assembly addressed the subject in 1970, noting that "attitudes toward abortion laws are shifting, and Christians are being asked to clarify where they stand and what light their Biblical faith sheds upon decision making in this area." It asserted that while abortion is "the willful destruction of the fetus . . . [and] the decision to terminate a pregnancy should never be made lightly or in haste," there were certain cases where circumstances justified such a step. The church itself needed to become more concerned about problem pregnancies and counsel women about the various choices, "in order that they act responsibility in the light of their moral commitments, their understanding of the meaning of life, and their capacities as parents."[84]

In 1971 a group presented a resolution to the Board of National Ministries of the PCUS asking that a "comprehensive Bible study on God and the unborn child, and a historical study of the teaching and practice of the primitive Church and of the Constitution of our own Church in regard to abortion be circulated to its counsellors on problem pregnancies, and to those who seek their counsel in this matter."[85] The General Assembly re-

---

82. Enoree Presbytery, April 7, 1959, 8D.
83. South Carolina Presbytery, August 1, 1974, 70.
84. General Assembly, 1970, 125-6.
85. Ibid., 1971, 140.

fused and reaffirmed the 1970 statement. However, the debate continued and the General Assembly requested guidance on abortion, its safety, its morality, its legality, and its relation to Presbyterian polity.

Governments were also addressing the issue of abortion. On January 22, 1973, in *Roe v. Wade*, the Supreme Court issued its decision legalizing abortion. South Carolina laws on abortion changed accordingly. On July 16, 1973, in *State v. Lawrence*, the South Carolina Supreme Court declared the current abortion laws unconstitutional. The following year the South Carolina legislature passed laws similar to the ruling of the US Supreme Court. The decision in *Roe v. Wade* caused the PCUS to affirm its commitment to the health and wellbeing of individuals and families, declining to "make decisions for persons," but instead deciding to "provide the moral and theological context and a supportive community in which discussion, decision making and compassionate ministry can occur."[86]

This stance did not satisfy everyone. Bethel Presbytery was quick to respond, declaring that "policies and activities governing abortion are not a part of the Constitution of the Presbyterian Church US." Members of the upper state presbytery asked the assembly to discontinue support of the Committee on Therapeutic Abortion. The General Assembly denied the request, and assigned its General Education Board to "establish or designate appropriate committees or agencies capable of, and equipped for, ministry to those in need of counsel and guidance relating to abortion, and that the Committee on Therapeutic Abortion be recognized as one of these."[87]

Opposition to denominational abortion policy grew. Pee Dee and Congaree presbyteries, led by First Presbyterian Church, Florence, and Shandon Presbyterian Church, Columbia, objected to the denomination's affiliation with the Religious Coalition for Abortion Rights and urged withdrawal of support. In 1981 Congaree Presbytery raised additional objections to abortion on demand.

The PCUS reiterated both its comprehensive statement on abortion, "The Nature and Value of Human Life" (1981), and the right of a woman to choose in consultation with her physician, based on "the freedom to struggle with just such awesome and difficult decisions." PCUS commissioners from Charleston, Congaree, and Piedmont presbyteries joined a formal protest against the denomination's statement.[88]

Among Presbyterians in South Carolina, the storm clouds of the abortion debate shadowed the next decade. Many were not content with the mainline PCUS policy advocating pastoral care and support for women while concurring with the legalization of abortion permitted by both the US

86. Ibid., 1973, 134–44.
87. Ibid., 1974, 164.
88. Ibid., 1981, 62, 286–304.

Supreme Court and state law. The debate over the right to life and women's right to decide was one of a number of issues that led many to join the conservative movement that formed the Presbyterian Church in America while the majority approved the merger to form the Presbyterian Church (USA) in 1983.

Homosexuality

Beginning in the 1970s, the church also started dealing with the issue of homosexuality. In 1972 the General Assembly received a resolution asking that it "reaffirm its conviction that homosexual behavior is a grievous sin, that marriages (so called) between two of the same sex are contrary to the divine plan and under divine wrath (Romans 1:27); but . . . that the church expresses its deep love and compassion for all those struggling with this problem . . . and offers its Christian help and counsel to assist them in making normal and wholesome adjustments to life."[89] By 1976 the General Assembly had expressed its "sense of urgency concerning this matter."

In 1977 the Council on Theology and Culture distributed a report entitled "The Church and Homosexuality: a Preliminary Study." Noting that no General Assembly report can speak for God, for the denomination, for all individuals, members or even a majority of those members, the Council presented its report as "a paper or statement by a particular assembly" to be used as "a basis for study."

After summarizing biblical interpretation, theological and ethical considerations, and clinical data, including the 1973 decision by the American Psychiatric Association to remove homosexuality from its diagnostic list of mental disorders, the report posed three broad positions that the church and its members might take on the subject of homosexuality. The first position was that homosexuality is a sickness or arrested psychosexual development; the second, that homosexuality is sinful; and the third, that homosexuality is a legitimate variety of human sexuality.

The statement confronted the disagreement among Christians about homosexual orientation and declined to propose any one position for the church. Instead it put forth some suggested guidelines to be used by church members, sessions, and presbyteries. The PCUS reflected the uncertainty of its members and fell short of decisive conclusions beyond urging compassionate pastoral care. The response did very little to quell division in the denomination.

At its April 1978 meeting, Pee Dee Presbytery objected to the General Assembly's study because it failed to "condemn the practice of homosexuality

---

89. Ibid., 1972, 182.

as a sin." The presbytery approved a resolution, asking the General Assembly to declare that homosexuality is a "grievous sin."[90] That same year, in an overture presented to the General Assembly, the Presbytery of South Carolina affirmed its "adherence to the clear Biblical teaching concerning the sinfulness of all homosexual acts." While confirming its "compassionate concern for this group," the presbytery asserted that homosexuality was not a lifestyle that should be acceptable in the eyes of God or his people. In regard to church officers, the presbytery felt that all "unrepentant" homosexuals should be barred from serving as elders, deacons, or teachers. Harmony Presbytery submitted a similar overture. The General Assembly declined to act on these resolutions, referring them to the Council on Theology and Culture, which continued to study the issue.[91]

In 1979 the Council on Theology and Culture submitted a report entitled "Homosexuality and the Church: a Position Paper." The paper presented a version of a policy statement previously issued by the United Presbyterian Church, "adapted to make it appropriate for use in this report and in our church." The paper included positions on several aspects of homosexuality. In regard to theology, their conclusion was that "homosexuality is not God's wish for humanity." In regard to the issue of church membership, the report concluded that "the church is not a citadel of the morally perfect, it is a hospital for sinners . . . Homosexual persons who sincerely make a profession of their faith and obedience should not be excluded from membership." Ordination, however, was a different matter: "For the church to ordain a self-affirming practicing homosexual person to ministry would be to act in contradiction to its charter and calling in scripture . . . Our present understanding of God's will precludes the ordination of persons who do not repent of homosexual practice." These actions, however, were not to be used "to affect negatively the ordination rights of any Deacon, Elder, or Minister who has been ordained prior to this date in the Presbyterian Church in the United States."[92] Discussion and controversy about homosexual ordination remained unresolved at the time of the reunion of the two main branches of the Presbyterians in the US and continued in the following decades.

Conclusion

In this survey of the consideration of social concerns in the Synod of South Carolina, a pattern emerges. During the 1920s James Henley Thornwell's doctrine, "the spirituality of the church," held sway. It observed "proper

90. Pee Dee Presbytery, April 11, 1978, 41.

91. South Carolina Presbytery, April 11, 1978, 38; General Assembly, 1978, 75–76, 190.

92. General Assembly, 1979, 201–9.

ministerial authority" by restricting the deliberations of the governing bodies of the church to matters of the preaching of the gospel for individual conversion and salvation, leaving the governance of the civil order to voting citizens and their elected officials.

During this time, Presbyterians tended to be concerned about such issues as dancing, observing the Sabbath, and the problems caused by alcohol. As Walter Edgar observed, during the rising affluence of the Jazz Age in the rest of the country, South Carolina was still trying to cope with economic recovery, and in the 1920s and 1930s, the insularity of the state caused many to seek refuge in traditional social and moral values.[93] In the case of Prohibition, the church entered increasingly into the political arena. Almost in spite of themselves, Presbyterians left Thornwell's doctrine of the spirituality of the church behind, both by joining other denominations in ecumenical organizations and in embracing the debate about the repeal of Prohibition.

This pattern of addressing public concerns and expanding ecumenical partnerships, though often contested, continued. In the 1930s, as World War II approached, Presbyterians became more open to solidarity with other members of the Christian church. North American society became more diverse and mobile, and traditional southern sectionalism diminished. These changes brought the denominations to clearer organized advocacy for social concerns.

The continuation of a concern for "worldly amusements" into the 1940s certainly shows that the socially conservative commitments of traditional Presbyterians had not died out in South Carolina. For many Presbyterians the church offered help and reinforcement in the face of modernization and challenge to the old ways. In the last half of the century, the PCUS expanded its agenda so broadly that it included such public issues as world food policy, the manufacture of high-mileage cars, the regulation of pesticides, economic justice, the establishment of a Martin Luther King holiday, the plight of the Cambodian people, the crisis in El Salvador, labor relations, and the boycott of Nestle products.

At this same time, Presbyterians became increasingly interested in other moral issues such as divorce and remarriage, abortion, and homosexuality. After careful consideration, the General Assembly gradually moderated its strict opinions on these subjects. As was the case with earlier issues, however, the more conservative Presbyterians in South Carolina were sometimes reluctant to follow the Assembly's lead.

---

93. Edgar, *South Carolina, a History*, 483.

4

A Work of Real Spiritual Power

Women and the Presbyterian Church

WOMEN HAVE ALWAYS MADE up a large part of the membership of the Presbyterian Church, and they have been very active in all of its programs. In the early days of the church, they were not allowed to speak in mixed groups, and they could not serve as church officers or pastors. Instead, they organized local women's societies to study the Bible or to support foreign missions and local causes. They often raised funds for equipping and improving their churches and sometimes even did the work themselves. They were active teachers in the Sunday schools and helped to organize young people's societies. In the nineteenth century, they were also able to serve as home and foreign missionaries, sometimes alone and sometimes with their husbands. In the 1920s, churches began to hire women as pastor's assistants or directors of Christian education. Gradually, they joined committees of the General Assembly and its synods. In line with the policies of the Presbyterian Church (PCUSA) to which they belonged, South Carolina's African American Presbyterian churches began to ordain women as deacons in 1923, and by 1956 they could become pastors. Finally in 1964, the presbyteries of the PCUS voted to ordain women as officers and ministers of the word and sacrament, and women finally were able to take their place as full members of the PCUS.

Women's Societies

Before 1964 and the ordination of women, one of the main arenas for women's leadership in the Presbyterian Church was through the women's auxiliaries. This movement started quite early. The first "Female Charitable Society" seems to have been established in Newark, New Jersey, in 1803.[1] By 1811 the organization of various missionary, tract, and Bible societies

---

1. Penfield, "Women in Presbyterian Church," 108.

by Presbyterian women prompted the General Assembly to observe, "It has pleased God to excite pious women also to combine in associations for the purpose of aiding by their voluntary contributions." The assembly went on to add, "Benevolence is always attractive, but when dressed in a female form, possesses peculiar charms."[2] By the 1880s there were a number of women's groups in both white and African American churches in South Carolina.

African American Congregations

Although women's societies existed in both African American and white churches, the first Presbyterian women to organize on the presbytery and synod levels were African American women who belonged to PCUSA churches in the state. On the local level, one of the first women's missionary societies organized in the Atlantic Synod was at Ladson Church in Columbia. Mrs. Mack G. Johnson, who was the wife of the church's first pastor, founded the society which was to become very significant in the church's life. Mrs. C. M. Young and Mrs. Gertrude Sanders were prominent leaders for many years.

Among organizations on the lower, or presbytery, level, McClelland Presbyterial was organized at the Second Presbyterian Church in Abbeville in 1886. Fairfield Presbyterial was organized a year later, and Atlantic Presbyterial in 1903.

Mrs. Lillie B. Nelson, Goodwill Presbyterian Church, who was prominent in women's work at all levels

2. Ibid., 108–9.

The synod-wide organization in the Atlantic Synod first met in November of 1885 in Macon, Georgia. The first president was Mrs. E. V. C. Williams, and early leaders from South Carolina included Mrs. B. F. McDowell, whose husband was the pastor of Matoon Presbyterian Church in Greenville; Clarkie Hughes Young of Rock Hill; and Mrs. William L. Metz, wife of the pastor of the Edisto Presbyterian Church. The development of these organizations largely preceded the development of non-religious women's groups dedicated to social reform, philanthropy, and education. The South Carolina Federation of Colored Women's Clubs (SCFCWC), for example, was not organized until 1909.

The local church groups initiated a number of activities. Hopewell Presbyterian Church in King's Creek, for instance, organized Bible studies, held fellowship services, sponsored youth programs, conducted workshops on such subjects as food preservation, provided counseling services for young married couples, and wrapped gifts for needy families at Christmas. Those at Pleasant Grove Church in York sponsored a Mother's Day program, a May fellowship, and a World Day of Prayer service. They also supplied clothing for newborn babies in the congregation.

Women of all races in the PCUSA were strong supporters of the schools that the denomination had set up for the education of freedmen. The Board of Missions for Freedmen created a separate sub-group for women, the Department of Freedmen (often called the "Women's Committee") in 1884. When the separate women's committee was disbanded in 1923, women continued to work through the Unit of Schools and Hospitals, which dealt primarily with boarding schools, and the Division of Work for Colored People, which dealt with the day schools. The women's groups raised large amounts of money for scholarships, teachers's salaries, and new school buildings. From 1918 to 1919, for instance, in the midst of World War I, 5,005 women's societies in the PCUSA contributed over $90,000 toward the cause.[3]

African American presbyterials collected supplies for schools and churches through the "Box and Barrel Project." The 35th Annual Report of the Women's Committee, written in 1919, reported that "the contents of boxes have helped clothe the needy children in many of our Schools and Churches. Sewing materials were needed and supplied in work-rooms. Little gifts have made the Negro boys and girls happy at the Christmas Season ... Every box sent, with nice clean garments and new material, carefully packed, is a help as well as an object lesson in neatness to our pupils in school and home."[4]

---

3. Parker, *The Rise and Decline of the Program of Education for Black Presbyterians,*" 3–4.

4. Thirty-fifth Annual Report, 1919, 223–4.

In addition the women organized a Colored Worker's Conference, provided literature for study classes and missionary education, and even published a study book, "The Negro, an American Asset." In 1919 despite the shortages of material and labor caused by World War I, they provided money for a farmer's house at Harbison College. The committee's report included an observation that sounds very familiar to our modern ears: "It costs $500.00 to put a Negro boy in a Christian School for ten years, but every one arrested and tried, costs tax-payers $2000.00. Let us think on this statement."[5]

The war also had its effect on social conditions:

> A new consciousness has come to these dusky defenders, from the experiences through which they have passed in these dark days of our conflict. The Negro women and girls at home have caught a new vision of life. If we are to be together in a *crisis*, as we have been, we must be together in times of peace in the broadest sense of mutual understanding and helpfulness. We must let them know that justice will triumph and that democracy shall indeed find its truest place in America. The only thing that will make our democracy safe is the practice by the white race and the black, of those principles Christ taught two thousand years ago. The Christian Church, better schools, and the home, must be given them.[6]

Many of the women leaders in the Synod of the Atlantic, which included churches in South Carolina, Georgia, and Florida, were from South Carolina. In 1924 eight out of the ten officers of the Atlantic Synodical were South Carolinians, including the president Mrs. M. M. Jones of McConnellsville, the first vice president, Mrs. G. W. Long of Cheraw, and the second vice president, Mrs. J. R. Pearson of Charleston. Other officers included Mrs. W. L. Metz of Edisto Island, Miss Lucinda White of Abbeville, Mrs. M. L. Pope of Abbeville, Mrs. J. D. Davis of Columbia, and Mrs. H. N. Usher of Sumter.

In later years, auxiliaries were also organized in African American churches in the PCUS. The North and South Carolina Presbyterial Auxiliary of Colored Women was organized at a meeting at New Liberty Presbyterian Church in Dillon on December 9, 1925; representatives attended from nine churches and one Sunday School. The Auxiliary next met in 1927, with nine churches and seven auxiliaries represented. Members of an affiliated auxiliary from the Dutch Reformed Church at Timmonsville also attended. By

---

5. Ibid.
6. Ibid., 225.

1928 presbyterial membership among black women in the southern church numbered between 200 and 275, two-thirds of whom were from South Carolina. South Carolina churches represented that year were Bishopville, Golden Hill (Dillon), New Liberty (Dillon), St. James (Kingstree), Hartsville, Timmonsville, and All Souls (Florence). Training schools for members of these auxiliaries were held at Stillman College from 1944 to 1958.[7]

Snedecor Memorial Synodical was organized for women in the PCUS's African American churches in 1948, and a synodical training school was held the following year. The synodical president was appointed a representative to the Women's Advisory Council, and she and the presidents of the presbyterials were included in the women's training school at Montreat.[8]

After World War II, the Board of Women's Work decided to hire an African American woman to help facilitate the organization of more women's auxiliaries in the black churches of the PCUS. This was a difficult task because the synod covered such a large geographical area that travel and communication among the auxiliaries was difficult. Arena Devarieste began this work in 1946 in partnership with Louisa Miller, a former missionary who planned to return to Korea. Devarieste took over all the work in Snedecor Synod in 1947 and continued until 1960. In the mid 1960s, the church began to integrate the black churches into the existing white presbyteries. While this had been a goal long hoped for, it resulted in a temporary loss of identity for those in the African American churches.[9]

On the presbytery level, a training school was held at Boggs Academy in Georgia for women from Georgia-Carolina Presbytery. The Women of the Church remained active in Georgia-Carolina Presbytery until the mid 1960s. In her report to the presbytery in 1962, presbyterial president Mrs. W. E. Hendricks noted that the presbytery boasted nineteen local women's organizations with 250 members. A number of members that year availed themselves of training opportunities offered at Montreat and Stillman. In 1964, with some of the organizations having been absorbed into the Athens and Atlanta presbyterials, membership had been reduced to 14 organizations and 156 members.

Organization of Women's Societies in the PCUS

Women in the southern Presbyterian Church (PCUS) began organizing local societies in the nineteenth century. By 1878 the idea had become so

---

7. Gist, *Presbyterian Women of South Carolina*, 784.
8. Batchelor, *Jacob's Ladder*, 111.
9. Alvis, *Religion and Race*, 39.

popular that the General Assembly encouraged all local congregations to have missionary societies. With the organization of local missionary unions in East Hanover (Virginia) and Wilmington (North Carolina) presbyteries in 1888, such societies moved onto the presbytery level. In South Carolina, Bethel and Enoree presbyteries were the first to organize Foreign Missionary Unions, or presbyterials, in 1899. South Carolina Presbytery followed in 1900, Pee Dee in 1905, Harmony and Charleston in 1907, and Piedmont in 1910. Congaree Presbytery did not organize a presbyterial until 1915, three years after the organization of the South Carolina synodical.[10]

By 1904 southern Presbyterian women had begun to establish synod-wide organizations called synodicals. By the time of the National Jubilee of Missions in 1911, however, it was becoming painfully clear that the women of the PCUS needed a more efficient organization. According to Hallie P. Winsborough, who was to become the General Assembly's first secretary for women's work, "a wave of unrest swept over our leaders as they realized how poorly the work of our scattered groups compared with the efficient work of other denominations. The Presbyterian Church US was the only evangelical denomination in America with no department of woman's work; with no systematic promotion of the missionary program of the Church among the women."[11]

This lack of organization was certainly not the result of lack of effort. In both 1907 and 1908, the General Assembly declined to appoint a woman secretary to supervise women's work in the church, in 1907 opining that it was hardly necessary "in view of the splendid work now being done by our women, through their Church Societies and Presbyterial Unions."[12] And this work was certainly splendid. In 1905 and 1906 the women of the PCUS raised over $350,000 to support the denomination's various causes. The organization of presbyterials only served to increase this amount, with $315,000 being raised in 1910 alone. In 1910, the assembly finally consented to allow synod-wide conferences, annual events where representatives from the synod's presbyterials could meet to share ideas. This was far from the systematic organization that the women were requesting.

In 1912 women from the Missouri Synodical presented the idea for an organized Woman's Auxiliary to the General Assembly. In their proposal they noted that women made up three-fifths of the membership of the church, and a large percentage of the money given to missions by the church came from the various women's societies. The women proposed the

10. Gist, *Presbyterian Women of South Carolina*, 118, 253, 415, 485, 631, 725.
11. Winsborough, *Yesteryears*, 20.
12. Alexander and Nicolassen, *A Digest*, 133.

establishment of an independent board intended to promote the benevolent work already being carried out by the church. They made it clear that they did not want a new agency or more control over how benevolent funds were handled, but were only asking for more organization and efficiency. The General Assembly appointed Hallie P. Winsborough as secretary for women's work in 1912. She began the effort to further organize women on the presbytery and synod levels.

That same year, the Synod of South Carolina organized its synodical. On April 11, 1912, representatives from each of the South Carolina presbyteries met at First Presbyterian Church in Columbia to discuss the organization of a state synodical. The women's auxiliaries in South Carolina held their first annual meeting in 1913, representing 137 societies and 3,241 women. (In the early days, all women were automatically enrolled in women's auxiliaries.) Mrs. J. O Reavis presided as the first Synodical President. By 1925, 213 of the 293 churches in the Synod had auxiliaries, numbering 9,309 members. Contributions that year totaled $94,693, almost a quarter of that amount going to foreign missions.[13]

Women's organizations supported other causes besides foreign missions. They also strove to do work closer to home. City churches were advised to start Sunday schools, sewing schools, or a kindergarten in a "little Italy" or "new Bohemia." They were also asked to provide weekly preaching in any "dark town" that was without a preacher. In small towns women were encouraged to investigate the living conditions of local mill workers and to see whether or not they had a Sunday school or a day school. In rural towns they were asked to improve the Christian social life in the community, including at Sunday school, in an attempt to keep young people from leaving the farms.[14]

At this same time, some local auxiliaries began to divide their members into smaller groups known as "circles." By 1904, for example, First Presbyterian Church in Spartanburg had established five neighborhood circles and a business circle. In 1914 local groups began to participate in Bible studies, at first organized around a series of studies of the men and women in the Bible. In 1919 the General Assembly encouraged all congregations to follow this circle plan.

Occasionally the Bible study curriculum caused controversy. At their meeting in September 1970, the members of Harmony Presbytery asked that their women not use the suggested study book, Kenneth Phifer's *In Christ*, but instead "employ alternative materials that are in harmony with the Holy

---

13. Gist, *Presbyterian Women of South Carolina*, 761–77.
14. "The Duties," *Prestyterian of the South*, 6.

Scripture and the Confession of Faith."[15] Members felt that Phifer denied "the existence of the soul" and failed to sufficiently treat sin, salvation, and judgment. They felt that his discussion exhibited an unacceptable "ethical relativism." In addition, his bibliography included works by Rudolph Bultmann, Paul Tillich, and Joseph Fletcher, which they felt were "writers who bear no relationship to our own tradition as Presbyterians and are known to be men far removed from the evangelical faith."[16]

Seven members of the Presbytery did not agree with this recommendation and filed an objection with the synod's judicial committee. The synod then organized a special judicial commission which concluded that "the action of Harmony Presbytery does bring implied charges of unsoundness in Church prepared and sponsored material without specific supporting charges."[17]

The circles also used study and prayer to concentrate on their own spiritual development and the church's broader concerns. In addition, they emphasized helping members create a Christian life for their families. They provided support for their members and the congregation at large in times of need and organized many church social events.

The projects of the various auxiliaries included all the causes of the church. To further support their foreign missions effort, in 1924 they established the White Cross program through which Presbyterian women at local churches made bandages, gowns, sheets, and layettes for medical missions. South Carolina women took to this project early. In 1925, only the second year of its existence, 116 of the 393 local auxiliaries in South Carolina were participating in White Cross work. In 1940 South Carolina women shipped over sixteen hundred pounds of White Cross supplies to hospitals in China and Korea.

It proved harder to maintain the program during World War II. In 1941 only three South Carolina presbyterials managed to get their supplies into China. Shipments to China ceased entirely in 1942, but resumed after the war. In later years, it was cheaper to buy supplies in bulk, and auxiliary members sometimes purchased supplies rather than making them themselves. Women in the PCUS also supplied missionaries through other avenues. In 1958, according to Synod Minutes, women from the Synod of South Carolina sent over 7,500 pounds of clothing to Church World Service and almost two thousand pounds to individual missionaries.

---

15. Synod of South Carolina, 1971, 59.
16. Harmony Presbytery Minutes, April 17, 1971, 7.
17. "Synod Annuls Harmony Action," *The Southern Presbyterian*, 2.

In another effort to support home and foreign missions, women established the annual Birthday Offering. In 1922, on the tenth anniversary of the Woman's Auxiliary, they decided to celebrate the birthday of the organization by giving a gift *to others*. That first year Mrs. Winsborough challenged women to celebrate their anniversary by giving a penny for each year of their lives to Miss Dowd's School in Kochi, Japan. In subsequent years, the women of the denomination would decide on different objectives for their gifts, with projects being selected from both the home and foreign mission fields. Between 1922 and 1972, birthday offerings from South Carolina women provided $572,434.06 for various causes at home and abroad.[18]

Women's Training Conference, Montreat, 1955 (Courtesy of the Presbyterian Heritage Center, Montreat, N.C.)

While there were separate organizations for women in South Carolina's black Presbyterian churches, women in the white churches also focused on race relations. A continuing highlight of the work of the Synodical Woman's Auxiliary was the Conference for Colored Women. Mrs. Winsborough organized a denominational conference for Negro Women at Stillman Institute in Alabama in 1916, "the first of its kind ever held by any denomination for Negro women."[19] Mrs. Winsborough's plan was prophetic; as she herself later said, "The question of interracial relationships is looming large on the horizon

---

18. Wright, "Some Fruits," 2.
19. Batchelor, *Jacob's Ladder*, 104.

of church discussions, and the modest effort made by the Auxiliary to really help our colored women has assumed an importance little dreamed of."[20]

Individual synods began offering similar programs in 1921. In 1923 Mrs. Frances L. Mayes, president of the South Carolina synodical, delivered a speech entitled "Our Heritage: A Challenge." While her text may seem patronizing and sometimes insulting to our modern ears, her ideas were revolutionary for the time. Noting that Presbyterian women had been "shirking our duty towards our brother in black," she urged them to face the interracial problem "squarely and deal with it wisely." African Americans, according to Mrs. Mayes, were "the child-race of the world, and need judicious leadership given kindly, but firmly." The program she envisioned would not contemplate "social equality in any measure; *they* do not want this any more than we." She urged the formation of a committee in each local auxiliary, mirroring committees on the presbytery and synod levels, to produce a program for "work in the home, the church, and the school." This program would be conducted through leaders in the African American community, "selecting always with care those who are conservative and reasonable."[21]

Mrs. Mayes's idea quickly bore fruit. That same year, Mrs. A. D. Calhoun, chairman of the Interracial Committee, organized a local conference at Brewer Normal Institute in Greenwood. The following year, the South Carolina synodical began holding its Interdenominational Conference at Benedict College in Columbia.

Interdenominational Women's Conference 1957 (Courtesy of the University of South Carolina)

20. Gibbins, "Christian Conferences," 666–7.
21. Gist, *Presbyterian Women*, xviii–xix.

Local churches selected African American women of all denominations and financed their attendance. This first conference, organized by Mrs. Andrew Bramlett and Mrs. Leslie Stribling, had an enrollment of ninety-two delegates sent by fifty-two different churches. The conference drew criticism from some: "This plan met with much disapproval and required most tactful handling and much work from Mrs. Bramlett and Mrs. Stribling. The result in winning the confidence and gratitude of these colored women who, for the first time in many years, realize that Southern white women are truly interested in their Christian welfare, cannot be overestimated."[22]

Conferences were also held on the local or district level; Greenville held such a regional conference beginning around 1936. Some of these took the form of one-day conferences which were more economical, could reach more women, and sometimes served as feeder schools for the annual conferences.

Over the years, attendees from other African American denominations, particularly Methodists and Baptists, sometimes outnumbered Presbyterians. The conferences spawned numerous Sunday schools and vacation Bible schools in African American communities throughout the state. In 1935 Rosa Gibbins described what these conferences meant to the women who attended: "What have the conferences meant to the Negroes in attendance? A changed attitude toward the values of the real things of life, increased knowledge of the solution of everyday problems, a wider outlook, the opening of doors of opportunity, a deepened Christian love for each other, and a new appreciation of the interest of white women in the problems of their race."[23]

There was a brief hiatus during World War II, when the overcrowded conditions in Columbia caused the synodical to cancel the conference. With the dawn of the civil rights movement, the synodical cancelled the conference again in 1960. Otherwise, annual conferences were held until 1968. The meetings provided courses ranging from family management and hygiene to Bible, teaching methods, and Christian witnessing. By 1967 the courses in Christian witnessing included presentations about working with problem drinkers and those who had been in prison. Approximately 75 percent of those who attended these conferences were school teachers who used the training they received to hold vacation church schools and to teach in Sunday schools and youth groups. In 1969 the annual women's conference in Montreat, previously all white, was "quietly" opened to "women of the presbyterials left homeless by the suspension of the Interdenominational Conference in Columbia . . . Nothing happened except the proving of

---

22. Ibid., 774.
23. Gibbons, "Christian Conferences," 667.

Christian love and interest to those fellow Christians in our own Synod. Not enough of them came but it was a beginning."[24]

Local churches also did interracial work. Women at First Presbyterian Church in York sponsored a Bible class for African Americans in 1925 and donated clothing to pupils at the black school. In 1937 women from Aveleigh Church in Newberry started a weekly Bible class at nearby Calvary, a black Presbyterian church started by the PCUSA. The Business Women's Circle at First Presbyterian Church in Anderson held what has been called the first vacation Bible school for African American children. The city-wide school, taught by teachers of both races, enrolled three hundred children.[25] The General Assembly also asked the women of South Carolina to support the assembly's endorsement of integration in their local communities. In 1955 the Women's Advisory Council recommended that women "in these days of crisis [pursue] an earnest cultivation and practice of the Christian graces of forbearance, patience, humility, and persistent goodwill."[26]

As David Reimers noted in his book *White Protestantism and the Negro*, the women were far ahead of the rest of the PCUS in their work with African Americans. Reimers cites several reasons for this activism among the women. With the ratification of the Nineteenth Amendment in 1920, women began speaking out more on social issues. They were also more active than men in the work of their local churches, and their various study groups enabled them to learn about a wide array of social problems. They had close daily contact with African American women, who often worked in their homes. Indeed, in the Presbyterian Church, as in other denominations, the church's men often left the women to serve according to their consciences in such matters as race and poverty.[27]

Other important facets of the women's program included funding Presbyterian student work at Clemson, raising scholarship money for students at Presbyterian College, supporting Thornwell Orphanage and Columbia Seminary, and contributing to the upkeep of the William Brearley (South Carolina) Home at Montreat. At the Seminary, the women's funds went mainly to support the library and Mission Haven, which provided apartments for missionaries on furlough.

---

24. Synod of South Carolina, 1969, 30.
25. Cathcart, *Yesteryears*, 186.
26. Minutes of Piedmont Presbytery, 1956, 25.
27. Reimers, *White Protestantism*, 91–2.

Sketch of Mission Haven, Columbia Theological Seminary
(Courtesy of Columbia Theological Seminary)

Presbyterian women began an additional program at the seminary in 1955, when they organized the Columbia Friendship Circle to add to the endowment and help with capital improvements. Women's groups provided crucial support to Thornwell Orphanage and Presbyterian College, especially during the Depression. In 1932, when the banks of Greer failed, the auxiliary of the First Presbyterian Church lost over half of its funds. Unable to send a financial gift to Thornwell, they sent food and clothing instead.[28]

The offerings collected at the annual meeting of the synodical were used to support a wide range of projects including the Synodical Scholarship Fund, the chair of Bible at Presbyterian College, the Presbyterian Guidance Center at PC, and the Presbyterian homes in Summerville and Clinton. In 1948 the synodical instituted Blessing Boxes into which each woman dropped coins of thanks for "blessings large and small." The proceeds were used to prepare young people for full-time Christian service through the Synodical Scholarship Fund. By 1972 these scholarships had helped over 450 young people by raising almost $192,000.[29]

The Woman's Auxiliary also played a major part in raising the morale of the troops during World War II. "Increasing numbers have answered the call to serve the men of the Armed Forces through the church," reported Mrs. J. M. Williams, president of the South Carolina synodical. "Letters, Bibles, pamphlets, and prayer lists have all been used to 'maintain the tie,'

28. Blackwell, *A People and their Faith*, 112.
29. Wright, "Some Fruits of Faith," 33.

and many groups meet regularly to pray for a just and enduring peace. In this ministry of prayer, the lives of our women have been enriched."[30]

The activities of the auxiliary at First Presbyterian Church in Greer were typical. Members adopted servicemen, writing letters, knitting socks, and sending food. They invited soldiers home for dinner or visits. The president of the auxiliary served on the board of the Greer Service Men's Center, an organization that served troops from Donaldson Air Force Base in Greenville and Camp Croft in Spartanburg.[31] Auxiliary members at First Presbyterian in Anderson made sure each of their 150 servicemen and women received a monthly letter and a birthday remembrance. They furnished a prayer room near the sanctuary so that people going to and from work could stop by to meditate and pray for those in the service. Presbyterian women supported military personnel again during the Vietnam War. In 1967 they began a new program called "Operation Home-Tie" to help local congregations maintain their ties with members in the service.[32] In 1968 the synodical president reported that "ditty bags," Bibles, and gifts had been sent to soldiers in Vietnam and that their home congregations were supporting them by sending letters and cards.[33]

In 1948 the General Assembly voted to change the name of the Woman's Auxiliary to the Women of the Church. While this may seem a minor change, it was done on the recommendation of the Committee on Woman's Work to "more clearly define the relation of the woman membership as an integral part of the whole church."[34] In other words, women's work was no longer considered "auxiliary" to the regular work of the church.

Changes also affected the Committee on Woman's Work. In 1950 it became the Board of Women's Work, one of the General Assembly's five boards. The board was incorporated in 1956, forty-one years after a similar action had been taken in the PCUSA. It served as an advocate for the position of women throughout the church, urging that they be adequately represented on boards, agencies, and councils, and lobbying for better pay for women employees. There was no corresponding change in structure at the synod level however, and one of the few committees to include no women was the three-member Committee on Women's Work. No woman would serve on that committee until the synods were restructured in 1973.

30. Synod of South Carolina, 1943, 44.
31. Blackwell, *A People and their Faith*, 154.
32. Synod of South Carolina, 1967, 23.
33. Ibid., 1968, 29.
34. General Assembly, 1948, 95.

Membership in the various auxiliaries and contributions by their members continued to rise steadily over the years. In 1945 the synod had 229 women's groups, boasting 14,967 members, responsible for $124,196 in total benevolences. By 1955, after a decade of rapid growth, there were 23,953 members in 292 groups, responsible for $275,787 in gifts.[35]

The Woman's Auxiliary also offered its members leadership opportunities. Among these was the annual Women's Conference at Montreat. According to Mrs. J. M. Williams's report to the synod, in 1941 alone, 139 women from the South Carolina synodical participated in some form of study at Montreat, "thus striving to learn more of the work of our church and the means of serving more acceptably."[36] One of the main avenues for training and leadership on the state level was the annual Synodical Training School.

Attendees at the Synodical Training School 1954
(Courtesy of Presbyterian College)

The first school, established by synodical president Mrs. O. A. Matthews, was held at Coker College in Hartsville in 1948. In 1954 Presbyterian College became the school's permanent home. Courses covered a broad range of subjects; for instance, in 1956 they included "Missions in the Local Church," "How to Study the Bible," "Organization and Program," "The Home and Church Working Together," "Christian Witnessing during the

---

35. Women of the Church, Synod of South Carolina, 1956, 11.
36. Synod of South Carolina, 1941, 19.

Platform Hour," and "Living the Life of Christian Love." PC hosted the training school until restructuring eliminated the synodical in 1973.

Many South Carolina women gained valuable organizational and leadership skills from this training and became leaders on the denominational level. Among early South Carolina chairmen of the General Assembly's Woman's Advisory Committee were Mrs. F. Louise Mayes (from 1922 through 1923) and Mrs. Andrew Bramlett (from 1924 through 1925). In 1931 Mrs. Bramlett was named to the Executive Committee on Assembly's Home Missions and thus became a member of the Committee on Woman's Work. Mrs. J. M. Williams Jr. of McConnellsville served on the Committee on Women's Work/Board of Women's Work from 1946 to 1953, and Mrs. Helen T. Vass of Clinton was appointed to the Board of Women's Work in 1954. Ann (Mrs. W. Rex) Josey of Manning served as chairman of the Women's Advisory Council from 1954 to 1955, was on the Board of Women's Work beginning in 1956, and served as its chairman from 1962 through 1963.

Mrs. W. Rex Josey (Courtesy of Presbyterian College)

By the 1960s, the Women of the Church in South Carolina had developed into a cohesive group that loyally and efficiently supported all of the church's various enterprises. In his centennial address delivered to the Synod of South Carolina in 1961, C. Darby Fulton called "the development of women's work from a maze of unorganized societies into a welded force enlisted in every good cause" one of the "conspicuous gains of the last half century." Fulton quoted Dr. Henry Sweets, longtime Secretary of the Executive Committee of Christian Education and Ministerial Relief, who once called the organization "the most highly developed and best articulated enterprise that I have ever seen. Why, if Mrs. Winsborough were to sneeze up there in St. Louis, the President of the Woman's Auxiliary in Key West would have a tickling sensation in her nose!"[37] By 1972, when the synods were restructured, the original 137 women's organizations in South Carolina had increased to 332, encompassing 26,667 members.[38]

When the synods were reorganized in 1972, pairing South Carolina with Georgia in the Synod of the Southeast, the entire structure of the Women of the Church was changed in the hope that women would at last be fully integrated into the life of the church. The Board of Women's Work endorsed restructure but expressed "their deep concern that integration of all boards could result in women's being integrated *out*."

They hoped that "women's full inclusion in church and society be assured and that women continue to have direct access to the General Assembly."[39] But according to Sidney West, a member of the Board of Women's Work and future member of the Committee on Women's Concerns, "We used to say that the church had nothing better to do than to restructure. It always put a bottleneck in the road for women and minorities, and the southern white men continued to rule ... The restructure allowed women who wanted change a tiny voice, but it left a huge void for what had been."[40]

To help fill this void, the General Assembly requested that each presbytery establish a task force on women "in order to study the role of women within the presbytery, inform local congregations, work toward adequate representation and utilization of women in presbytery's affairs, and assist in implementing the church's concern for the personhood of women."[41] By 1983, however, only thirty-eight of the sixty-one presbyteries in the PCUS had a task force on women's concerns. Examination of available records indicates that no South Carolina presbytery established such a task force.

As a result of restructuring, the Board of Women's Work was disbanded and women's work was joined with men's work, youth work, and

---

37. Synod of South Carolina, 1961, 84.
38. Synod of the Southeast, 1973, 26.
39. Farrior, *Journey toward the Future*, 64.
40. West, Email correspondence, April 2, 2002.
41. General Assembly, 1972, 179.

voluntary service under the Mission to Laity Office. Staffing and program budgets were drastically reduced. The annual Women's Conference at Montreat, which had drawn as many as six hundred women annually, was discontinued, not to resume until 1977. Some of the traditional functions of the Women of the Church were transferred to other offices. The White Cross program, for instance, was moved to the Division of International Missions. The problems with this decision were voiced in the General Assembly in 1977:

> Women had little voice in the decision to integrate all boards, including the Board of Women's Work. This restructure decision meant that at a critical time in history, just as the Church was acknowledging a commitment to the inclusion of women as full partners in the Church, especially in the area of decision making from which they had been excluded, the voice that had been raised on behalf of women, the Board of Women's Work, would speak no more. Women and men serving on the Board of Women's Work . . . feared a future without an advocate for women.[42]

The synod's structure was also drastically altered; indeed, only on the congregational and presbyterial levels was the program unchanged. The position of synodical president was done away with, and the Women's Advisory Council was disbanded. Instead there was a Women's Coordinating Committee made up of the presbyterial presidents which served under the synod's Coordinating Council.

In the face of all of these changes, Presbyterian women strove to remain optimistic. In 1973 Mrs. J. Beaty Smith, Field Director of the General Assembly's Board of Women's Work, addressed the women of Enoree Presbytery on the topic "Alert—We are Going out of Business." Despite the rather pessimistic title of her speech, Mrs. Smith asserted that the dissolution of the Board would represent "a joyous day moving into something greater than we have ever had before." She foresaw the new structure as a precursor to the wholeness of the church, "all people working together in the congregation to accomplish what God expects us to accomplish."[43]

In 1973, in an attempt to ameliorate some of the destructive results of reorganization on women's programs, the General Assembly established the Committee on Women's Concerns (COWC), which included one woman from each synod. Its responsibilities were to "develop a national strategy for expressing concerns of women," to "identify major issues involving women,"

---

42. Ibid., 1977, 347.
43. Women of the Church, 1974, 10.

and to "develop increased responsiveness in the Church to the resources of women for the mission of the church."[44] In addition, the committee was to provide women direct access to the General Assembly. Its placement under the Office of the General Assembly assured it a measure of independence from other agencies, which was "considered necessary for effective functioning of advocacy and monitoring."[45]

In 1974 the new Synod of the Southeast (produced by the merger of the synods of South Carolina and Georgia in 1973) formed its own Women's Coordinating Committee consisting of the thirteen presbyterial presidents plus a coordinator. The Committee held both a retreat and a seminar that year to "help the women understand the new organization and program of the Church." They recommended that each presbytery should elect a woman delegate to the General Assembly if they didn't have a woman commissioner and establish a Task Force on Women if they hadn't already done so. In coming years, several other women's advocacy groups were formed within the denomination: the Church Employed Women Office (1973), which was supplanted by the Committee on Women Employed by the Church (1975); the Joint Committee on Women, designed to include women from both the PCUS and UPCUSA (1979); and the Committee on Racial and Ethnic Women (1981). According to Sidney West, "We . . . realized that our work must be multi-faceted because so many groups were left out. Women of color, women seminarians, the few women who were ordained, and women who had worked as secretaries and musicians for years without any retirement were reasons to step up to the plate, to make our voices count."[46]

Some members of the Women of the Church were ambivalent about these various advocacy groups. "By temperament and training many members were uncomfortable with what they perceived as strident and confrontational tactics . . . "[47] The older women's organization did not want to give up part of its influence with the General Assembly, and the agendas of the various groups were never integrated. Indeed, Sidney West asserted, "Whether by design or neglect, and I believe it was design, the way restructure actually came to be meant that women were split apart. The traditional against the 'radical feminists' . . . Divide and conquer. So for those of us in the midst of it all, we had to walk a tight rope designed to help us fall! . . . In a way, looking back, it was perfectly designed for failure. And beautifully

---

44. General Assembly, 1980, 385.
45. Ibid., 384.
46. West, Email correspondence.
47. Boyd and Brackenridge, "Study of the Current Status of Women Pastors, 55.

orchestrated as well. What do women want, they asked? We gave you an advocacy group, and you still are not satisfied."[48]

The Synod of the Southeast also expressed reservations, particularly about COWC. In 1978 the synod's coordinating council recommended "that the General Assembly be urged to give thoughtful consideration to the counter-productive impact of some aspects of the work of the Committee on Women's Concerns as it presently functions." The Council asked the General Assembly to "instruct the Committee on Women's Concerns to clarify its role for the Synod of the Southeast. This response will include: (1) Definition of what 'monitor' and 'advocacy' mean to the Committee on Women's Concerns; (2) What the Committee on Women's Concerns sees as its task with the General Assembly, Synods, Presbyteries, Sessions and Churches; and (3) How the Committee on Women's Concerns intends to fulfill its task with the above–named groups . . . "[49] The General Assembly declined to do this, noting that these matters had already been dealt with in existing reports and manuals.

The Synod of the Southeast was slow to create a Committee on Women's Concerns. As Sidney West noted in an Email, "As far as South Carolina was concerned, it was just another of the states where the COWC was definitely not loved, and whatever we did in Atlanta, there were people from South Carolina who were appalled." It was not until 1982 that the synod established a committee.

In 1964 the PCUS decided that women were eligible for church office and could be ordained as ministers of the word and gospel. Shortly after this decision, participation in the Women of the Church began to decline. The membership of the WOC was aging, and with an increasing number of younger women working or attending school, there were fewer women available for daytime activities. It was especially difficult for those with jobs or young children to organize and serve at church dinners and other functions. Some younger women felt that the WOC concentrated too much on social events and spent too little time on the problems of society at large. Other young women noted an emphasis on family, making it difficult for single women or married women without children to fit in. Between 1977 and 1988, membership in the Women of the Church decreased by 17 percent across the denomination.[50]

A study of presbyteries and churches in South Carolina reflected in Presbytery minutes illustrates this trend. Harmony Presbytery clearly saw a

---

48. West, Email correspondence.
49. Synod of the Southeast, 1978, 26.
50. Boyd and Brakenridge, "Study of the Current Status of Women Pastors," 63.

drop in participation. In 1972 the presbytery boasted thirty-nine local organizations with over two thousand women gathered into 103 circles. By 1985 membership had dropped to just under 1,600 scattered among 27 churches. It should be noted that by this time, a number of churches in the presbytery had left the PCUS and joined the more conservative Presbyterian Church in America. Charleston Presbytery also saw a drop. In 1971 there were 107 circles in the presbytery, with 2,915 members. By 1985 membership had dropped to 1,748.

The experience of First Presbyterian Church in Greer typified this situation. By 1983 the number of circles had dropped from an all time high of nine in the 1960s to only three. While the evening circle had seventy-five people on its roll, the average attendance at meetings was only two or three. This placed an undue burden on the few active members: "This left the twenty-odd women in the other two circles with the responsibility of all the women's work—an intimidating list encompassing mission work, fellowship events, decorating, visiting the sick and bereaved, and welcoming new members... It had become physically impossible for twenty faithful women to "care for" all their circle members and tend to all the needs of the church. Something had to change."[51] Finally the officers set up committees to cover the work that women had formerly done through their circles. Women were allowed to choose the committee or committees on which they wished to serve, leaving the circles free to pay more attention to Bible study.

Working Towards Reunion and an Improved Structure

In the midst of all this change, Presbyterian women were also working to prepare for anticipated Presbyterian reunion. By 1971 some women's groups from the UPCUSA and the PCUS in the synods of Arkansas, Kentucky, Missouri, Texas, and Virginia had already united or had plans to do so. By 1976 union presbyterials were being established in Alabama, Florida, Oklahoma, and the District of Columbia. The first joint Bible study for both memberships, "Praise God—Worship through the Year," was prepared for use in 1979. By 1983 women had established a WOC/UPW (United Presbyterian Women) Working Team to begin working toward reunion. With the formalization of reunion in 1983, the new Presbyterian Women devoted themselves to a new purpose: "Forgiven and freed by God in Jesus Christ, we commit ourselves: To nurture our faith through prayer and Bible study, To support the mission of the church worldwide, To work for justice

---

51. Blackwell, *A People and Their Faith*, 335.

and peace, and To build an inclusive, caring community of women that strengthens the Presbyterian Church (USA) and witnesses to the promise of God's Kingdom."[52]

Women in the new denomination were to be governed by the new Churchwide Coordinating Team; the traditional Thank Offering of the UPW and Birthday Offering of the WOC were to be continued. The General Assembly ultimately established a Women's Ministry Unit which reported directly to the assembly; it included the Presbyterian Women, the Committee of Women of Color, Justice for Women, and Women Employed by the Church. Thus, after over a decade of transition, reunification served to restore much that had been lost in the restructuring of 1972.

"Acceptable" Church Vocations for Women

Beginning in the nineteenth century and continuing until women's ordination was approved in 1964, there were two important fields of church work in which women could use their talents: the mission field and Christian education. In many ways women had unique qualifications for the mission field. In many countries women were kept at home and could not be reached by male missionaries. In some cultures it was impossible for a male doctor or nurse to treat a female patient. In these cases, women were indispensable both in treating the sick and spreading the Gospel.

In 1890 the General Assembly noted that there were many young women who wished to be missionaries, and as they would need special training, especially in the field of medicine, Presbyterian schools and colleges should make special provisions to provide it. In 1909 the assembly decided that any woman who hoped to become a missionary (except for those trained as nurses) would be required to have an AB or a BS or equivalent and at least one year of special training.

One source that trained women to serve in these areas was Assembly's Training School (later the Presbyterian School of Christian Education) in Richmond, established in 1914 to train lay people for work at home and abroad. The student body was predominantly female, the first full-time male student not enrolling until 1938. Thornwell Orphanage also produced a number of missionaries and from 1893 until 1903 had a Mission Training School that educated between forty and fifty women. Several graduates of Thornwell served in the mission field. Ava Patton Anglin of Laurens County served with her husband L. M. Anglin in Mexico and later in Shantung, China. Rhoda Carolina "Carrie" Kilgore of Newberry, a graduate of

---

52. General Assembly, 1986, 384.

Winthrop College, served in Brazil for over twenty-eight years. Cassie Lee Oliver of Lowndesville entered the mission field in China in 1923, where she met and married fellow missionary Reverend A. A. Talbot. They served as missionaries at Tsing-Kiang-Pu, where she was the primary nurse at the hospital for twenty years.[53]

Many of the synod's female missionaries attended institutions besides Thornwell or the training school. They were graduates of schools like Converse, Winthrop, Mary Baldwin, and Columbia College, and many had advanced degrees from hospitals and Bible colleges. Beginning as early as the late nineteenth century, South Carolina sent many capable women into home and foreign missions. Some accompanied their husbands and assisted in their work, while others went on their own. One of the early single female missionaries from South Carolina was Dr. Mattie Ingold (later Mrs. Lewis Tate) of Rock Hill, who graduated at the top of her class from Women's Medical College in Baltimore. In 1897 she went to Korea as a doctor and later, after her marriage to fellow missionary Lewis Tate in 1905, as a missionary. Ella Davidson Little of York, wife of Reverend Lacy Little, served with her husband in China and established the first women's Bible school in the mid China region. Charlotte Dunlap of Sion Church in Winnsboro served as a medical missionary in China and Formosa for thirty-seven years.[54]

Women also worked in home mission work. Zoulean Anderson of Florence, who graduated from Assembly's Training School in 1918, worked in the mining camps of West Virginia. Other South Carolinians engaged in home mission work were Cornelia McLaurin of Sumter (Appalachian Mountains), Mae Blackwell of Abbeville County and Virginia Neville of Clinton (Rabun Gap/Nacoochee School), Alice Winn Brownlee of Abbeville County (Highland Institute), and Claudia Fraser of Sumter, who worked in several mill communities in North and South Carolina.

In addition to working in home and foreign missions, women gradually began to find employment in their local churches. The training available at Assembly's Training School made it possible for them to serve as pastor's assistants, Directors of Religious Education, and Directors of Christian Education. First Presbyterian Church in Spartanburg was one of the first South Carolina churches to employ a trained worker when the congregation hired Marion Wilcox as a pastor's assistant in 1922. She was followed by Irene Hudson who served from 1923 to 1929. Margaret McElwee began her work as Director of Religious Education at First Presbyterian Church in Rock Hill

---

53. Gist, *Presbyterian Women of South Carolina*, 754.
54. Missionary Biographies, Presbyterian History Center.

in 1923. Gladys Pugh followed her for one year and was succeeded by Janie Lord Garrison who served from 1924 until 1930. Another longtime educator at Rock Hill was Ora Mast Glenn Roberts who had earlier served as a missionary in Brazil. Other churches were slower to use women in such positions. First Presbyterian Church in Greenwood hired Euphemia Gordon as its first female Director of Christian Education in 1939. Aveleigh Church in Newberry followed suit in 1949 when Anne Kelley was hired.

Women also worked as educators on the synod level. In 1927 the synod hired Mrs. George W. Sheffer of Atlanta as the Director of Religious Education for the Synod of South Carolina, a position she had held previously in Arkansas. In 1961 the synod employed two Area Directors of Christian Education, Mrs. Helen T. Vass of Clinton for the upstate, and Mrs. E. G. Beckman for the lower portion of the state. Before campus ministers became common, women were also involved in student work on South Carolina's various campuses. Mrs. John C. Hayes worked with students at Winthrop College as early as 1939. Ten years later Mrs. Florence Pardew was working with students at the Citadel, and Jane Chamblee was working with the Westminster Fellowship groups on campuses statewide.

Seen But Rarely Heard

Despite the large number of women engaged in women's organizations, mission work, and Christian education, leadership roles for women in the church as a whole remained carefully circumscribed. Over the years the General Assembly had engaged in a continuing debate about whether or not women should be permitted to speak at public meetings. The 1916 General Assembly forbade women to "publicly expound God's Word" from the pulpit or to be ordained or licensed. The preaching of the gospel by women was considered "opposed to the advancement of true piety and to the promotion of the peace of the church," and was "an irregularity not to be tolerated." As for their speaking in mixed assemblies, this was "left to the discretion of the sessions and the enlightened consciences of our Christian women themselves."[55] Sixty-one delegates to the assembly, including eight from South Carolina, objected even to this minor concession, asserting that it conflicted with both scripture and church polity.

These restrictions also applied to General Assembly meetings. In the early years of the Woman's Auxiliary, the annual report was always presented by a man. President Hallie Winsborough was the first to present her own report at the General Assembly in 1920. However, the controversy over

---

55. General Assembly, 1916, 175–9.

women speaking in mixed assemblies continued, causing such a furor that in 1925 Mrs. Winsborough deputized H. H. Sweets to read her report to the General Assembly for her. A man also read the report the following year, but that assembly made the decision that as an "authorized and responsible agent of the assembly . . . she [the president of the Woman's Auxiliary] has a natural right to read her report to the Assembly." They were careful to add, however, that "this privilege does not carry any implication of membership in the Assembly or of participation in its discussions."[56]

In the meantime, the General Assembly opened up other opportunities for women. In 1923 delegates voted to include women on executive committees. A number of South Carolina delegates, including J. J. Brown of the Fishing Creek and Van Wyck churches, R. C. Reed of Columbia Seminary, and A. H. Key of Smyrna Church in Newberry, protested this action. Noting that their protest was "not based upon any want of recognition of the ability, good judgment, or consecration of women nor upon any failure to appreciate the magnificent work the women are doing," they nevertheless asserted that no one should be a member of an executive committee who could not be a member of the General Assembly itself. They also declared that membership on such a committee constituted "a position involving authority to rule" and that the Bible "expressly forbids the woman to exercise ecclesiastical authority over a man."[57] The General Assembly rejected this protest, however, noting that neither God's word nor church governance prevented it from putting women on its executive committees, and the inclusion of women served to recognize their "loyal and faithful work."[58] Mrs. Andrew Bramlett of South Carolina was one of the first women appointed; she served on the Home Missions Committee.

In October 1923, the Synod of South Carolina asked the General Assembly to rescind the action as unconstitutional "because the Assembly itself is charged with the duty of selecting the members of its committees and cannot delegate this duty to any other body, and . . . especially because to invest women with governmental powers is contrary to the explicit doctrine of our form of government."[59] This overture was soundly defeated, but the sentiment lingered.

The subject of women preaching or expounding God's word from the pulpit resurfaced in 1926 when the General Assembly considered an overture from several presbyteries including Enoree, "asking that the assembly

56. Ibid., 1926, 43.
57. Ibid., 1923, 69.
58. Ibid., 701.
59. Synod of South Carolina, 1923, 21.

reaffirm its deliverance of 1916 forbidding women to preach and leaving their other activities to the discretion of the sessions."[60] The General Assembly responded positively, declaring that "inspired Scripture" prohibited preaching by women.[61] Purity Church ignored the assembly's decision and decided on October 11, 1926, that "consecrated women" would be permitted to speak in the church's prayer meetings.[62]

While progress was slow at the denominational level, it was even slower in South Carolina. Over ten years after Mrs. Winsborough first presented her own report to the General Assembly, the reports of the synodical president were still presented to the Synod of South Carolina by a man. In 1935, in a break with this tradition, Dr. James W. Jackson, chairman of the synod's Committee on Woman's Work, suggested that the president of the synodical present her own report the following year; this was done when Mrs. Mason L. Carroll addressed the meeting in 1936.

An interesting situation arose in South Carolina in 1931 when Miss Janie McGaughey, the General Assembly's Secretary of Woman's Work, was asked to speak to women of the presbytery at First Presbyterian Church in Anderson. The pastor, Dr. R. F. Kirkpatrick, felt that since a large crowd was expected, and Ms. McGaughey held such an important position, she should be allowed to speak from the pulpit in the sanctuary. Some of the elders, however, felt that the pulpit should be reserved for use by ordained ministers. The session ultimately agreed with Dr. Kirkpatrick, and Miss McGaughey spoke from the pulpit.[63]

Even in the face of sometimes strong opposition, the increasing significance of women's work necessarily caused a gradual change in attitudes towards the role of women in the church. Almost ten years after the General Assembly added women to some of its committees, the Synod of South Carolina began to do the same. In 1932 the Trustees of the William Brearley Home in Montreat recognized the support provided by the Synodical Woman's Auxiliary and requested that Mrs. C. E. Graham of Greenville be added to the Board of Trustees, along with the president of the synodical, ex officio. The synod concurred. In 1934 the synod recognized the Auxiliary's significant support of young people's conferences and the conferences for African American women and added three women to be nominated by the synodical to its Executive Committee on Religious Education. The synod added Mrs. J. M. Williams to the Board of Trustees

60. General Assembly, 1926, 26.
61. Ibid., 52.
62. Dawson, *Purity and Its People*, 146.
63. Cathcart, *Yesteryears*, 177-8.

at Queens College in 1941, and by 1946 officers of the synodical auxiliary served ex officio on the Home Missions Committee, the Religious Education Committee, the William Brearley Home Board of Trustees, and the Committee on Student Work.

With the end of World War II, some South Carolina Presbyterians began to notice the significance of the women's "quiet, unobtrusive" ministry. In 1945 the synod's all-male Committee on Woman's Work noted that during the war years,

> in nearly all departments of the Church's work greater loads have fallen upon the women . . . Although that last retreat and inner sanctum of Presbyterian men, the Diaconate and Session, has not yet been graced by the presence of women members, we think it is only fitting that we humbly acknowledge that many of the functions of these offices are fulfilled and made effective because there are women who set the example of godly conduct and character and assist the pastor in his ministry to the people . . . We commend the Women's Work to the Presbytery as a work of real spiritual power . . .[64]

Progress Toward Ordination

Despite this increasing recognition of the role of women in the church, there continued to be opposition to the ordination of women. In 1953, as part of the abortive plan to unite the Presbyterian Church in the United States of America, the Presbyterian Church in the United States, and the United Presbyterian Church of North America, it was proposed that women be ordained. In their response to this plan, the members of Enoree Presbytery declared their "opposition to the election, and/or ordination of women as Ministers, Elders, or Deacons, recognizing the magnificent service rendered to the church through the ages and to the present time by women in their appointed sphere."[65] No mention was made that this "appointed sphere" included most of the functions performed by the church.

In 1955 the Presbytery of Granville in North Carolina asked the General Assembly to allow women to serve as elders and deacons "on a permissive basis." The assembly referred the issue to an Ad Interim Committee for "thorough Biblical study" and in 1956 sent the matter to the presbyteries

---

64. Pee Dee Presbytery Minutes, April 1945, 15.
65. Enoree Presbytery Minutes, October 1953, 37.

where it lost by a close vote of 44 to 39.⁶⁶ At its fall stated meeting in 1956, the Presbytery of South Carolina voted against the measure by a vote of 25 to 5. Other South Carolina presbyteries also voted against the amendment. Piedmont Presbytery's vote was close, 15 to 11, but Enoree defeated the amendment by a vote of 57 to 18.

In 1963 the General Assembly's Permanent Judicial Committee recommended women be eligible to hold church offices. At their meeting in January 1964, the members of Enoree Presbytery, whose members had so vehemently opposed ordination only eight years earlier, received an interesting report from a special committee appointed to study the proposed changes. As background, the committee explained that

> the New Testament does not present a clear picture of the role of men or women in the life of Christian congregations. The picture that is presented often has to do wth matters which have long ceased to be of direct application to our day and time . . . The doctrine of ordination played the most decisive role in determining our recommendation to you. We asked ourselves, "Is the Spirit of God *calling* women to positions of leadership in the institutional church?" If the answer is "Yes," then we felt the institutional church was under obligation to recognize this call of God's Spirit and to put its stamp of recognition and acceptance on the person or persons so called.⁶⁷

The presbytery approved ordination by a very close vote of 41 to 40.

Most other South Carolina presbyteries failed to imitate Enoree in its careful study of the issue, and some voted soundly against the ordination of women. Only two South Carolina presbyteries, Enoree and Piedmont, approved the amendment. A majority of presbyteries in the PCUS did approve, and in 1964 the General Assembly amended the church's constitution. The reluctance of many churches to accept this reinterpretation of what they considered scriptural truth was evident only a few years later when a score of churches from the Synod of South Carolina left the PCUS to join the newly organized National Presbyterian Church (which later became the Presbyterian Church in America) and other more conservative denominations. The overwhelming majority of these churches were from Harmony, Congaree, and South Carolina presbyteries, none of which had approved the decision to ordain women.

On July 5, 1964, Clara D. Williams of Covenant Presbyterian Church in Tuscaloosa, Alabama, became the first woman ordained as a ruling elder

---

66. Boyd and Brackenridge, "Study of the Current Status of Women Pastors," 130.

67. Enoree Presbytery Minutes, January 1964, 6–8.

in the PCUS. On May 12, 1965, Reverend Dr. Rachel Henderlite of Hanover Presbytery, Virginia, became the first woman ordained by the PCUS to the ministry of Word and Sacrament.

Some churches in South Carolina persisted in questioning ordination. According to the *South Carolina Presbyterian*, "Many who favor the change look upon it as permissive, allowing women officers where needed."[68] Among these was Covenant Presbyterian Church in Columbia, which asked Congaree Presbytery the following question: "If a congregation nominates its officers by mail ballot from a list of qualified members submitted by the Session, is it mandatory that the names of women, otherwise qualified by age, residence, etc., be included?" The General Assembly replied that "it is mandatory that women be considered eligible for election as officers, and this requirement extends to ensuring that the processes of election shall be designed to provide for women on the same basis as men."[69]

South Carolina churches began to ordain women very shortly after the changes in the *Book of Church Order*. By 1965 Mrs. E. A. Wright was an elder at Grace Church, Congaree Presbytery; she represented the church at a meeting of the synod in May 1965. At the First Presbyterian Church in Anderson, Lois Young was installed as an elder on February 6, 1966, and Eunice Major on January 21, 1968. Columbia's Shandon Church elected one female elder (Gene Lindler) and two female deacons in 1967. Women were still asking for a larger role, however. At the meeting of the Presbytery of South Carolina on April 2, 1968, a resolution was introduced recommending "that the attention of the members of the Sessions and Presbytery be called to the fact that there is a large reservoir of informed leadership among the women which might be more fully used to strengthen the work of the church, since women form such a small percentage of the membership of Sessions, boards, and committees of our Presbytery and its churches."[70]

By 1972 there were twenty-nine female elders in the synod, but there was still a desire for more opportunities to serve. Synodical president Irlene V. Cannon noted in her report that "the Church as the people of God must value all persons within its fellowship as God's own and regard both men and women as full members of the body of Christ ... We have talents, skills, and unique contributions that are needed by society. The time is now to use this leadership as church officers."[71]

68. "Women's Ordinations Practically Approved," *South Carolina Presbyterian*, 1.
69. General Assembly, 1965, 30, 96.
70. Women of the Church, 1968, 47.
71. Synod of South Carolina, 1972, 37.

Progress continued to be slow. Purity Church in Chester ordained its first women deacons in October 1975. In his history of the church, Dawson notes that "Purity seemed to have been willing to elect women before women were ready to serve."[72] The First Presbyterian Church in Greer ordained its first female deacon, Helen Holladay, in 1975. She served two terms as deacon and in 1981 was the first woman in that congregation to be elected elder. According to the church history, "She served wisely and well. Breaking new ground was not always easy, but she neither exploited her position as a woman nor allowed herself to be exploited. She simply served as a member who had the best interests of her church in mind. In doing so, she earned the respect of her colleagues on the Session."[73]

However, South Carolina and Georgia continued to lag behind other states. In 1979 only 11.7 percent of ruling elders and 9.9 percent of deacons in the Synod of the Southeast were women. This was by far the lowest percentage for any synod in the denomination. That same year, 33.4 percent of elders and 44.5 percent of deacons in Mid-America Synod (which included parts of Missouri and Kansas) were women. The synod most similar to the Synod of the Southeast was North Carolina, with 13.7 percent women elders and 14.7 percent deacons. By 1983, within the bounds of the former PCUS, only 25.2 percent of elders and 27.4 percent of deacons were women. By comparison, only five years later women made up 57 percent of elders in African American Presbyterian churches in the South Carolina low country. This was probably in part because, as members of the PCUSA, they were able to begin ordaining women elders much earlier.[74]

Changes were also taking place at the presbytery and synod levels. Inez Mitchum served as the first moderator of a South Carolina presbytery, Charleston Presbytery, in 1976. She had formerly headed the Women of the Church of Charleston Presbytery (1960 through 1962). Dr. Elizabeth Davidson of Hartsville moderated the meeting of Pee Dee Presbytery in July 1977. Mrs. Marvin Ellison of Piedmont Presbytery served as a commissioner to the General Assembly in 1975, apparently the first from South Carolina. In 1982 the report of the Executive Coordinator noted a 10.5 percent increase in woman officers. That same year a woman, Ms. Betty Cotton Brantley, served as synod moderator. She had come to her leadership through the opportunities offered by the Women of the Church, having served as president of that organization in Savannah Presbytery and as director of the 1978 Synod Women's Conference. By this time the General Assembly had had

---

72. Dawson, *Purity and Its People*, 146.
73. Blackwell, *A People and Their Faith*, 298.
74. Clarke, *Our Southern Zion*, 284.

two women moderators, both of whom had been chairs of the Board of Women's Work: Sarah B. Moseley (between 1978 and 79) and Dorothy G. Barnard (between 1981 and 82).

The churches of the PCUS were also slow to call women ministers. The first woman to be ordained as a minister in South Carolina was Elizabeth H. Dunlap, who had received an MCE degree from PSCE in 1959 and an MDiv from Columbia Theological Seminary in 1973. She was ordained by Bethel Presbytery on April 15, 1973, and apparently left immediately to serve as a missionary in Zaire. This was almost ten years after the first female minister had been ordained in the PCUS.

In 1977 women accounted for 1.4 percent of the denomination's pastors. By 1980 the number was only 3.3 percent. Figures on seminary enrollment were not very heartening either. In 1980 only 21 percent of the students in PCUS seminaries were women, the lowest percentage of any denomination.[75] In 1981 minutes from the meeting of the Synod of the Southeast indicate that there were only two female ministers and ten elders from South Carolina in attendance. The outlook improved in the PCUS as a whole, however. In 1986 there were three hundred female ministers within the bounds of the former PCUS, 53 percent of whom were in the pastoral ministry. That same year women accounted for 42 percent of seminary graduates; by 1989 the PC(USA) boasted 1,098 female ministers.

Conclusion

The position of women in the PCUS changed dramatically between 1925 and 1985. Their journey began with the significant contributions they made to the church's programs through their missionary work and their work in the Woman's Auxiliary. At first unable to speak in mixed gatherings, they eventually gained their voice. They were named to synod committees and were employed as pastor's assistants and Christian educators. In 1964, in a vote by its presbyteries, the denomination ruled that women could be ordained as deacons, elders, and ministers of the word and sacrament. In the twenty years that followed, they slowly took their place in positions of leadership. In 1985 Pat Hilliard, President of the Women of the Church in Harmony Presbytery, presented the following eloquent summary:

> More and more women are elected and appointed to positions of service on the Session, Diaconate, and church committees. Women are taking responsibility for and accepting the results of

---

75. Carroll, *Women of the Cloth*, 6.

the ideas, thoughts, and desires of their hearts in the church as they have done in their homes and the business world . . . Within the next few years we will have a slightly changed structure. This happened many times in the past seventy-eight years. Our obedience to the commands of our Lord and Savior remains unchanged. Our response to His love shows forth in our lives and identifies us as Christians.[76]

---

76. Harmony Presbytery, Women of the Church Minutes, April, 1985, 16.

5

African American Ministries

Initiatives and Partnerships

THE PURPOSE OF THIS chapter is to tell the story of how the two Presbyterian denominations, the Presbyterian Church in the United States (PCUS, from 1865 to 1983— southern Presbyterians) and the Presbyterian Church in the United States of America (PCUSA until 1958; UPCUSA, from 1958 to 1983) developed African American Presbyterian ministries in South Carolina. To develop this aim, the chapter first describes some congregations and Presbyterian parochial schools established after the Civil War by the northern Presbyterian mission in South Carolina, second describes home mission outreach to African Americans in South Carolina by the PCUS, and third considers ways some Presbyterian leaders in the Synod of South Carolina responded to the Civil Rights movement.

PCUSA Congregations in South Carolina

After the Civil War, the PCUSA commissioned missionaries to go to the South to establish churches and schools for the freed slaves. This evangelical work, shared by members of both white and black races, gave African American Presbyterians in the South a strong and distinctive regional Presbyterian identity that lives on today within the larger Presbyterian church.

In 1864 the PCUSA (Old School) Committee for Education of Freedmen began with three areas of responsibility: 1) organizing churches, presbyteries, and synods with the understanding that churches would be established by ordained missionaries and ministers who could train catechists; 2) providing education by establishing parochial schools with congregations; and 3) providing higher education for lay people and pastoral training for "native" ministers and teachers.[1] The PCUSA organized "the Committee on Freedmen" on June 21, 1865, within six weeks of the surrender at

---

1. Murray, *Presbyterians and the Negro*, 163–5.

Appomattox. With the Freedman's Bureau, established by the United States Congress in March 1865, the Presbyterians joined other denominations in a collaborative mission to the South to respond in evangelism and service to the former slaves.

The denomination established synods and presbyteries in the South to provide regional organization. Atlantic Synod, founded in 1868 for Southern Virginia through Florida, encompassed three South Carolina presbyteries: Atlantic Presbytery (founded in 1868) for the coastal area around Charleston; Fairfield for the central counties (1872); and McClelland (1885) for the Piedmont. Fairfield-McClelland Presbytery was established in South Carolina from the two previous presbyteries in 1959, and congregations in Clarendon, Lee, and Sumter counties were realigned from Fairfield-McClelland and taken into Atlantic Presbytery.

After the Old School and New School streams of the PCUSA reunited in 1869, the mission to the former slaves became organized as the Board of Missions for Freedmen in 1882. This Board continued until 1923 when the name was changed to "Board of National Missions Division of Work for Colored People." Though "Colored People" sounds racist now, at the time it reflected the progressive usage incorporated by the National Association for the Advancement of Colored People founded by W. E. B. Dubois in 1909. The office of the Board established in Pittsburgh in 1885 remained there until 1938, when Dr. John M. Gaston (chairman from 1911 to 1938) retired. Mindful of paternalism in the previous administration and to begin a move toward incorporating African American work into the regular offices of the denomination, the Reverend Albert B. McCoy became the first African American Field Secretary for the PCUSA, and the title of the department was changed to "Unit of Work with Colored People." In 1951 the Reverend Jesse B. Barber, former dean of the seminary at Lincoln University in Philadelphia, became head of PCUSA work with African Americans. African American support and programs were gradually dispersed among various denominational departments without regard to race, and in the United Presbyterian Church in the United States of America (UPCUSA), African American mission and programs were included in the regular organization of the denomination.[2]

After they were free, the majority of African American Presbyterians affiliated with Baptist and Methodist congregations. The former slaves left the PCUS, most of them never to return, but thousands were ready to welcome the ministry of northern Presbyterian missionary pastors and lay people establishing congregations and schools.[3] African American congregations in the synods of the Southeast developed their own strong iden-

---

2. Swann, *All-Black Governing Bodies*, 88–94.
3. Ibid., 41–2.

tity in leadership and programs with a determination that issued in a large Presbyterian witness concentrated in the Carolinas.

By 1916 the PCUSA had established 113 parochial schools in the Southeast and administered 67 public high schools and 27 boarding schools in South Carolina. North Carolina Scotia Women's College in Concord (renamed Barber-Scotia College in 1932) and the Henry J. Biddle Memorial Institute and Seminary in Charlotte, North Carolina (renamed Johnson C. Smith University in 1923), offered college and seminary nearby.

Year	Communicant Members	Churches	Ministers
1925	6,682	106	62
1930	7,037	96	50
1940	7,298	86	50
1950	7,244	74	54
1960	6,464	69	43
1970	7,153	62	41
1980	6,351	57	45
1985	6,025	31	

South Carolina Membership in Synod
of the Atlantic Congregations

Selecting a few of their congregations illustrates the remarkable story of how African American Presbyterian churches in great relative strength were established and continue to serve today in the PC(USA). These congregations in South Carolina, formerly in Atlantic and Fairfield-McClelland presbyteries, now are in the presbyteries of Charleston-Atlantic, New Harmony, Providence, Trinity, and Foothills in the Synod of South Atlantic. Selected from available local histories, these churches show the patterns of planting and growth that were typical of the PCUSA home missions in the South.

St. James Presbyterian Church on James Island is today one of the largest African American Presbyterian churches in North America. Records show that in the period from 1833 to 1845, there were 34 white members, 153 slaves, and one black free man; between 1853 and 1862, there were 234 black members.[4] When the church building burned soon after the Civil War, black members began to worship under a large oak tree on a parcel of the Ephraim Clark plantation. Clark gave them the land, and the members constructed a brush arbor as their forebears during slavery had done to seek their own worship. Atlantic Presbytery licensed Paul Campbell, a former slave "watchman" for the black members of the James Island Presbyterian

4. Ibid., 153.

Church, as pastor. In 1866 Reverend Hezekiah Hampleton Hunter came as a missionary from the North, and the African American congregation was organized as St. James Presbyterian Church by Catawba Presbytery in 1867 and then transferred to Atlantic Presbytery when it was formed for the PCUSA South Carolina congregations in 1868.

St. James Presbyterian Church was among the earliest of the northern mission Presbyterian churches in the Charleston area. For twenty-eight years until 1894, Reverend Hunter led the church. Under his leadership the congregation grew to four hundred members, the largest membership of any Presbyterian Church in the low country. The long pastorates of A. P. Frayer (from 1894 to 1917) and Marion A. Sanders (from 1924 to 1962) lent great stability in the church and its parochial school, and in 1965 the church reported a membership of 1,030 members, 15 Sunday school teachers, and 250 Sunday school students. In 1969 St. James called the Reverend Cornelius Leroy Campbell as pastor. Under his leadership the church constructed a large sanctuary to accommodate the membership and nurture the community ministries of the congregation. At the time of Presbyterian reunion in 1983, Campbell served on the Task Force for Presbytery Boundaries, and the St. James Presbyterian Church was the host congregation for the First Stated Meeting of Charleston-Atlantic Presbytery, February 6, 1988. The Reverend Charles and the Reverend Carolyn Heyward are strong pastoral leaders today in this church which has now come into the greater Charleston urban area.

The Reverends Carol and Charles Heyward

On Edisto Island, the separate African American Presbyterian Church was established when white members of the southern Presbyterian congregation, returning to the community after the Civil War, evicted its black members from the old church building where they had continued to worship. Ishmael Moultrie, a remarkable freedman who had learned to read from his owner, was ordained by Catawba Presbytery, worked with Hezekiah Hampleton Hunter on the Sea Islands, and organized the African American Edisto Island church in 1866.[5] The Larimer Presbyterian school was also established about the same time.

Reverend McKinley Washington Jr. began serving the Edisto Presbyterian Church, Faith Presbyterian Church, and St. Paul's Presbyterian Church, Hollywood, South Carolina, in 1962 as a student and accepted their call as pastor in 1964.

Reverend McKinley Washington, Jr. and his wife, Beulah

In 1976 Reverend Washington was elected to the South Carolina State House of Representatives where he served District 116 from 1975 to 1990 and as state senator from 1990 to 2000. Since Ishmael Moultrie, Edisto Presbyterian has had only eight ministers. This tradition of stability, long service, and strong commitment to the congregation and community has also characterized the history of St. Paul Presbyterian Church where Reverend Audrey O. Deas has served as pastor.

The largest number of African American Presbyterians in the Charleston area came from the Johns Island Presbyterian Church, which reported 510 slave members in 1860.[6] H. H. Hunter and Ishmael Moultrie were also instrumental in gathering them together after the Civil War, establishing

---

5. Parker, *The Rise and Decline*, 142–4.
6. Raynal, *Johns Island Presbyterian Church*, 50–2.

churches on Wadmalaw and Johns Island. The Mary A. Steele Memorial School served the community on those islands until 1933.

Zion-Olivet Presbyterian Church came from the joining in 1958 of two African American congregations in Charleston. The Zion Presbyterian Church was established as a church for African Americans in 1847 as part of the southern Presbyterian ante-bellum mission to the slaves. Zion thrived under the leadership of prominent South Carolina ministers John B. Adger and John Lafayette Girardeau. Girardeau was a native of James Island, whose lively preaching from 1853 to 1861 attracted large crowds of African Americans and white patrons to the balcony in its sanctuary on Calhoun and Meeting Streets, the largest church building in Charleston.[7] Olivet was established as a mission on George Street by the Wallingford Presbyterian Church.[8]

Wallingford Presbyterian Church and Wallingford Academy were established by the PCUSA in 1867. The church and academy, named by a gift to the PCUSA Committee on Freedmen from Mrs. E. G. Wallingford of Pittsburgh, Pennsylvania, in memory of her husband, shared a building on Meeting Street. The school was the first of the Presbyterian boarding academies established in South Carolina, and like the Congregational denomination's Avery Normal Institute, it became a model for other boarding academies for African Americans.

The Wallingford church mission became Olivet Presbyterian Church in 1879, located with its manse on Beaufrain Street where the congregation ministered for a half century. Joseph R. Pearson was its pastor from 1906 to 1943. He was from Walterboro, came through the Presbyterian school there, and was educated at Biddle Memorial Institute and Seminary in Charlotte, North Carolina. His education shows how the PCUSA developed second generation leaders from the African American community in South Carolina.

In 1958, during the pastorate of Simon H. Scott, the Session of Zion voted to unite with Olivet, and the two celebrated their joining August 16, 1959. F. Perry Metz, the son of William Lee Metz of the Edisto Island Presbyterian Church (from 1916 to 1946), served at Olivet from 1944 to 1959 and then the united congregation until 1984. The congregation began worshipping at its new sanctuary and educational building on Cannon Street in 1964. Sidney E. Davis has been pastor of Zion-Olivet since 1992. These long pastorates show again the gifts of remarkable stability and commitment in the African American Presbyterian community in South Carolina.

7. Clarke, *Our Southern Zion*, 108–9.
8. Swann, *Congregational Histories*, 271–2.

The intertwining of the histories of Zion Presbyterian Church, Wallingford Presbyterian Church and Academy, and Olivet Presbyterian Church is a good example of how the PCUSA through Atlantic Presbytery carried out its evangelical mission to establish congregations and schools in the city, where this strong heritage bears faithful witness today through Charleston-Atlantic Presbytery.

Several congregations, formerly in Fairfield-McClelland Presbytery, indicate how the mission moved inland from the coast. The Ladson Presbyterian Church in Columbia represents an example of an early African American congregation that grew out of the mission in the city. The PCUSA in 1838 established it as a Sabbath School on a tract of land on Sumter Street donated by Colonel Abram Blanding to First Presbyterian Church for "the religious training of Negroes."[9] George Whitfield Ladson, who died in 1864 while he was the pastor, was born in 1830 in Liberty County, Georgia, and came to serve the mission as a student at Columbia Theological Seminary (from 1859 to 1862). The church was named for him.

After the Civil War, the PCUSA resumed and renewed its ministry, establishing it as an independent African American congregation. First Presbyterian Church, Columbia, transferred the title to the property to the Trustees of Ladson Presbyterian Church in 1876, soon after the organization of Fairfield Presbytery, and in that year the church called the Reverend Mack Johnson, a graduate of Howard University, to be the pastor. The fifty-one year service of this dedicated pastor carried the church through the period from Reconstruction into the third decade of the twentieth century until he died in 1921. Ladson Presbyterian Church remains an important congregation in Trinity Presbytery.

Salem Presbyterian Church in Anderson and Second Presbyterian Church in Sumter show how the mission of congregations and parochial schools in local African American populations responded to particular needs in the third and fourth generation. Both Sumter and Anderson are county seats. Their economies depended upon the industrial development of the Piedmont and the agricultural black loam belt of the state. Anderson and its neighboring counties were both agricultural and industrial, but the Piedmont textile mills in South Carolina were prohibited by South Carolina law from employing African Americans. Reverend Charles Lawton established Second Presbyterian Church in Sumter in the second generation of leadership in Atlantic Presbytery in 1880. After Watkins's twenty-two year pastorate, A. U. Frierson became pastor. He came through the Goodwill School in Mayesville, received his BD and MA from Biddle Seminary, and

---

9. Ibid., 137.

in 1885 resigned a teaching position at Biddle to become pastor at Second Presbyterian Church and principal of Kendall Institute, where he remained until 1916 when he went to Salem Presbyterian Church and Salem Industrial School in Anderson. The move of A. U. Frierson from teaching at Biddle, serving at Sumter, and then exchanging calls with John Peter Foster in Anderson shows how networks of friendship, collegial ties, and the work of Fairfield and McClelland presbyteries assured continuity of strong leadership. The introduction of industrial courses at the Kendall Institute prepared lay people for jobs outside textile employment. The evangelical and social program of worship and education equipped a Presbyterian lay and pastoral leadership well into the twentieth century. Second Presbyterian Church in Sumter received strong pastoral leadership from Reverend Dr. Robert E. Bligen Jr., and the congregation serves as an important part of the ministry of New Harmony Presbytery today with the leadership of its pastor the Reverend Gloria Jones Williams, a graduate of The Interdenominational Theological Center in Atlanta, Georgia.

Carmel Presbyterian Church, Chester, South Carolina, with Brainerd Institute (from 1869 to 1939), and George W. Long Memorial Presbyterian Church, Cheraw, South Carolina, with Coulter Memorial Academy (from 1881 to 1949), deserve particular mention.

Carmel Presbyterian Church has a distinguished and well documented history.[10] The Chester Mission was founded in 1868 as part of the New School Presbyterian southern outreach in the first generation by Reverend Samuel Loomis, a white minister. After the twenty-year service of Reverend and Mrs. Loomis, Professor and Mrs. John S. Marquis from Washington, Pennsylvania, served the institute until 1928 as administrator and teachers. Prominent African American ministers served both Carmel and Brainerd Institute in long tenures. It is appropriate that today the congregation is named George W. Long Memorial Presbyterian Church in honor of the devoted pastoral and educational leader who came in 1908 and served until his death in 1943.

After the Depression, the PCUSA established larger parishes, networks of support for groups of churches in rural areas for the efficiencies of cooperation and resources.[11] Fairfield Presbytery established the Goodwill Larger Parish between 1948 and 1949.[12] It was a gathering of eight congregations in Clarendon, Lee, and Sumter counties. The larger parish reinforced the connections among the congregations established through the previous generations. It offered strengthened leadership where congregations needed cooperative pastoral and educational work, and it enabled the consolidation of parochial schools into the 1960s.

10. Parker, *The Rise and Decline*, 152–6.
11. Murray, *Presbyterians and the Negro*, 207.
12. Adair, "Goodwill Larger Parish," 1951.

All around the formal congregational structures of southern white Protestantism, African Americans developed their own religious life. The very significant translation of the Christian gospel by the slaves and freed people in their own language and ethos is well known and documented.[13] We should recognize that the personal redemptive power of Christian faith expressed in the African American churches came from the movement and energy of the Holy Spirit in the lives of the African American people. We can see the signs of it in their testimony. The references to the building of a brush arbor for their own secure place for gathering and worship, the eloquence of the slave spirituals and the gospel music, the ready and competent preaching, teaching, pastoral care, church building and leadership, Sunday School missions, and broad and deep hunger for education in church related schools all bear ample testimony to personal faith and life that go beyond the testimony of official records. So in describing the history of church institutions, we barely touch the surface of the African American Presbyterian heritage.

School	Location	Grades	Enrollment
Ebenezer Grade School	Dalzell	6 Elementary	325
Goodwill School	Mayesville	9 Elementary	320
James Island	James Island	8 Elementary	155
Larimer High School	Edisto Island	12 Elem. & High School	76
Lincoln High School	Due West	6 Elem.	72
Brainerd Institute	Chester	5 Elem. & High	88 boarding
Coulter Memorial Academy	Cheraw	11 Elem. & High	366 some boarding
Harbison Agricultural and Industrial Institute	Irmo	8 High School and College	76 boarding

PCUSA Schools Remaining in South Carolina in 1933

Home Missions and the PCUS Negro Work Campaign in the Synod of South Carolina

From its founding in 1861 as the Presbyterian Church in the Confederate States of America and its continuation after 1865, the Presbyterian Church in the United States (PCUS) affirmed strong support for both foreign and domestic missions, including home mission work among African Americans. The first Assembly appointed a committee to prepare a plan for "the

---

13. Clarke, *Our Southern Zion*, 34–6.

religious instruction of the colored people," affirmed its wish to be united in worship with them, and promised its support. Dr. John Leighton Wilson (1809 to 1886) gave the report for the Executive Committee on Domestic Missions saying, "Our churches, pastors, and people have always recognized this claim to Christian equality and brotherhood and have rejoiced to have them associated in Christian union and communion in the public services and sacraments."[14]

Though sincere, these words failed to recognize that African Americans freed from slavery did not want to return to the balconies of white churches, and so in large numbers they flocked to their own churches. Nor did Wilson's promise early after the Civil War estimate fairly the meager financial resources nor summon sufficient commitment for a vigorous ministry among African Americans.

The PCUS reflected the increasing segregation of the races in society. Between 1874 and 1917, the PCUS erected three different racially segregated organizational structures for the few remaining African American members and new congregations. In 1874 it established Tuscaloosa Institute in Alabama to train African American pastors and lay members. Charles Allen Stillman (pastor in Tuscaloosa) was the moving spirit that led the effort to establish the Institute. He was born in Charleston, attended Oglethorpe University, and graduated from Columbia Theological Seminary in 1844. In 1895 the Institute was named in his memory.

First the PCUS approved the establishment of separate African American presbyteries. In 1898 the PCUS formed the Afro-American Presbyterian Church, with its own ministers and ruling elders, a racially separate southern Presbyterian denomination. In a day when public facilities were thoroughly segregated, African Americans could not travel easily or safely, meetings were poorly attended, and the denomination was not able to build up a substantial membership. In 1916 the PCUS General Assembly recognized the failure of the two previous organizations and reaffirmed its intention to support the southern Presbyterian African American churches.[15]

So the PCUS again established and incorporated into its life a racially segregated synod from all the presbyteries which had been established for African Americans. The Snedecor Synod was named in memory of Reverend James G. Snedecor (1855-1916), the denomination's Superintendent of the Committee of Colored Evangelism and principal of Stillman Institute. The synod reported 1,492 members in 1918. It sent commissioners elected by its presbyteries to the PCUS General Assembly, the highest governing

---

14. Thompson, *Presbyterians in the South*, Volume II, 97-8.
15. Alvis, *Religion and Race*, 14-5.

body. They voted. They led prayer in worship. Still they were seated in a group down toward the front of the meetings, and they roomed and took their meals separately from the white commissioners. Painful memories of this and other official discrimination linger today.

South Carolina Membership in Snedecor
Memorial Synod Congregations, 1925–1970

Year	Members	Churches	SC Ministers
1925	343	8	5
1930	356	8	5
1940	364	8	5
1950	321	8	5
1960	398	8	2
1970	316	6	1

Presbytery of North and South Carolina (1925–1952), Presbytery of Georgia–Carolina (1952–1967), Presbytery of Carolina, 1967–1968)

The Synod of South Carolina placed its work among African Americans in the home mission evangelical effort to bring new members and establish new congregations. In 1924 the synod heard about the home mission work with African Americans in Pee Dee Presbytery: "Reverend R. B. Strong, a Negro Presbyterian Minister, began work Nov. 1, 1923. Half of his salary is paid by the Assembly Home Mission Committee. His work is among the large number of spiritually destitute Negroes of this Pee Dee section and largely in the counties of Dillon and Marlboro. A few small churches have been organized with some thirty-five added to the membership."[16]

As the decade of the 1920s moved toward the Great Depression, church resources diminished. The cotton crop failed and devastated the rural economy of South Carolina years before the Great Depression affected the whole nation. The Presbyterian Church became poorer, and synod's institutions lost funding. Home Missions reported losses throughout much of the decade. In the five years from 1929 to 1933, the synod's commitment to Home Missions dropped from $12,396 to $4,173, a loss of 56.1 per cent.[17] Reverend R. B. Strong resigned from Pee Dee Presbytery in 1926. No one took his place in African American home missions.

---

16. Synod of South Carolina, 1924, 43.
17. Ibid., 1933, 26.

In 1934, when the synod was beginning to recover from the Depression, Daniel M. McIver, pastor at Bishopville, reported for Assembly's Home Missions that the churches were encouraged to study E. T. Thompson's *Presbyterian Missions in the Southern United States*. Thompson was Professor of Church History at Union Theological Seminary in Richmond, Virginia, from 1922 to 1964. His book had a historical account of African American Presbyterians in a chapter "Early Wards of the South," which considered denominational practice until about 1930. The choice of *ward*, implying parental guardianship, was an unfortunate paternalism; however, the spirit of Dr. Thompson's work encouraged sympathy for the application of the gospel to social concerns and a relatively progressive view of race relations. He urged the southern Presbyterian Church to meet the missionary challenge of the whole New South. His outlook was shared by colleagues, and his students and leaders in the denomination moved to address social concerns as a part of Presbyterian witness. Thompson's advocacy contributed toward the PCUS ministry of evangelism with African Americans.

In 1945 the Synod of South Carolina heard advocates for evangelism in the African American Community. Reverend F. T. McGill, pastor in Greer who became the Secretary of Home Mission in South Carolina Presbytery (1950–62), reported that the General Assembly had set up the Ad Interim Committee to study Negro Work. He called the synod's attention to "a growing interest and an awakened Christian conscience among the membership of our Church in regard to our responsibilities towards the many millions of un-saved Negroes in our very midst." As local examples, he reported, "In our own synod, Florence First and Spartanburg First are doing outstanding work among the Negroes; and all our churches are urged to enlarge their work among our Negro friends at our very doors."[18]

A group of twenty African American ministers representing the denomination signed a request for supporting Negro Work, and in 1946 the PCUS General Assembly established a campaign designating a committee with "our Negro constituency" given representation and providing $100,000 budgeted each year.[19] It envisioned a program of evangelism and organized Sunday Schools and mission points under African American leadership incorporated into Snedecor Synod. It urged cooperation with the Presbyterian Board Executive Committee for Religious Education, calling a director of religious education for Snedecor Synod and providing college scholarships for outstanding African American youth. The emphasis on higher education included reorganization and a capital campaign of $1,000,000 for Stillman

18. Synod of South Carolina, 1945, 50.
19. Alvis, *Religion and Race*, 13–45.

Institute, developing it into a four-year college with special provision for training church leadership.

Several members of the denomination's committee for evangelizing African American people came from the Synod of South Carolina. Dr. J. McDowell Richards had been the President of Columbia Theological Seminary since 1932 and attended nearly every meeting of the Synod of South Carolina. The committee was interracial. George Washington Gideon, born in Fairplay in 1874, had attended Ferguson and Williams College in Abbeville and Stillman Institute. Gideon came from the Afro-American Presbyterian church into the PCUS and in 1917 was the first moderator of the Snedecor Memorial Synod. While pastor of Rice Memorial Presbyterian Church in Atlanta, he served in the same office twice more in 1937 and 1944. The task of evangelism brought white and black Presbyterians together in South Carolina in spite of the pervasive acceptance of racial segregation in the church and society.

In 1950 the Reverend Alex R. Batchelor became the Secretary of the Division of Negro Work of the PCUS Board of Church Extension.

Reverend Alex R. Batchelor
(Courtesy of Presbyterian College)

Originally from Geneva, New York, he graduated from Presbyterian College, completed his MA at the University of South Carolina and his BD at Columbia Theological Seminary. Batchelor's enthusiasm for the work among African Americans is apparent in his book *Jacob's Ladder: Negro Work of the Presbyterian Church in the United States*. He gives an account of the move to develop the Negro Work Campaign. He celebrated the decision of the Presbyterian Church in the United States "to make an exhaustive study of the whole field of our Assembly's evangelistic and educational work among the Negroes within the bounds of our Assembly."[20] He was convinced that the change in 1946 was a decisive corporate shift and new commitment.

When Batchelor died, his assistant Dr. Lawrence W. Bottoms, originally from Selma, Alabama, became his successor as the Secretary of the Division of Negro Work. In 1974 Dr. Bottoms was elected the only African American Moderator of the Presbyterian Church in the United States. When the previous moderator placed the official cross around his neck, Bottoms famously quipped, "Any time any white person puts anything around my neck, it makes me nervous."[21]

The Negro Work Campaign showed clearly that segregation provided no wholesome environment for the spirit of evangelism. Dr. Walter L. Lingle, president emeritus of Davidson College, spoke at the 1950 General Assembly meeting to urge incorporating the African American presbyteries into the geographical synods of the church: "The time has come when we will have to abolish the color line in our religious work if we wish to reach the present generation of Negroes."[22] African American presbyteries would remain apart until received by the synods and presbyteries in their respective geographical areas. After debate, Ruling Elder Francis Pickens Miller in a forceful word appealed for the adoption. "The question we ought to face," he said, "is what do you mean by the church? Is it a race thing? God forbid! The Church of our Lord Jesus Christ is a community of all believers."[23] So in 1951, three years before the action of the US Supreme Court to set aside the segregation of public schools, the southern Presbyterian Church Assembly voted to integrate African American Presbyterians into the governing bodies of the denomination.

In its own life and organization, the denomination espoused cooperation and equality of authority of black and white members in the General

---

20. Batchelor, *Jacob's Ladder*, 1.
21. "Report on Early Steps," *Time Magazine*, July 1, 1974.
22. Thompson, *Presbyterians in the South*, Vol. 3, 421.
23. Ibid., 422.

Assembly, synods, and presbyteries; however, the lower church judicatories, especially presbyteries and local church sessions, often opposed this early move toward inter-racial partnership in the denomination. The presbyteries of the Synod of South Carolina moved very slowly to incorporate African American congregations. There were only seven PCUS African American congregations in the state, all located in Harmony Presbytery and Pee Dee Presbytery in Williamsburg, Dillon, and Clarendon counties. Gathered in 1952 in Georgia-Carolina Presbytery, they remained apart until 1967 when the presbyteries finally received them.

Meanwhile the Negro Work Campaign continued, and the Synod of South Carolina responded. The goal the General Assembly designated for the Synod of South Carolina was $206,216, over 10 percent of the goal of $2,000,000. In 1951 Arthur Martin, pastor of Sion Presbyterian Church in Winnsboro and from 1952 to 1972 the Executive Secretary for the Synod, urged study of Batchelor's *Jacob's Ladder* and recommended "that churches and presbyteries explore the possibilities for establishing churches for Negroes, specially [sic] in the cities."[24] In 1952 James C. Wool, Chair of the Negro Work Subcommittee of the synod, urged the Committees on Church Extension of the presbyteries "to survey the possibilities on the development of Negro Work within their bounds and report to synod's Church Extension Committee such projects as in their judgment should be initiated." He called on local churches to "face their responsibility for Negro Evangelism."[25] Edward G. Lilly of Charleston, Chair of the Negro Work Campaign in the synod, gave a report of the result. By August 21, 1953, the Synod had subscribed 61 percent of its goal. Of the 312 PCUS churches in South Carolina, 199 (64 percent) had participated.

A few new initiatives in local churches followed. The synod answered a request from Lawrence Bottoms, Secretary of the denomination's Division of Negro Work, with funds for the support of Allen E. Fortune, the pastor of Bethel Church and St. James Church, Kingstree. Bottoms acknowledged the funding with kind words: "This interest on the part of your Synod will do a great deal to strengthen Negro work in South Carolina. We are grateful for your interest."[26]

In 1954 the Division of Negro Work helped bring about a call to the Reverend Charles Coles to organize a new Presbyterian church in a cooperative mission among African American people started by the Presbyterian Council of Greater Greenville.

24. Synod of South Carolina, 1953, 24.
25. Ibid., 1954, 3.
26. Ibid., 1958, 40.

Reverend Charles Coles (Courtesy of
Columbia Theological Seminary)

However, Enoree Presbytery by a close vote (31 to 30) refused to receive Coles and admonished him: "Presbytery suggests to the Reverend Charles Coles (colored) . . . that he seek membership in the Georgia-Carolina Presbytery, colored, of the Synod of Georgia."[27] Georgia-Carolina Presbytery, meeting October 19, 1954, at Bethel Presbyterian Church in Hamer, South Carolina, assigned Coles to the Greenville Mission. In 1954 Enoree Presbytery missed by one vote the opportunity to be the first South Carolina presbytery to receive an African American pastor as a member. However, the effort in Greenville established Nicholtown Presbyterian Church in 1961.

In 1953 the Religious Education Committee made a request for synod to approve a Negro Youth Conference as a part of the Negro Work Campaign. H. Dockery Brown, minister in Rock Hill reporting for the Stewardship Committee, urged the churches to raise their goal for the Negro Work Campaign. The Men of the Church conducted the youth conference July 5–10, 1954, and W. Ted Jones, the synod's Regional Director of Religious Education, reported that seventy-eight Negro High School students attended from all eight presbyteries. Interracial leadership came from both

27. Enoree Presbytery Minutes, September 14, 1954, 36.

PCUS and PCUSA churches. Jones characterized the 1954 youth conference this way: "The Negro ministers all agreed that this was the best youth conference they ever attended, and the Regional Director has about ten 'letters of appreciation' from Negro young people. We believe such a conference conducted annually, as in several other synods, will have far reaching effect both on the Christian leadership among Negroes and on relations between the races."[28]

The Georgia-Carolina Presbytery cooperated in other ways with the Division of Negro Work to strengthen the churches. It recommended that congregations be yoked together to make calling a pastor more feasible. In 1955 Mt. Pelier Presbyterian Church in Rowland, North Carolina, New Liberty in Dillon, and Bethel in Hamer were brought together, as were Mt. Hebron in McColl and New Bethel in Florence. In 1956 that presbytery grouped together St. James in Kingstree and New Bethel in Florence. In spite of the synod's failure to achieve all its goals, the General Assembly's program to develop African American Presbyterian churches and leadership gained strength in South Carolina.

Through the evangelistic efforts of the Negro Work Campaign, the PCUS brought several thousand African Americans into the denomination, revitalizing existing churches and developing new ones. In 1946 approximately three thousand African American members were reported; in 1955 the number was five thousand; in the 1960s the number increased to seven thousand. The program renewed Stillman College. Dr. Sam Burney Hay had been called in 1948 from First Presbyterian Church in Auburn, Alabama, to become its president, where he remained until 1965. Presbyterian Women of the Church supported it six times with its substantial Birthday Offering, continuing a long tradition of its sense of mission with African Americans. When the Negro Work Campaign ended, the Civil Rights movement was establishing a new basis for the relationship of the white and black races in both society and the churches. In spite of racism and segregation in church and society, the Negro Work Campaign strengthened PCUS partnership with African Americans.

Further changes in policy and attitudes about race relations followed the Negro Work Campaign. The Reverend Charles Coles met with the all-white Enoree Presbytery in January 1963. He had been serving the Nicholtown Presbyterian Church in Greenville while remaining in Georgia-Carolina Presbytery, still left from the dissolution of Snedecor Synod. Finally on April 13, 1965, eleven years after the first request, the congregation and its pastor came into Enoree Presbytery.

---

28. Synod of South Carolina, 1954, 38.

In 1965 Arthur Martin, Executive Secretary of the Synod, reported that five presbyteries (Bethel, Enoree, Pee Dee, Piedmont, and South Carolina) voted in favor, and three presbyteries (Charleston, Congaree, and Harmony) voted against the General Assembly amendment to the *Book of Church Order* declaring that all Presbyterian Church congregations should welcome all persons.[29] In 1966 he again reported that the four Negro churches in the bounds of Pee Dee Presbytery and the two in the bounds of Harmony Presbytery had not been received. The Presbyteries objected to the policy of the General Assembly to unite the African American congregations with the presbyteries even though the Synod was obliged to conform to the governance of the denomination.

In 1967 Thomas J. James, representing the Presbytery of Georgia-Carolina and the seven remaining South Carolina African American churches, reported to the Judicial Committee appointed to deal with the dispute of 1964 between Pee Dee and Harmony presbyteries and the General Assembly:

> Mr. Moderator, Fathers, and Brethren, I bring you greetings and goodwill from the Synod of Georgia, in behalf of the Presbytery of Georgia-Carolina and the seven churches in its bounds: Cousar Memorial at Bishopville, St. James at Kingstree, Mt. Pisgah at Hartsville, New Bethel at Florence, New Bethel at Dillon, Old Bethel at Hamer, and Mt. Hebron at McColl. These churches have been organized some eighty or ninety years ago by our fathers of both races. These churches desire to come under the banner of the Synod of South Carolina, where they can have communion and fellowship with the saints. We beg your prayers that we might grow in grace and in the knowledge of our Lord and Savior, Jesus Christ.[30]

James, who was eighty-six years old when he spoke these words, was born in Bishopville. He had studied at Columbia Seminary between 1918 and 1919, at Stillman Institute between 1919 and 1921, and was ordained by North and South Carolina Presbytery (Snedecor Memorial Synod) in 1922.

29. Ibid., 1965, 20.
30. Ibid., 1967, 55.

Reverend Thomas J. James

He organized and served Mt. Pisgah Church in Hartsville from 1926 until his retirement in 1958. His eloquent request persuaded the Committee. Finally in 1968, eighteen years after the PCUS moved to receive them, Pee Dee and Harmony Presbytery received the few African American congregations that had been segregated since the nineteenth century. The synod offered tribute to Thomas J. James who had served most of these years and "who at age eighty-seven is still preaching, and continuing his work among the Negro Presbyterians of our Synod."[31]

The synod continued its work through the Church Extension Committee to enlarge and strengthen its witness among African Americans. Presbyterian College admitted its first African American student in 1965. Thornwell Orphanage integrated its admission policy in 1970. New energy for the denomination's program for church extension among African Americans shows in reports in the 1960s and into the 1970s.

For example, in 1964 Reverend Cecil D. Brearley Jr., Chair of the Negro Work Subcommittee for Church Extension, reported cooperative work with General Assembly's Board of Church Extension and Pee Dee Presbytery to construct a sanctuary for New Bethel Presbyterian Church in Florence. The synod accepted $3,000 out of $28,340 of the estimated cost, and "an anonymous friend in Chicago has given $5,000 for building and $4,000 for equipment." Brearley also reported, "The Nicholtown Church in

---

31. Ibid., 1968, 46.

Greenville and the missions in Spartanburg are the chief activities in Negro Work participated in by churches in this Synod. The Dillon Church is helping the New Liberty Church of Negroes in that city, too.[32]

Another instance of cooperation and sharing came when Dr. James E. Cousar challenged Cousar Memorial Presbyterian Church in Bishopville with $2,000 to build an educational building. That same year William McLeod Frampton reported for the Standing Committee on Judicial Business that Allen E. Fortune had become a member of Congaree Presbytery, along with pastors Leroy Horsley, William I. H. Reeves, and James L. Robinson. Roy A. Booten was ordained and installed as pastor of Mt. Pisgah and New Bethel. In partial response to Cousar's challenge gift, the synod in 1969 designated $1,000 for the educational building of the Cousar Memorial Church and an additional $1,000 for the building of Mt. Pisgah Church in Hartsville. Arthur Martin, Executive Secretary, took over supplying pulpits of some African American churches and worked with others to hold Sunday services. The personal interaction brought concrete cooperation in ministry and program.

Presbyterian Women provided helpful joint work with African Americans. Mrs. Pricilla S. Sheppard, President of the Women of the Church, reported, "While arguments were still going on in our Synod, the women quietly opened Synodical Training School last year to the women of the presbyterials left homeless by the suspension [in 1967] of the Interdenominational Conference in Columbia." She observed, "Nothing happened except the proving of Christian love and interest to these fellow Christians in our Synod. Not enough of them came, but it was a beginning."[33]

Arthur Martin's annual reports emphasized the progress in unity and fellowship. In 1971 he said that in connection with Church Extension, "four of our Black Presbyterian churches are presently in the midst of building programs." Meanwhile the implications of the civil rights legislation moved ahead in the state, and the social context of change had bearing on the synod. Martin reported, "There have been several causes for disturbance in the Synod. During 1970 the Federal Government commanded complete integration of public schools. Our churches and members have generally taken a positive, sympathetic, and helpful stance toward the problems involved. The Thornwell Board of Trustees revised their charter in line with the desires of the General Assembly, Synod and Government."[34]

32. Ibid., 1964, 49.
33. Ibid., 1969, 30.
34. Ibid., 1971, 32.

Confirmation of Martin's judgment came from within Harmony Presbytery which just two years before had been reluctant to receive African American churches. James E. Graham, chair of the Harmony Presbytery Committee on National Ministries, told the synod that the work at Cousar Memorial, Bishopville, was progressing under the leadership of the pastor of the Bishopville church. Cousar Memorial was providing day care for sixty children with support from the denomination's Board of National Ministries ($1,800) and Presbytery's Committee ($2,400). In addition, Presbytery gave $1,000 for Cousar's indebtedness. That same year, Reverend Ben F. Ormand, Executive Secretary of Pee Dee Presbytery, recounted three significant events. 1. Parkwood Presbyterian Church was organized. 2. Mt. Pisgah Church, Hartsville, and New Bethel Church, Florence, called as pastor Chester B. Johnston from Charlotte in August 1971. Mt. Pisgah was planning new construction. 3. The New Bethel Church, Dillon, under the leadership of Sandy A. Dingle, completed a new building in 1971, dedicated on January 16, 1972. The cost was over $45,000; the congregation owed $20,000.

The PCUS Division of Negro Work, under the persistent and quiet leadership of Dr. Alex R. Batchelor from 1947 to 1955 and Dr. Lawrence W. Bottoms from 1947 to 1973 moved the PCUS to greater openness to full African American participation. Lawrence Bottoms gave effective and gracious leadership as Moderator of the PCUS General Assembly in 1974 and 1975. In contributing to the Negro Work Campaign, establishing Nicholtown Presbyterian Church, giving pastoral and program sustenance, and at last including the remaining PCUS African American congregations in regular ties with the Synod, South Carolina congregations and pastors were finally together in one body. The Synod moved toward a new structure in 1973, and the next step of inclusion was the uniting of the PCUS and the UPCUSA in 1983.

The Synod of South Carolina Responds to Civil Rights

At the beginning of the 1920s, the synod largely confined ethical deliberations to matters of personal morality, and when it addressed public issues, it most often restricted its deliberations to prohibition and beverage alcohol. South Carolina Presbyterians increasingly addressed broader social concerns when the Great Depression, the outbreak of World War II, and racial inequality set vast moral perplexity before the nation. The PCUS was a member the Federal Council of Churches (reorganized in 1950 as the National Council of Churches). Although the denomination withdrew in 1931 on charges that the Federal Council was sympathetic to communism, it rejoined in 1941 in the midst of the mobilization for World War II.[35] In spite of continuing hesitancy about corporate advocacy for social justice, the Synod of South Carolina heard the ecumenical voice during the 1930s and early 1940s in reports from the South Carolina Synod's Committee on Social and Moral Welfare. The national emergency overcame the denomination's socially conservative reluctance to participate in the mainline Protestant witness in the United States.

For example in 1941, the Committee on Social and Moral Welfare addressed a broad array of social questions and emphasized justice in race relations:

> Only by God's Grace can we escape the shackles of deep and abiding hate. The church must keep ever before the minds of our people that the boys of German and Italy and Japan are immortal souls who must stand in the presence of the eternal God—that the Christ who gave his love and life for us died that they too might have life and love. It may be our responsibility to be God's agents to restrain and even destroy the vicious systems of life and government in which they find themselves and restore human liberty to earth—yet must there be no hate. Hate can only make tragic confusion and bitterness more tragic.
>
> In a time like this our hearts and prayers need as never before to be centered in God's Kingdom on earth which transcends national and racial lines and embraces all God's people everywhere.[36]

Reverend J. W. Jackson, minister of First Presbyterian Church in Columbia from 1931 to 1958, reported for the same committee in 1942 and drew a parallel between Nazi racism and race prejudice in the South. He cited a report in *The Charlotte Observer* of a white racist rumor that African Americans were forming "Eleanor Clubs," named after Eleanor Roosevelt, to rise up against white women: "This problem calls for church people to be rumor spikers wherever possible. It likewise calls upon us when opportunity presents itself to exercise a ministry of reconciliation. Here is a call for education, enlightenment, and an understanding. Surely those who believe in the Gospel of Christ which refuses to recognize barriers of race, color, class, or nations have something to give to this problem."[37]

The practice of considering broader social concerns came before the 1947 synod meeting when the Reverend Samuel S. Wiley, pastor of First

---

35. Thompson, *Presbyterians in the South*, Vol. 3, 1973, 272–3.
36. Synod of South Carolina, 1941, 51.
37. Ibid., 1942, 49.

Presbyterian Church Anderson from 1946 to 1951, recommended a new name, "Committee on Christian Relations" instead of "The Committee on Social and Moral Welfare" to follow the PCUS General Assembly's move in reorganization. Wiley called attention to the areas of employer-employee relations and civil rights. He urged the people of the church not to be deterred by "the red herring of intermarriage." Wiley's report was reflecting the influence of Gunnar Myrdal's *An American Dilemma* (1944), which showed that the main issue for African Americans was equal and just claim on civil rights. Wiley's report was consistent with the voice of the Federal Council of Churches, and his statement came during the time that President Harry Truman advocated new measures in civil rights for African Americans.

While the PCUS Negro Work Campaign was moving forward, the decade of the 1950s brought out into the open pain and public conflict in race relations in South Carolina. In 1953 the PCUS General Assembly urged that the Church practice no discrimination in ministering to the needs of people and called on churches to observe Race Relations Sunday to promote good will. In "The Church and Segregation" (1954), the denomination encouraged the desegregation of church institutions of higher education and church conferences, and it asked all churches to admit people to membership and fellowship in the local church.

The 1954 report affirmed "that enforced segregation of the races is discrimination and is out of harmony with Christian theology and ethics, and that the Church, in its relationship to cultural patterns, should lead rather than follow. In this time of crisis and concern, we commend to all individuals in our communion and especially to all leaders of our churches the earnest cultivation and practice of the Christian graces of forbearance, patience, humility and persistent good will."[38] In South Carolina, at the 1954 meeting of the synod at Presbyterian College, Carl Pritchett, minister in Anderson, introduced Reverend Malcolm Calhoun, PCUS Secretary of Christian Relations, who presented the concerns of the denomination.

The response was cautious: "We recommend that the recent action of the Assembly on segregation be studied by our institutions, Sessions and churches and that they take such action as they think consistent with the will of God. We recommend that all of us make a genuine effort to cultivate understanding and promote good will in human relations in our communities."[39]

In 1954 the desegregation of Presbyterian College and Thornwell Orphanage was unacceptable to the majority of the ministers and lay people

---

38. General Assembly, 1954, 54, 187.
39. Synod of South Carolina, 1954, 24.

in the synod. The synod adopted this push-back resolution offered by John McSween: "It is the sense of the Synod of South Carolina that it is in the best interest of harmonious relations between the white and Negro races in this section at this time that the present enrollment policies in the institutions under the control and support of the Synod be continued."[40]

The decision by the synod on a vote of 136 to 83 made the news. The *Greenville News* and *The State*, on September 1, 1954, carried headlines that told the story: "S. C. Presbyterians Favor Segregation" and "Presbyterians on Record for Segregation." The action served to notify the trustees of Presbyterian College and Thornwell Orphanage that the Synod did not expect the General Assembly declaration to cause change in their policies for the foreseeable future. Presbyterian College admitted its first African American student in 1965. Thornwell desegregated when the public schools integrated in 1971.

Many South Carolina Presbyterians continued to favor the old policies of segregation of the races. For example in 1956, Harmony Presbytery, joining East Alabama Presbytery, sent an overture to the 96th General Assembly to protest the stated policy of "opening our churches, schools, and colleges to all races."[41] Again in 1957, Congaree Presbytery petitioned the General Assembly, meeting at South Highland Presbyterian Church in Birmingham, not to break the Jim Crow law restricting integration of Alabama public facilities. The effect would have been to ban African American commissioners from the meeting in that church. In 1958 the Presbytery of Pee Dee joined with the Presbyteries of Mississippi and Tuscaloosa in an overture to dissolve the denomination's Council of Christian Relations, denying "that the Council on Christian Relations, or any other Committee or Council, has any authority to tell us what is Christian and what is not Christian."[42] Some South Carolina Presbyterians were expressing deep resentment for the denomination's rejection of segregation in its own governance and in the society beyond the church. At the higher governing level, George H. Vick, Chair of the General Assembly's Committee on Christian Relations, recommended a negative response to the overtures from South Carolina and Alabama.

Amid the turmoil of the 1950s, a few clear voices of local pastors and church members spoke out from pulpits and in public meetings for racial harmony, understanding, and justice. Prominent among South Carolina Presbyterians were John S. Lyles, pastor in Marion; Lucius B. DuBose, pastor in Mullins; and James McBride Dabbs, elder living near Mayesville. Lyles and four other South Carolina ministers edited a pamphlet, "South

40. Ibid., 25.
41. General Assembly, 1956.
42. Ibid., 1958, 38.

Carolinians Speak" (July 1957). It gathered together twelve essays by prominent church members of several denominations who advocated a path of openness and moderation by citizens of South Carolina in response to the civil rights movement. The publication sparked notice. George Bell Timmerman Jr., governor from 1955 to 1959, tried to dismiss the message.[43] Later in October, after Lyles preached a sermon on race relations, the elders of the Marion Presbyterian church met while the minister was out of town and upon the pastor's return reported to him that he had "disrupted the leadership." At the next stated meeting, Lyles agreed to seek another position. After serving in West Virginia, Virginia, and Florida, sixteen years later he returned to the Lake City Presbyterian Church.

The 1960s brought further conflict and also progress in the Civil Rights movement. Lucius B. DuBose was pastor for two years at Mullins. He spoke against the policy of his officers not to seat African American visitors at church services. In September 1963, racists bombed the Sixteenth Street Baptist Church in Birmingham, Alabama, killing four little girls and injuring a score of other people. DuBose responded in a sermon: "Because Birmingham was my home town, I felt that I could and must speak a personal word growing out of my own sense of involvement in this horrible tragedy."[44] After his sermon, when he was out of town, the officers met and decided that he should seek a call elsewhere.

James McBride Dabbs, a ruling elder, was a distinguished writer and public figure in the state. He was President of the South Carolina Council of Human Relations from 1948 to 1953, the President of the Southern Regional Council from 1957 to 1963, and a lay member of the Presbyterian Church in the United States General Assembly's Permanent Committee on Christian Relations. In a 1964 address to a Georgia presbytery, Dabbs contrasted the good in southern culture with its failures: "As I see the racial revolution in the South, then, it is the Spirit of God working for freedom against bondage, and it is the spirit of the South discarding old evils, creating new goods. We should welcome the revolution, both as Christians and as southerners—as southern Christians."[45]

Dabbs represented a progressive voice in the southern Presbyterian Church. The synod heard this more progressive approach to social concerns through its representation in the South Carolina Christian Action Council. The Council was interracial, and it spoke for social justice in the wider South Carolina community. Presbyterians were active in its work. Reverend Neil Truesdell, pastor of Aveleigh Presbyterian Church, Newberry, South Carolina, was President from 1960 to 1964. Dr. Joseph T. Stukes, a Presbyterian

---

43 Edgar, *South Carolina, a History*, 528.
44. Shriver, *The Unsilent South*, 85.
45. Ibid., 98.

elder, originally from Manning, South Carolina, professor of history at Francis Marion University in Florence, South Carolina, was president from 1969 to 1972.

Joseph T. Stukes

Reverend Arthur M. Martin, Executive Secretary of the Synod from 1952 to 1973, took an active part in the work of the Council, joining other denominations calling for support of African American civil rights, for example in the 1960s at the time of the application of Harvey Gantt to Clemson University and a protest of segregation in Orangeburg in 1968.[46]

At the time of Harvey Gantt's application to Clemson University, the Council worked in connection with President Robert C. Edwards of Clemson and many other church and public figures to encourage a peaceful admission. South Carolina avoided the violent reactions that occurred at the admission of James Meredith to the University of Mississippi in the fall of 1962.

However, such peace did not always obtain. On February 8, 1968, a tragic outcome followed the student protest of segregation at a bowling alley in Orangeburg. Samuel Hammond and Henry Smith, South Carolina State University students, and Delano Middleton, a student at the Orangeburg Wilkinson High School, were shot dead by a police force of National

---

46. Spears, *The South Carolina Christian Action Council*, 6–7.

Guard and state patrolmen after a policeman was injured. Other bystanders were hurt, including a pregnant woman, Louise Cawley Kelly, who lost her child.[47] The South Carolina Christian Action Council asked state officials to work for reconciliation. Governor Robert E. McNair, a Southern Baptist, called it "one of the saddest days in the history of South Carolina."

Four years later, Governor John C. West, a Presbyterian from Camden, appointed Dr. Stukes to the new South Carolina Human Rights Commission, serving with James E. Clyburn, the Governor's appointed human affairs commissioner. Clyburn, a member of the African Methodist Episcopal Church, now serves as a US Congressman.[48] Through participation in the South Carolina Christian Action Council, members of the synod provided leadership with other denominational leaders to support social justice and racial reconciliation in the 1960s and 1970s.

Meanwhile, members of the United Presbyterian (UPCUSA) congregations in South Carolina were active in civil rights work. In an interview in 2008 at Second Presbyterian Church, Sumter, several African American Presbyterian pastors and lay people reflected on their individual church memories of Presbyterian parochial schools, the Civil Rights era, and other church matters. Reverend Dr. Robert E. Bligen Jr. served as pastor of Second Presbyterian Church, Sumter, from June 1970 to September 1998.

Reverend Dr. Robert E. Bligen

47. Ibid., 15–7.
48. Edgar, *South Carolina Encyclopedia*, 1014–5.

He grew up on Edisto Island, was educated in the schools on the Island and then at Johnson C. Smith University and Seminary (BA, 1959; BD, 1962) and McCormick Theological Seminary (DMin).

Bligen recalled the struggle for Civil Rights in the 1960s when he was pastor near Mayesville: "We had meetings and so many people came they were hanging out the windows. We were talking about voter registration and the schools." A prominent white citizen sent word that Bligen was not to have mass meetings at his church and charged a messenger "to tell me that he would be sure I didn't get paid. I sent a message back that the Board of Mission of the Presbyterian Church would pay my salary. After that I didn't hear any more."[49]

Others confirmed the theme. Dr. Franklin Colclough, Executive of New Harmony Presbytery, said, "The Presbyterian churches supported Civil Rights. J. Herbert Nelson and Ed Miller were jailed for sit-ins at lunch counters. Nelson helped organize the NAACP chapter."

Reverend Dr. Franklin Colclough

Mrs. Frances D. Singleton, elder at Second Presbyterian Church, Sumter, remembered, "In the Oakdale Community we were observers at the polls."[50]

49. Charles Raynal, Interview at Second Presbyterian Church, May 2008.
50. Ibid.

An excellent example of the leadership of African Americans in and beyond the civil rights era is Reverend McKinley Washington Jr., pastor at Edisto Island United Presbyterian Church from 1962 to 2012.[51] During his fifty-year pastorate, he was elected as South Carolina state representative from 1976 to 1990 and state senator from 1991 to 1994. He served as Chair of the South Carolina State Employment Security Commission and the Sea Island Comprehensive Healthcare Corporation. During his time in the state senate, the legislature appropriated funds for the new bridge connecting Edisto Island with the mainland and named it after him. At the time of his retirement, he reflected on his many years of dedication to progress in civil rights. He confirmed that members of his congregation and his friends in the United Presbyterian Church gave him full support for his election and service in the state legislature. His remarkable combination of leadership in service to church and state grew from the skills and sense of calling that he drew from the Presbyterian Church.

These memories from African American Presbyterians illustrate how the members of the United Presbyterian Church worked together in the civil rights struggle. Steven Hahn in *A Nation Under Our Feet: Black Political Struggles in the Rural South from Slavery to the Great Migration* has presented persuasive evidence showing that public responsibility and political skills flourished through generations of African Americans in a society that tried to deny them their part. Hahn demonstrates that grassroots political work by African Americans in local organizations, especially in churches, contributed to the civil rights movement in the twentieth century, and the testimonies of these African Americans in Sumter is consistent with his discovery.

Unfortunately, most PCUS members of the Synod of South Carolina ignored the possibilities of mutual accountability and support that might have come from connections with the United Presbyterian congregations. Over six thousand African American Presbyterians in the Presbyterian denomination were near at hand in all areas of the state. However, southern Presbyterians defeated the proposal to unite the PCUSA and the PCUS in 1955. The union would not come to pass until 1983.

In conclusion we can see that even during the 1950s, the Synod of South Carolina heard and entered into record voices from its leaders who espoused openness to the civil rights movement. The synod wanted to encourage the establishment and support of African American congregations. Various presbytery and congregational actions during the 1950s and 1960s opposed the welcome of African Americans to their worship services or

---

51. Ibid., Interview with McKinley Washington, 2012.

membership. During the same period, some South Carolina pastors who preached about race relations in their churches found their leadership rejected by their sessions. John Lyles in Marion and Lucius DuBose in Mullins provided examples of pastoral courage in the struggle for racial equality. Many other pastors of good will of both races worked steadily, seeking to be faithful to the message of the gospel in race relations. The PCUS advocacy for enfolding African American congregations into the regular regional governing bodies of the denomination and its advocacy of the principle that any person should be welcome in any congregation was a prophetic voice. The southern Presbyterian church became more open and welcoming to African American brothers and sisters. This increasing openness and partnership contributed to the reuniting of the largest branches of the Presbyterian churches in the United States in 1983.

Presbyterian Restructure and Reunion

In the late 1960s and early 1970s, the PCUS reorganized its boards and agencies. One feature of this new organization was the redrawing of synod lines. As the Synod of South Carolina with the Synod of Georgia formed the Synod of the Southeast, African Americans became a part of the governance and work of the governing body in a new way. The Presbyterian Church in the United States established a policy requiring the church to include women, racial-ethnic people, and persons under thirty years of age, groups formerly excluded from the regular work of the deliberative bodies of the church. The new structure required that these constituencies be represented in the committees and programs. The new synod took affirmative action in hearing new voices and acting upon minority concerns.

Meeting at Peachtree Presbyterian Church in Atlanta, Georgia, July 1-2, 1973, the Synod of the Southeast adopted standing rules which showed how minorities would figure in the organization. The rules required at least eight at-large members, including two persons from each constituency who were African American, women, and young people under the age of thirty. The synod's Coordinating Council elected the chair of the Coordinating Committee for Black Concerns from among its members. In turn the Committee recommended an African American member to represent it on the Coordinating Council. In 1975 Reverend John Talford, the chairman, was the first African American representative.

The Committee found nineteen black churches in Georgia, with seven active ministers serving and six black churches in South Carolina with three active ministers serving.[52] "The Committee found no new initiative for establishing black churches . . . [and that] blacks had no vehicle for expressions, concerns, or direct involvement in policy-making decisions."[53] The Committee proposed several recommendations to Synod's Coordinating council: placing blacks on policy level in presbytery, synod, and General Assembly; evangelizing the poor and disadvantaged; placing ethnic concerns in church literature; establishing a black campus ministry; establishing more black churches; and equipping blacks and minorities to deal with Presbyterian polity.

The Black Concerns Committee expressed its understanding this way: "We are very much interested in Synod having the knowledge that this body is not created as a separatist group, but as an ongoing part functioning within the total life of the church. This means that this committee is charged with the responsibility of heightening the black witness of the Synod of the Southeast."[54]

The denomination's policy had taken new form. Whereas before, African American ministries had been considered home missions, the new guiding policy espoused partnership in mission with present and active African American church leaders. This understanding would carry forward into the 1983 reunion of the Presbyterian denominations.

The Committee also recommended a convention of blacks and other minorities in which they "would be able to gather and express concerns, map strategies, and find handles for complete involvement in the total system of courts in the church."[55] The Coordinating Council authorized the gathering in March 15–16, 1975, in Montreat, North Carolina. From 1976 to 1983, the Black Concerns Committee reported on its two primary concerns, strengthening of existing black ministries and establishing new ones. In February 1978, twenty-two black leaders from the Synod gathered in Charleston at a meeting sponsored by the UPCUSA. The conference led to a five-year program of emphasis for developing leadership and a series of annual conventions. As the plans worked out, only four of the conferences took place, the last on Youth Ministry in October 1982. The report concluded, "The General Assembly is taking on more of the program leadership and will continue in this capacity."[56] The point of future reference was the reunited Presbyterian Church (USA).

52. Synod of the Southeast, 1975, 52–3.
53. Ibid.
54. Ibid.
55. Ibid.
56. Ibid., 1982, 47.

In the decade of the 1970s, as the Presbyterian Church in the United States developed a new alignment of its governing bodies, it noted that "the old establishment of Negro work" had ended. A full embrace of the needs and concerns of African American Presbyterians became an integral part of the organization and the program of the denomination. In the Synod of the Southeast, the initiative for inclusion and advocacy of the work of African Americans, along with so many other denominational programs, was moving toward the centralized work of the General Assembly. This movement of responsibility for Black Concerns to the General Assembly was occurring while the denomination was evaluating its structure and mission. The reunion of the two main Presbyterian denominations in the United States was underway.

6

South Carolina Presbyterians and Higher Education

AMERICAN PRESBYTERIANS, SPURRED BY their need for an educated clergy, have had a long-standing commitment to higher education. William Tennant founded the Log College in Neshaminy, Pennsylvania, in 1728; a number of its graduates and trustees went on to establish the College of New Jersey (now Princeton University) in 1746. Over the next 125 years, the Log College was followed by over five hundred similar institutions, although half of these survived for only a short time.

The earliest denominational colleges fit the pattern of other church-related colleges across the country. They frequently had presidents who were also ordained ministers, the curriculum included required courses in Bible and moral philosophy, and attendance at daily chapel and local church services was required. Faculty were expected to be church members. The remainder of the curriculum, however, was secular, including courses in science, mathematics, and the classics.

South Carolina Presbyterians placed great emphasis on church-related higher education, supporting by their benevolences and their leadership a seminary and two colleges. Columbia Seminary, established in 1828 by the Synod of South Carolina and Georgia to train southern Presbyterian ministers, was originally located in Lexington, Georgia. In 1830 it moved to Columbia, South Carolina, where it remained until 1927 when it moved to Decatur, Georgia. In 1880 the Clinton Presbyterian Church, under the leadership of Reverend William Plumer Jacobs, founded Clinton College, which became Presbyterian College (PC) and was taken over by the Synod of South Carolina. The synod established Chicora College for Young Ladies in Greenville in 1893. Chicora was relocated to Columbia in 1915 and in 1930 was united with Queens College, the Presbyterian women's college in Charlotte, North Carolina. Spurred on by concerns about increasing secularism on the campuses of the state's public institutions, the denomination also established campus ministries on public campuses across the state. While the synod provided financial support for its programs in higher education, the relationship was far from one-sided. In return, the colleges provided a Christian education which included study of the Bible and training for lives of service. They produced many pastors, missionaries, and church leaders for the PCUS. Examination of the institutions and programs supported by South Carolina Presbyterians indicates the importance they placed on preparing educated and enlightened persons who could go on to lead the church as pastors and lay leaders.

Columbia Theological Seminary

In 1925 Columbia Seminary, like the synod's other institutions, was feeling the effects of the Depression. The economic downturn hit South Carolina earlier than it did some parts of the country. Per capita wealth in the state stood at $1,499 in 1925, placing it forty-fifth among the forty-eight states.[1] The Depression caused all church programs to suffer, particularly the synod's commitment to higher education.

Columbia Theological Seminary, Columbia, S.C.
(Courtesy of Columbia Theological Seminary)

---

1. Brown, *Report of the Survey,* 59.

Columbia Theological Seminary had been in a precarious financial situation for a number of years. During the 1921/1922 session, the seminary's deficit was over $5,000, and predictions were that it would more than triple the following year. It was the most poorly equipped seminary in the denomination and needed a new library, dormitory, social center, and dining facility that would cost over $350,000. An additional $300,000 was needed for the endowment. The new dining facility, which was completed in 1923, was the first new building on the campus in fifty years. The seminary's investment in each student was lower than that of any PCUS seminary.[2]

That same year, the seminary's board recommended that the institution either merge with Union Theological Seminary in Richmond or relocate to a city that could provide the necessary financial support. The *Atlanta Constitution* reported on October 18, 1923, that meetings had already been held in Atlanta "with prominent laymen and ministers and the Columbia management and some members of its board and that there was a distinct desire upon the part of many to remove Columbia Seminary to Georgia and locate it in Atlanta."[3]

The Synod of South Carolina, meeting in Clinton in 1924, overwhelmingly approved the plan to be executed as soon as a $500,000 fundraising campaign was completed and a suitable site had been selected. Atlanta Presbyterians immediately embarked on a campaign to secure the necessary funds. It ended in December 1925, with pledges totaling a little over $600,000. The board approved plans for a campus costing $500,000 and consisting of an administration building, a heating plant, and a dormitory. The new campus was to be situated on sixty acres in the southeastern section of Decatur. The first classes were held on the new campus in the fall of 1927.

Once the seminary was situated on its new campus, President Richard Thomas Gillespie began to strengthen the academic program.

Seminary enrollment grew from thirty-three in 1925 to seventy-five in 1928. The school's financial condition, although improved, remained unsteady. The seminary continued to run an annual operating deficit of roughly $15,000. By 1929 the Columbia debt had reached $212,166, with interest payments making up more than half of the annual deficit of $19,000.[4] The operating budget was reduced by 35 percent in the two academic years of 1929 and 1930, but receipts also decreased. The seminary received only $35,000 from all sources in 1932, a reduction of nearly $14,000 from the previous year.[5]

2. Ibid., 35.
3. "Presbyterians May Establish Seminary Here," *Atlanta Constitution*, 1.
4. Synod of South Carolina, 1929, 71–4.
5. Ibid., 1932, 62.

Despite financial hardships however, in 1930 the synod's Committee of Christian Education concluded that the move of Columbia Seminary to the Atlanta suburbs had "saved that institution from extinction, put behind it the strength of the powerful Presbyterian constituency of Atlanta, and won for it the allegiance of Synods further west."[6] The Synod of Mississippi joined with the Synods of South Carolina, Georgia, Florida, and Alabama in the control and support of the Seminary.

In 1932 Reverend James McDowell Richards replaced Gillespie as president of the seminary.

Dr. J. McDowell Richards (Courtesy of Columbia Seminary)

Richards inherited an institution that had been hit hard by the expenses of its move, the construction of its new plant, and the deepening economic depression. It was difficult to collect pledges. Indeed, 10 percent of the promised donations in the Atlanta campaign and 25 percent of those in the Synod of Georgia were never realized. The Depression also resulted in a decreased number of students; for a number of years, annual enrollment was less than fifty students. Local congregations were having financial difficulty resulting not only in decreased giving but also in fewer available jobs for seminary graduates.

Dr. Richards, however, worked hard to stabilize the financial situation. By 1934 the seminary's debt had been pared to $100,000, and the school ended the year with an operating surplus, the first in many years. The

---

6. Ibid., 1930, 43-4.

curriculum was expanded from twenty-seven courses to fifty-one in the first three years that Columbia was in Decatur. Subsequently, a Rural Ministers Institute (which enrolled sixteen ministers in 1935) and a Pastors Institute (enrolling forty-six) were added. In 1934 graduate courses leading toward the ThM degree were offered for the first time, and a non-residential Extension School was opened for Presbyterians in the Atlanta area.

In 1937 a successful campaign in the Atlanta area cleared the seminary's debt and increased its endowment. South Carolinians continued their support. Among the seminary's staunchest supporters during this time was D. W. Robinson, an attorney in Columbia, South Carolina, and an elder in the Arsenal Hill Presbyterian Church. He had chaired the seminary's Investment Committee before the move to Decatur and continued to handle the seminary's investments after the move. Another loyal supporter from Columbia was Mrs. Fannie J. Bryan. When she died, she bequeathed $30,000 to fund fellowships for outstanding seminary graduates.

With the end of World War II, returning soldiers swelled enrollments at all of the denomination's seminaries, and housing was crucially needed. Columbia added more courses in social ethics, pastoral counseling, and ministerial practice. The seminary also began to offer broader opportunities for field education. "The vision of ministry broadened; the necessary skills multiplied; specialization and professional criteria were prized."[7]

The 1950s were years of expansion and building at Columbia.

Campbell Hall, Columbia Theological Seminary
(Courtesy of Columbia Theological Seminary)

7. Coalter, Mulder, and Weeks, *The Re-forming Tradition*, 213.

The seminary was engaged in a $350,000 campaign to fund a new library, with South Carolinians expected to provide 10 percent of this amount. Seminary enrollment soared as more young men chose to become ministers. Indeed, while seminary buildings could hold only 125 students comfortably, the enrollment in 1950 had reached 164. In 1953 the John Bulow Campbell Library was dedicated, and the seminary began planning two new dormitories for married students. By the end of the decade, Columbia was once again involved in a fundraising campaign. By May 1959, presbyteries in South Carolina had pledged over $1 million, with half of this amount already in hand. Preparations were underway for the construction of a new dormitory and apartment building to be completed by September 1960.

During this period, there was increasing pressure to eliminate segregation in schools and public places. Columbia Theological Seminary led the way among the synod's institutions when in 1951 it admitted its first African American student. This was probably Reverend E. E. Newberry, who began as a day student at Columbia and then went on to receive his degree from Atlanta University. He later served as moderator of both Snedecor Synod and Mecklenburg Presbytery in North Carolina.

The seminary entered the 1960s on a high note, having raised $3.5 million toward a $5 million campaign goal. This effort was spurred by the promise of a matching amount from an anonymous donor. New buildings, including two new dormitories and a student center, were under construction. The seminary's annual budget was balanced. There were, however, concerns about declining enrollments and synod support, which was significantly below the desired $.50 per church member per year.

After initial success, the seminary's campaign faltered somewhat. By 1963 an additional $1 million in pledges was still needed to claim the challenge grant. While Columbia had been able to meet its building needs, the institution still needed funds to increase the endowment. In 1965 the board launched a ten-year, five million dollar capital campaign. The funds were intended to increase the endowment, support the faculty, increase student aid, fund continuing education, and perform preventive maintenance.

Throughout the 1970s, Columbia, like the rest of the synod's institutions, was dealing with an uncertain economy. In 1971 the trustees asked the Synod of South Carolina to support a $1.2 million campaign. When Dr. C. Benton Kline took over as president in 1972, he was faced with continual budget deficits caused by inflation, the oil embargo, and the collapse of the stock market. The precarious economic situation affected many areas including fundraising, the value of the endowment, and enrollment. The seminary was also affected by increasing unrest in the church. Fundraising efforts continued, however, and by the spring of 1974, South Carolina presbyteries had pledged over $600,000.

After the synods of South Carolina and Georgia were combined into the Synod of the Southeast in 1973, the synod's institutions came under the supervision of the Institutional Coordinating Committee of Synod's Coordinating Council. In 1974 the Coordinating Committee recommended that the synod increase its gifts to all of its institutions. Columbia, which had received $138,000 in 1974, was to receive $190,000 in 1975. In 1975 when these amounts proved to be unrealistic, the synod decided to allocate fixed percentages of the total budget for institutions to each school. Columbia was to receive 15.89 percent, only slightly less than PC's 18.22 percent.[8]

By 1975 when J. Davison Philips became the seminary's president, donations from the Synod of the Southeast were down 8 percent, and the seminary had an annual deficit of almost $64,000.

J. Davison Philips (Courtesy of Columbia Theological Seminary)

---

8. *Synod Handbook*, 1975, addendum.

In 1976 South Carolina giving fell yet again and was $23,000 below expectations. The $5 million fundraising campaign begun in 1965 was finally completed in 1976. Enrollments were increasing, with a student body of 254 students in 1977. Sixty of these were enrolled in the MDiv program, the most in many years. The budget was balanced, with 25 percent of the funds coming from the sponsoring synods.

In the spring of 1978, the seminary's board approved yet another fundraising campaign, a capital campaign with a goal of $7 million. The Synod of the Southeast phase, to be conducted from 1980 through 1981, was intended to raise $4.5 million of this amount. Meanwhile, however, annual support from the synod began to drop. In 1978, which was the seminary's 150th year, only 17 percent of the seminary's budget came from the supporting synods, down from 37 percent in 1952 and 25 percent200 the year before.[9] This declined to 14 percent in 1979.

By 1982 enrollment stood at 378, and the seminary's endowment had reached $10 million. By 1983 the campaign in the Synod of the Southeast had concluded, slightly exceeding its goal. There was, however, some concern about the seminary, which reflected larger concerns in the denomination as a whole. First Presbyterian Church in Columbia was asked to contribute $81,000 to the campaign over three years. Some of the church's elders, however, lacked confidence in the institution. A group of session members visited the Decatur campus and recommended that the church's money be given directly to the establishment of an endowed chair in Old or New Testament to be filled by an "outstanding conservative scholar-teacher."[10] The seminary declined this offer, saying it was too restrictive.

By 1985, with the completion of the fundraising campaign, the seminary was on firm financial footing. In addition, Columbia's enrollment had increased significantly, spurred in large part by a tripling of the number of students in the Doctor of Ministry program and significant growth in the Master of Theology and Master of Divinity programs.

Presbyterian College

Aside from the short-lived Adger College, Presbyterian College, founded in 1880, was the first Presbyterian college in South Carolina. While it was originally founded by the Clinton Presbyterian Church and governed by an independent Board of Trustees, by the 1890s it had come under the control of the various South Carolina presbyteries. The standards governing PC in

---

9. Synod of the Southeast, 1978, 87.
10. Calhoun, *The Glory of the Lord*, 296.

1925 were a result of actions taken by the General Assembly of the PCUS in 1914 and 1916. According to these standards, two-thirds of trustees were chosen or at least ratified by one or more presbyteries or synods; the president or chief officer was required to be a member of the PCUS; all faculty members were expected to be active members of an evangelical church, with the majority being Presbyterian; colleges were to provide courses in the Bible and to require two of these for graduation; and teaching was to conform with the doctrines of the PCUS.[11]

Neville Hall, Presbyterian College (Courtesy of Presbyterian College)

In 1925 Presbyterian College's future seemed promising. Indeed, in 1926 the synod declared that PC was well cared for. The Committee on Educational Institutions reported that "Presbyterian College is more handsomely supported not only than any other church college in our denomination but is better supported than any church institution with which we are acquainted."[12]

At this time, the PCUS undertook a Million Dollar Campaign to improve finances at its various institutions. Money pledged (but not yet given) to PC through this campaign was used to obtain funds from a challenge grant issued by the General Education Board, founded in 1902 by John D. Rockefeller and Frederick T. Gates to support higher education. The board

11. Longfield and Marsden, "Presbyterian Colleges in Twentieth Century America," 107–8.
12. Synod of South Carolina, 1926, 46.

agreed to give the college $125,000 for its permanent endowment if the college could raise twice that much on its own.

At this point President Davison McDowell Douglas resigned as PC's president to become president of the University of South Carolina and was replaced by Dr. Burney L. Parkinson. Dr. Parkinson faced a financial situation that was suddenly quite threatening. According to the annual reports of PC presidents, by 1925 only a total of $60,000 to $70,000 had been received from the Million Dollar Campaign, and although the college was supposed to receive 8.5 percent of the synod's benevolence budget, it received only $17,000, or 5.5 percent, in 1925. This failure in the Million Dollar Campaign meant that the college was able to claim only a portion of the funds promised by the General Education Board.

In light of the worsening economy and the rising cost of education, sentiment grew for the church to get out of the business of education. To make matters worse, Presbyterians were supporting state schools through their taxes and then being asked to support Presbyterian colleges to do the same work. Indeed, more Presbyterian students were attending state schools than denominational colleges. In 1927 the Synod of South Carolina established the Ad Interim Committee to Study the Relation of Synod to Education. Their report in 1928 raised two questions: 1) Is there a continuing need for the church college? 2) What "educational load" could the Synod of South Carolina reasonably hope to carry successfully?

Committee members expressed their profound conviction that "the church positively has a permanent and definite mission in the sphere of college education . . . It is to illustrate and provide a distinctive type of higher education—an education in which the spiritual culture accompanies and crowns intellectual culture—in which Christian character is no less a goal than sound scholarship—in which devotion to Jesus Christ and loyalty to His Kingdom are the dominant motives."[13]

The practical question of the appropriate educational load for the synod was more difficult. Available statistics suggested that the average church college in the United States was supported by a constituency of 63,000 members. The Synod of South Carolina had just over 35,000 members and was supporting two colleges, an orphanage, and a seminary. Worse, experience suggested that even though contributions to education were higher per capita in South Carolina than in any other state, the synod still bore an educational load heavier than its members had "ever shown a disposition to carry." The committee noted that the synod's institutions were in debt

---

13. Synod of South Carolina, 1928, 50–1.

by almost $900,000 and were operating with annual deficits totaling about $30,000.

Indeed, by 1927 PC's total indebtedness was $237,000, and the college took measures to stem the tide of red ink. A report given to Congaree Presbytery in 1927 stated, "There has been a tightening up by the management that is hoped will remove all cause for the criticisms that have been made."[14] The college's Board of Trustees elected to use endowment funds to liquidate its bonded debt of $263,000, offering bondholders fifty cents on the dollar. By the end of 1927, this process was complete with accrued interest having been cancelled, but the endowment had been reduced to just $52,000. Meanwhile, the church had fallen short in its support of the college. An internal college report from this period, apparently intended for fundraising among the various presbyteries, noted that of the $147,820 that the synod had promised PC since 1924, only $80,706.38 had been received. Adding to the College's financial problems was the fact that approximately 56 percent of the student body (including the sons of ministers, candidates for the ministry, and Thornwell graduates) was attending tuition-free because of their various connections to the church.

In 1928 the Synod acknowledged that the college's condition was "decidedly critical." The 1928 report of the ad interim committee found it "plunging so rapidly down into the abyss of debt that only the most vigorous measures can save its existence."[15] In light of this dire situation, Dr. Parkinson resigned as president after only one year. In 1928 Reverend John McSween succeeded him. Reverend McSween had previously served churches in Dillon, Clemson, and Anderson, South Carolina, and Robeson County, North Carolina. His vigor and his popularity within the synod were to contribute enormously to the good will shown to the college by Presbyterians throughout the state.

The synod immediately took a number of actions to address PC's financial situation. It decided to allocate twice as much (17.5 percent) of its benevolence budget to PC than to any of its other institutions. Further, the Synod of South Carolina asked the synods of Georgia and Florida to join in the control and support of PC. Georgia agreed in 1928. The synod also established a Permanent Committee on Christian Higher Education with nine members, four of whom were to be "outstanding business men who shall be asked to give the same broad vision and successful service to the Master's work in this realm that they have given to their own business."[16]

14. Congaree Presbytery Minutes, October 24, 1927, 16.
15. Synod of South Carolina, 1928, 53.
16. Synod of South Carolina, 1929, 17.

Recognizing the difficulty of securing adequate endowments and annual support for all of its institutions, the Ad Interim Committee asked the synod to make the elimination of PC's debt its first priority. In his 1929 report to the college's Board of Trustees, President McSween recommended that the synod raise $300,000 in South Carolina by the fall and that a fundraising professional be hired to oversee the campaign.

Unfortunately this "Program of Deliverance," launched with much fanfare in September 1929, was drastically affected by the subsequent collapse of the stock market.

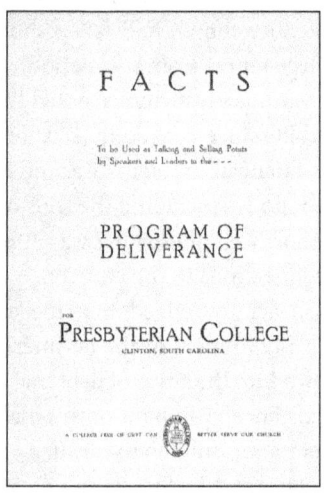

Program of Deliverance Brochure
(Courtesy of Presbyterian College)

The Depression hit South Carolina hard. Between 1920 and 1933, over three hundred banks failed.[17]

Unemployment reached 44 percent in some counties, and mills were operating on reduced hours or not at all. Agricultural production fell from a worth of $446,000,000 in 1918 to $156,000,000 in 1929 and $63,000,000 in 1932. Per capita income fell from $261 in 1929 to $151 in 1933.[18] By the summer of 1933, one quarter of the population of the state was on relief.[19]

These developments spelled disaster for the Program of Deliverance. According to letters found in the files of President John McSween, contributions from both churches and individuals were received in amounts as

---

17. Edgar, *South Carolina, A History*, 489.
18. Lander, *A History of South Carolina*, 72.
19. Edgar, *South Carolina in the Modern Age*, 71.

small as $3.00. According to a press release dated November 30, 1929, the date when the Program was to be completed, only $170,000 of the desired $350,000 had been pledged and only $25,000 of this had been received in cash. Accordingly, the college was forced to cut its budget by 20 percent between 1928 and 1930.

During the 1930s, PC continued to experience financial difficulties. In 1932 the synod requested another $5,000 reduction in operating expenses. Salaries were reduced substantially for the 1931/1932 academic year, and in 1932 the Permanent Committee on Education recommended that future salaries be paid only in proportion to the income received. By 1935, when Dr. McSween resigned to accept the pastorate of Purity Church in Chester, the College had accumulated $117,000 in annual operating deficits over eleven years, with a total debt of $335,000—a debt $60,000 larger than its total endowment.[20]

Following President McSween's resignation, the college chose William Plumer Jacobs II, grandson of the college's founder, as the new president.

William Plumer Jacobs II (Courtesy of Presbyterian College)

20. Synod of South Carolina, 1935, 34.

He promised to raise pledges totaling $20,000 per year for three years in order to preclude further operating deficits. President Jacobs's report in February 1936, however, was slightly more pessimistic. On the issue of fundraising, he made note of the "passive attitude of some of our churches and the outright resistance of others."

A brochure entitled "The Place of Presbyterian College in the Program of S. & P. [synod and presbytery] Home Missions," published around 1936, made it clear that the relationship between the synod and PC was not just a matter of governance and financial support from the synod; it was a reciprocal one. Of the college's 832 total alumni, 151 had become ministers and thirteen were foreign missionaries. The YMCA, the center of social life at PC, was sending out teams of leaders and ministerial students to churches in the synods of South Carolina and Georgia to conduct Bible courses and evangelistic meetings among the young people of the church with a view to reviving their interest in church work.

By the 1940s, the colleges of the PCUSA were beginning to move away from their Presbyterian roots. According to a survey taken in 1941, however, the twenty-four junior and four-year Presbyterian colleges in the south were able to take "justifiable pride in the effectiveness of their religious emphasis." Students reported that faculty members, Bible instruction, and religious programs on campus all contributed to their religious development. This was certainly the case at Presbyterian College, which continued to hold an important place in the life of the church.[21]

The financial situation at PC was gradually improving. In 1940 the college reported a slight deficit but a growing endowment. Because of an accumulated operating deficit of $90,000, however, the college launched the Perpetuation Campaign to pay off the debt and add $400,000 to the endowment.[22] In addition, the college asked the women of the synod to sponsor an ongoing annual campaign intended to raise $1.00 per member. Between 1941 and 1943, this "Perpetuation Campaign for PC" received $100,000 for the endowment from the Synod of South Carolina and $40,500 from the Synod of Georgia.[23]

During this period, world affairs had a huge impact on the college. After the US entered World War II, the college began operating on a twelve-month schedule, enrolling one freshman class in June and one in September. In addition, the use of the campus by the military to train aviation cadets gave the college's finances a boost. In 1943 Reverend C. T. Squires, chairman

---

21. Works, *Report of a Survey*, 145, 121–23, 135.
22. Synod of South Carolina, 1940, 12.
23. Hammet, *The Spirit of PC*, 87.

of the synod's Committee on Educational Institutions, reported that "Presbyterian College has rendered a laudable service to both Church and State ... Under the hectic conditions which obtain, we regard the increase in endowment and reduction in debt as an achievement worthy of our unstinted commendation. PC is still clouded by debt, but for the first time in two decades, we can see the light."[24]

In 1944 President Jacobs was able to assure the synod that the college was finally out of debt. He resigned in 1945 to become the president of the American Cotton Manufacturer's Association and was succeeded by Marshall W. Brown. Dr. Brown had been a professor of history at the college since 1925 and since 1928 had served as Dean. He had taken on an increasing number of administrative duties during the last years of William Jacobs's presidency.

In 1945 the synods of South Carolina and Georgia approved a $350,000 campaign to increase the endowment at PC, the first general campaign since 1929. By 1949 the endowment had increased over 100 percent to $473,272.29, and the synods of South Carolina and Georgia had pledged $332,000. The eventual increase in the endowment to $509,098.49 by May 1949 was enough that the Southern Association of Colleges and Schools, which had placed PC on its non-member approved list, returned the College to full accreditation.

Meanwhile, the field of Presbyterian higher education was shifting. By 1955 the number of colleges associated with the PCUS had dropped to seventeen. The others had fallen victim to what Guy Snavely calls the "unrelenting pressure of economic conditions."[25] Presbyterian College, however, was experiencing a housing shortage brought on by increased enrollment. The college began a fund drive for new dormitories designed to raise $150,000 from the churches in the synods of Georgia and South Carolina. In 1954 the Synod of South Carolina increased its annual contributions to PC by $20,000 to $76,000 and voted to support any development plans launched by the Board of Trustees. The college subsequently launched the Diamond Jubilee Campaign, a ten-year program designed to raise $2 million. The churches contributed liberally. Of the $1,033,335 eventually raised in the capital campaign, South Carolina presbyteries accounted for $605,932.[26]

Throughout this period, PC's ties with the church remained strong. The Student Christian Association was a major factor in campus life, sponsoring such activities as Sunday vespers, Religious Emphasis Week (which

---

24. Synod of South Carolina, 1943, 35.
25. Snavely, *The Church and the Four-Year College*, 107.
26. Hammet, *The Spirit of PC*, 117.

brought prominent speakers to campus), the annual Christmas party, a spring picnic, and a reception for new freshmen each fall.

Speaker at Religious Emphasis Week, Presbyterian College
(Courtesy of Presbyterian College)

SCA was even responsible for the intramural program, sponsoring teams in numerous sports. Members of the Ministerial Club organized service projects, served as supply preachers to area churches, taught Sunday school, and formed evangelistic teams. Many PC graduates went on to attend Columbia Seminary. In fact in 1956, fully a quarter of Columbia's students were PC graduates.[27] The college continued to play host to such church-wide events as the Young People's Leadership Training School, meetings of the synods of South Carolina and Georgia, and the Synodical Training School, which was moved to PC in 1954. There was one change in campus life, however, which would presage changes to come. Since 1887 students had been required to attend daily chapel as well as the church or Sunday school of their choice. In 1950 required chapel services were reduced to three days a week, although students were still encouraged to attend church.

In the midst of these prosperous times for the synod's various institutions, there were still divisive issues. Beginning in the 1950s, all of the synod's institutions were faced with the issue of integration. The issue of integrating South Carolina's public schools came to the fore when a group of parents in Clarendon County brought a suit about school busing in 1950. (This suit was eventually bundled into the landmark *Brown v. Board*

27. Ibid., 101.

of Education litigation.) The church itself was beginning to suggest that its institutions be integrated. Columbia Seminary led the way when it admitted its first African American student in 1951.

At the General Assembly meeting in 1953, Reverend Jack W. Ewart proposed that church institutions be open to students of all races. The assembly referred this resolution to the Council on Christian Relations for its consideration. The following year, the council recommended that the Assembly "affirm that enforced segregation of the races is discrimination which is out of harmony with Christian theology and ethics."[28] Recognizing that it could not require any action by the educational institutions, the council asked the Assembly to urge trustees of its institutions to "adopt a policy of opening the doors of these institutions to all races."

The Synod of South Carolina subsequently voted to continue its policy of segregation. Among those opposed to integration was former PC president John McSween, who sponsored the resolution that was eventually passed 136 to 83: "It is the sense of the Synod of South Carolina that it is in the best interests of harmonious relations between the white and Negro races in this section at this time that the present enrollment policies in the institutions under the control and support of the Synod be continued."[29] The synod did, however, agree to further consider the assembly's recommendation.

On the PC campus there was increasing discussion of school desegregation and integration in general. As early as 1956, when those on campus were asked, "What can the college student do to help determine the 'racial issue,'" most, including President Marshall Brown, suggested thorough study and consideration of the matter. Many felt that integration was sure to come, but that a hasty decision "could possibly set back the education of both races many years."[30] The issue was not to be settled for Presbyterian College until almost eight years later.

In the midst of this ongoing controversy, the synod again decided to examine its relationship to its institutions, with special attention to its financial responsibility. In 1958 the Ad Interim Committee to Study the Relationship of Synod to its Institutions of Higher Education reported that churches in the synod were setting aside less than 2 percent of their total giving for higher education, and gifts from the Synod of South Carolina accounted for 29 percent of Columbia Seminary's budget, 24 percent of PC's budget, and only 7 percent of the budget at Queens.[31] In 1957 the Board of Christian Education of the PCUS authorized a group of studies of Presbyterian institutions of higher education. They allocated $5,000 for a survey

28. General Assembly, 1954, 193.
29. Synod of South Carolina, 1954, 24–5.
30. McElveen, "The Collegiate Answer," 4.
31. Synod of South Carolina, 1958, 50–1.

of Presbyterian College to be carried out by Dr. Rufus Henry Fitzgerald, Chancellor Emeritus of the University of Pittsburgh, and five other educators. The study was designed to focus on the entire operation of the college and to recommend a long-range program of development. At the first meeting of the survey commission on March 25, 1957, college president Marshall Brown charged the committee with considering further provision for female students, the size of future enrollments, and plans for a new auditorium. The commission, however, considered much broader issues than these.

The first of their recommendations was that the college should admit more women. Members of the committee felt that the inclusion of more women at PC would balance the curriculum by providing more emphasis on the fine arts. It would also make the college more attractive to male students and raise the "intellectual level of the student body."[32] They also recommended that the college increase its enrollment to 900 while still maintaining its tradition of academic excellence.

Even though PC had recently raised faculty salaries, committee members felt that professors were "making a heavy financial sacrifice because of their devotion to the College."[33] Turnover was high, amounting to 25 percent of the faculty during the current year, and some faculty members were forced to seek outside employment. In addition, with only 40 percent of the faculty having the PhD, "the degree qualifications . . . are certainly not those of a superior institution."[34] Committee members also raised the issue of student scholarships and their relationship to the athletic program. Of the $75,000 in scholarship aid granted during 1957, $50,000 was earmarked for athletes; $35,000 of this amount was granted to football alone. The amount of aid to athletes was "nearly equal to the funds received from the various presbyteries of the two states."[35] The committee recommended the discontinuation of football and a reduction in scholarships for other sports. The issues raised by this far-ranging report would not be addressed until the 1960s.

Another development at this time came in the area of Christian education. In 1957 the General Assembly asked church-related colleges to train Associates in Christian Education. The Assembly provided challenge funds of $5,000 per year for five years to any college that would offer the necessary program and secure an additional $5,000 from their sponsoring constituency for this purpose. PC responded quickly, introducing this course of study in 1960. The curriculum included courses in Christian education, church school teaching for all ages, and the church and the home. The program was designed

32. "Survey of Presbyterian College," 1957, 14.
33. Ibid., 15.
34. Ibid., 16.
35. Ibid., 18.

to serve both those students who desired to go directly into churches and those who wanted to pursue graduate study in the field.

In 1958 the synod established a Guidance and Counseling Center at PC similar to those already in operation in Virginia, North Carolina, and Kentucky. The center was designed to provide career counseling and aptitude and personality testing for high school and college students. In addition, it offered a vocational guidance library and a limited counseling service for those with non-vocational problems.

As the turbulent sixties began, PC was still dealing with the Fitzgerald committee's recommendations on athletic scholarships. The prospect of change caused a huge outcry among the college's constituency. After several studies by the Board of Trustees and others and amidst steadily rising costs, the trustees finally decided in March 1963 to reduce the number of annual athletic scholarships to thirty-five, with a maximum of twenty-five to be allotted to football. This was a reduction from a high of fifty-two scholarships for football alone. The Walter Johnson Club, an athletic booster group, was asked to raise a minimum of $30,000 to support the athletic program during the coming year. While this was a compromise with the Fitzgerald committee's recommendation, it indicated a major change in emphasis.[36]

The committee's report also produced other changes. The administration was asked to adopt an organizational chart and to abide by it. The president was to delegate more responsibility accordingly. In addition, the committee recommended that the college expand its public relations program and revise the campus plan. They asked that the college require a fine arts course of all students, improve the classes in Romance languages, develop the programs in the sciences (including the construction of a new science building), and add senior honors work and courses in Latin, geology, and geography. Increased emphasis was to be placed on teacher education, philosophy, and sociology.

These changes were in line with what was happening with denominational colleges across the country. Pressure on enrollment from large public universities was increasing, and in the face of declining support from the churches, colleges needed to secure grants and other outside funding. In order to do this, denominational colleges had to offer more academic specialization, professionalization, opportunities for research, and a more rigorous academic program overall.

In the area of finances, the committee suggested that both tuition and fundraising efforts be increased to provide additional income for instructional expenses and the library. The committee described the holdings of the library as very weak in some areas and suggested that the library budget be increased from $11,000 to $25,000. The college adopted many of these

36. Hammet, *The Spirit of PC*, 123.

recommendations, and the report served as a blueprint for development over the next decade.

The college was also planning a major fundraising campaign. In December 1960, the committees on Stewardship and Educational Institutions met at PC and proposed a $3 million campaign. This would be phase two of the twenty-five year development campaign begun with the Diamond Jubilee Campaign in 1955 and was intended to provide $1.5 million to the endowment, with additional funding for renovations and the construction of a new science building, a dining hall, and two dormitories.

The synod eventually approved a capital campaign of $1.8 million, the largest fundraising effort in PC's history. The campaign was launched in Clinton, with local residents hoping to raise $300,000 for a women's dormitory. A group of women chairmen served with the ministerial and lay chairmen in helping to direct this synod-wide program of development. By the spring of 1963, the synod had pledged a total of $1,816,215.

At this point, Dr. Marshall W. Brown chose to take early retirement. In 1963 Dr. Marc C. Weersing, pastor of First Presbyterian Church, Spartanburg, who had been the Ministerial Chairman for the campaign, became president.

Dr. Marc C. Weersing (Courtesy of Presbyterian College)

One of the first issues to confront President Weersing was integration. The climate across the South was changing, as was federal law, and the synod's educational institutions would have to adjust accordingly. Indeed, Columbia Seminary and Queens College had already changed their admissions requirements.

The University of Georgia changed its policy in 1961, as did Wake Forest University. Following the rather turbulent transition at Georgia, PC's newspaper *The Blue Stocking* conducted a random poll asking students, "Should we sacrifice our education to keep integration?" According to the poll results, most students viewed integration as inevitable and, in the words of Jim Monroe, felt that "every man has the right to be educated to the best of his ability and should not be denied his right to freedom because of the color of his skin."[37]

In January 1963, Clemson University desegregated by court order, and that May the Synod of Georgia began to encourage desegregation in its colleges and universities. Furman University became the first institution of higher learning in South Carolina to pass voluntarily a racially non-discriminatory policy in October 1963 but encountered opposition from the South Carolina Baptist Convention and delayed implementing the new policy. In 1964 both Wofford College and Winthrop admitted their first African American students.

The University of South Carolina also desegregated under court order in September 1963. That same month, in an editorial in *The Blue Stocking*, editor Bob Phifer commented on the "note of urgency surrounding the integration issue." He declared that the goals of African Americans were "not going to be accomplished now," nor were they going to be achieved "merely by social reform." These goals were the responsibility of the black race itself, and due to "an almost innate cultural, intellectual and moral gap" which African Americans apparently could not, or did not want to bridge, this transition was not going to happen quickly.[38]

In April 1964, the General Assembly of the PCUS instructed its presbyteries to desegregate. That same month, PC's *Blue Stocking* revealed the results of a poll that Dr. Eduard Patte had taken in his sociology class since 1950. According to Dr. Patte, the opinions of PC students were becoming more liberal. Indeed, according to *The Blue Stocking*, it was the main supporters of the school and the trustees who were mumbling "that students here are nowhere nearly ready for integration." A further analysis of the poll results makes one wonder, however. Although most students said they

37. "Shall We Sacrifice Our Education?" *The Blue Stocking*, January 13, 1961, 1.
38. Phifer, "The Other Reform," *The Blue Stocking*, September 20, 1963, 2.

would be willing to attend an integrated college, 64 percent of those polled said that they "would make no attempt to be friendly to Negroes but would accept their presence in good grace." And a startling 16 percent declared that "they would organize to make life as miserable as possible for the Negroes on campus."[39]

In October 1964, in one of a set of opposing editorials in *The Blue Stocking*, PC student Raymond Summerlin declared that it was time for PC to heed the advice of various Presbyterian governing bodies and "no longer sit on the fence." Dee Hodges, on the other hand, urged the college not to stir up trouble by declaring a specific policy, but to wait until an African American student applied. "Time has a quality for healing wounds, and though PC's segregated days are numbered, let us take this time to try to study all the ramifications . . . If we do so now, when integration comes we will be better prepared to receive it."[40]

The Civil Rights Act of 1964 increased pressure on those institutions that had not yet changed their admissions policies. Colleges applying for federal assistance, including grants from such entities as the National Science Foundation and the Department of Health, Education, and Welfare, were asked to provide assurance of compliance with Section 601 of Title VI of the act. This prompted Furman to reinstate its non-discrimination policy. The executive committee of PC's trustees, meeting in January 1965, looked at the various federal monies received by the college, including student loans, support for ROTC, work study funds, funds for veterans, and grants from the NSF and HEW. They also considered the stances taken by the General Assembly and the Synod of Georgia, which was the college's other sponsoring synod. Much of the extensive discussion centered around whether to continue to seek and accept such federal funds would ultimately influence such requirements as compulsory Bible and the expectation that members of the faculty be Christian. They decided that the college should continue its longtime custom of making "a Constitution, Laws, Rules, and Regulations for the government of said college . . . not inconsistent with the laws of the land," and they voted to sign the Civil Rights Act of Compliance.[41] The board as a whole voted to endorse this policy at its March meeting.

There were a number of "no" votes, and as revealed in the correspondence of Stanley F. Morse, two trustees resigned outright and one opted

---

39. "Polls Indicate Changing Attitudes of Students," *The Blue Stocking*, September 1957, 6.

40. "Integration: Open Stand Now?" *The Blue Stocking*, October 2, 1964, 2.

41. Minutes of the Executive Committee, January 27, 1965.

not to seek another term. Morse, a prominent elder from the low country, wrote to Dr. Weersing to express his concern about the decision to integrate the college and about possible Federal influence in the college's affairs. At the time, Morse was president of the white supremacist Grass Roots League in Charleston, an organization created in response to Brown v. Board of Education ten years earlier. In the end, Morse's opinions had little influence on the actions of the college.

In the next several years, Columbia College, the Citadel, Newberry, Erskine, Converse, and Coker admitted their first black students. Although PC accepted several black students between 1965 and 1968, no one actually enrolled until Barbara Green entered the freshman class in 1969. This made PC the last institution in the state, except for Bob Jones University, to actually enroll an African American student. Progress remained slow. Judging by the class photos published in the college annual, the *Pac Sac*, by the time Barbara Green graduated in 1973, there were only six additional African American students on campus.

Other big changes were coming to the PC campus. While women had always been admitted in small numbers, the Fitzgerald report had recommended full coeducation, and the college decided to follow their recommendation.

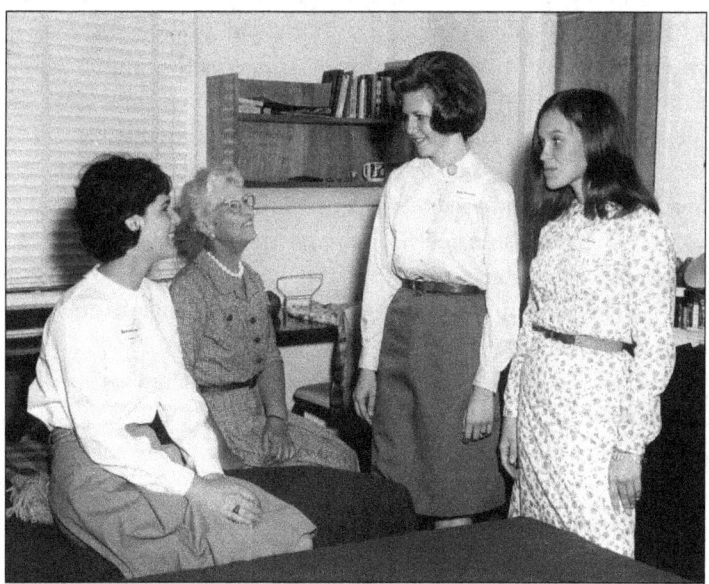

Presbyterian College Goes Coed 1965 (Courtesy of Presbyterian College)

Several single sex institutions in South Carolina had already opened their doors to women. Clemson began admitting female students in 1955; women at Furman began taking classes on the new campus in 1958 and began living there in 1961. This was in line with what was happening across the country. According to Claudia Goldin and Lawrence F. Katz, "By the 1960s, the only force holding coeducation in check was alumni (and alumnae) support for retaining the prior gender identity of the school. For the celebrated period of change in the late 1960s and early 1970s, institutions that switched early or were always coeducational increased enrollments faster than those that switched later, if at all."[42] PC at first housed women residential students off campus and then became fully coeducational when ninety-four residential women students were admitted in the fall of 1965.

Throughout the early 1960s, PC's ties with the church remained strong. The college remained a Presbyterian center serving as the location for women's conferences, synod meetings, and meetings of ministers and lay leaders. PC began to hold an annual Youth Day in 1963 with over 1,600 members of senior high youth fellowships from the Synod of South Carolina visiting in October.

The sixties did usher in some changes in the college's requirements, however. In the midst of increasing activism on campuses across the country, students at PC began to question the college's longtime practice of requiring chapel attendance of all students. An editorial published in *The Blue Stocking* on Feb. 22, 1963, summarized student concerns this way: "Although it involves beating one of the oldest of PC's dead horses, something should be said about required chapel, which is currently a completely ridiculous situation. A speaker must be appalled to look out upon a sea of sleeping and reading people; and no doubt the people are equally appalled at being there . . . A religion is a chosen discipline, not a dictated one . . . Many of the students we contacted felt that the religiously associated compulsion placed on them three times a week was more than enough to quell a desire to attend further sessions."[43] In September 1969, the faculty voted to reduce the number of required assemblies to one weekly; assemblies later became totally voluntary.

There were other changes in the religious life of the college. The influence of the Student Christian Association lessened, and it was eventually disbanded in 1969. In 1971 Religious Emphasis Week was replaced by Winter Conference, a popular off-campus retreat which continues to this

---

42. Goldin and Katz, "Putting the 'Co' in Education," *Journal of Human Capital*, 413.

43. "Horse Whipping," *The Blue Stocking*, 2.

day. In 1970 the religion requirement was reduced from nine to six hours, consisting of required courses in both Old and New Testament. However, the college resisted taking the path of many Presbyterian schools, including Davidson, when it came to faculty recruitment. Faculty members were still expected to be active members of a Christian church; this requirement was to remain in force for many years after Presbyterian reunion in 1983.

In 1966 PC enhanced its commitment to service by starting a program that was to grow into Student Volunteer Services. The initiative began with after-school and tutoring programs in local churches. With support from individual churches and the Presbytery of South Carolina, disadvantaged children were sent to camp for the first time in their lives. A grant from the General Assembly's boards of Christian Education and National Ministries provided a full-time director for three years starting in 1972; this responsibility was later taken over by the college chaplain. By 1985 more than one quarter of the student body was participating in more than twenty projects each year.

Officials at PC, however, were concerned about the level of synod support. In his report to the synod in 1967, President Marc Weersing noted that in 1966 the college received only about $109,000 of the $150,000 budgeted. In response, the synods of Georgia and South Carolina embarked on a fundraising effort dubbed EXCEL, with a goal of $2 million for a physical education center, library, infirmary, and the endowment. The campaign was completed in 1970, having raised a total of $3 million.

Throughout the 1970s, Presbyterian College maintained its strong ties to the church. When the synods of Georgia and South Carolina were combined into the Synod of the Southeast in 1973, the College reaffirmed its desire for a continuing relationship with all the churches and presbyteries in the expanded synod. Trustees who had previously been elected by the different synods were now to be elected by the Synod of the Southeast in the same geographical proportions.

In 1971 an interesting situation arose at PC when an accusation of heresy was lodged against religion professor Lewis Hay. The minutes of Charleston Presbytery indicate that G. Aiken Taylor, the editor of the *Presbyterian Journal*, had made charges against Hay concerning doctrinal matters. These were communicated to the presbytery in May and referred to the Commission on the Minister and his Work. According to a communication issued by the presbytery of which Hay was a member, "the charges of heresy grew out of articles written by Dr. Hay in the *Presbyterian Outlook*, which were criticized in the editorials of the *Presbyterian Journal*. Formal charges were presented in a letter to Charleston Presbytery from Aiken Taylor, editor of the latter publication." The charges were that Hay had publicly espoused positions that supported universalism, denied the deity of Christ, and promoted "secularism, and a distortion of the Christian view of the soul of man."

After studying the allegations and interviewing Dr. Hay, the presbytery found the charges unwarranted and declined to pursue further action against him. They affirmed Hay as "a fellow Christian and Presbyterian Minister in keeping with the requirements of the *Book of Church Order*." Hay's positions continued to be controversial, however, especially with the more conservative wing of the church. In an article published in *Contact*, a newsletter issued by Presbyterian Churchmen United in December 1972, Paul Settle criticized Hay's statement in a 1970 issue of the *Outlook*, declaring that Hay's "concept of the soul as the immortal, spiritual part of man's being is very much out of accord with the view of the Bible."[44]

The 1970s brought the lean financial times fueled by the energy crisis, recession, unemployment, and the stock market decline. By early 1975, the college's utility costs were running 75 percent ahead of the previous year, 50 percent of this attributable to inflation. Food costs for the dining hall increased 25 percent between 1973 and 1974 and rose another 10 percent in 1975. The value of the endowment slumped along with the stock market. In addition, the church was not able to fulfill its financial pledges to the college. After the restructuring of the synods and the creation of the new Synod of the Southeast, the institutions came under the supervision of the Institutional Coordinating Committee of Synod's Coordinating Council. While the committee budgeted $189,000 for PC in 1973, only $166,293 was received. The college engaged in a "general belt-tightening" to reduce costs by 5 percent in most areas. In 1974 the Coordinating Committee recommended that the synod increase its gifts to all of its institutions. PC, which had been allotted $195,000 in 1974, was to get $225,000 in 1975. These figures, however, were unrealistic, and in 1975 the Committee recommended that each of its institutions receive a certain percentage of the money budgeted for all institutions. PC was to receive 18.22 percent, the highest among the group. At the 1976 Synod meeting, the College reported a substantial deficit, the first in seventeen years.

In 1976 the Division of Institutional Ministries approved a $10 million campaign in conjunction with the college's 1980 centennial. The goal for the Synod of the Southeast was $5 million. By 1978 the campaign had brought in almost $6,050,000. In his annual report, however, President Weersing noted that while the synod had provided 12 percent of the college's operating budget between 1963 and 64, the amount was only 4 percent between 1976 and 1977. He asked that PC be included in the 1979 benevolence budget for $193,000.

---

44. Settle, "Why PCUS Evangelism is Sterile," *Contact*, 3.

In early 1978, Dr. Weersing announced that he would retire in June 1979. He was succeeded by Dr. Kenneth B. Orr, president of the Presbyterian School of Christian Education in Richmond.

Dr. Kenneth B. Orr (Courtesy of Presbyterian College)

In 1980 Dr. Orr launched a limited Centennial Campaign to raise the remaining $3.5 million for the Second Century Fund, and by early 1981, the $10 million goal had been exceeded by $1.3 million. Synod contributions totaled over $2.3 million and came from 286 churches. The entire Program of Progress launched in 1955 had raised the college's assets from $2 million to $25 million, which provided for eleven new buildings and a major increase in the endowment.

PC continued to offer programs that reflected its close ties to the church. In April 1978, the college, in conjunction with Columbia Theological Seminary, held its first Minister's Conference "to provide a short but intensive program under the leadership of one of the noted scholars of our Church," aimed at providing "fresh and stimulating insights for preaching and pastoral work."[45] In 1979 PC started a missionary-in-residence program through which missionaries on furlough could spend a year on the campus, teaching and counseling those interested in the mission field. This program led a number of students to go into mission work either in the church's

---

45. "Ministers' Conference Offers Fresh Insights," *The Presbyterian College Report*, 4.

summertime "youth-in-missions" program or after graduation. The church continued to operate a popular guidance center at the college. In 1980 the center served 328 non-PC students and 284 PC students. In 1982 the college established its own Career Planning and Placement Center and withdrew support from the synod's center. A synod task force proposed that the Guidance and Counseling Center remain in Clinton for at least the next three years, with the situation to be re-evaluated prior to preparation of the 1986 budget. PC offered to let the center use a house near the campus for a token rent. The center remained open until 1997.

Through all these years, PC maintained its close relationship with the church. The 1985 preamble to the faculty's terms of employment describes this relationship clearly: "Presbyterian College is a servant of the Presbyterian Church. The College frankly recognizes its purpose to build on Judeo-Christian faith as the faith which best underlies the search for knowledge in every field of learning. It roots its understanding of life in the revelation of God in the Scriptures and in Jesus Christ as Lord and Savior. It moves from this base to both personal commitment and dynamic freedom." Abiding by these principles, by 1987 PC had provided more than six hundred ministers, missionaries, and church educators to the denomination.

Chicora College

The Synod of South Carolina established Chicora College for Young Ladies in Greenville in 1893. Later, in 1915, Chicora moved to Columbia.

Chicora College, Columbia S.C. (Courtesy of the University of South Carolina)

By 1920 the prospects for the college looked good, with capacity enrollment. This seemingly rosy situation led Chicora's trustees to plan a new campus in Columbia in the developing Wales Garden suburb. The Synod showed its confidence in Chicora's plans by approving bonds to secure a $250,000 land purchase.

In his report to Enoree Presbytery in October 1925, President S.C. Byrd noted that enrollment had increased beyond the college's capacity, and a number of students had to be turned away. In 1927 President Byrd reported to Congaree Presbytery that "Chicora College is lengthening her skirts and broadening her phylactories. She has invaded the old Seminary campus and taken possession of its ancient buildings. The halls and dormitories are being worked over and where once was heard lectures and debates will reverberate with music and song. The enrollment is the largest in its history. The faculty is stronger than ever. If this school could once get out of debt, so that its income could be spent upon itself, its permanent success is assured."[46] The debt, however, was very troublesome, and instead of working toward a new campus in Wales Garden, Chicora had taken over the old Columbia Seminary campus.

In 1928 the Ad-Interim Committee to Study the Relation of Synod to Education expressed doubts that South Carolina Presbyterians could continue to support both PC and Chicora. Chicora had almost no endowment and there was little chance of raising one. While committee members reaffirmed the church's commitment to the education of women, they wondered if the synod should merge Chicora with another institution. They recommended establishing a Permanent Committee on Education to prepare an overall plan for the support of higher education. In 1929 ownership and control of Chicora was transferred from the presbyteries to the Synod of South Carolina, and the Synod assumed Chicora's bonded indebtedness and pledged "its full faith and credit to the prompt payment of the within bond and interest on same."[47]

On March 24, 1930, the synod held a called meeting at First Presbyterian Church in Columbia to consider merging Chicora with Queens College in Charlotte. According to this proposal which Chicora's trustees had already endorsed, the new college would be located on the Queens College campus and be known as Queens-Chicora (until the Board of Trustees deemed it advisable to change the name of the institution, which occurred in 1939). Half of the members of the board were to be elected by the Synod of South Carolina. Equity in Chicora's property in Columbia was to be transferred to the new institution.

---

46. Congaree Presbytery, October 24, 1927, 16.
47. Synod of South Carolina, 1929, 21.

As a part of the agreement, the synod relieved Queens-Chicora from all liabilities on debts, claims, and demands arising out of the transactions of Chicora's board or its agents. They also voted to liquidate the assets of Chicora, pay off all indebtedness, and transfer the surplus to the trustees of Queens-Chicora. They committed to place the new institution in the synod's budget for "a fair percentage of the benevolence for Christian education," but the new college was not to expect the Synod of South Carolina to engage in any major campaign. Clearly the synod expected to meet its obligation to the new institution by selling Chicora's real estate, thus enabling it to deal with the financial emergency that the Depression had caused at PC.

The synod instructed Chicora's board to appoint a liquidating committee which found that the assets of Chicora (primarily real estate valued at $422,500) exceeded the liabilities (principally the bonded indebtedness of $233,000) by $79,000—a handsome sum to present to Queens-Chicora. The property had not been sold, however, and Chicora and the liquidating committee did not have sufficient cash on hand to pay almost $100,000 in debts past due or soon to be due. Noting that the synod had guaranteed payment of these obligations, the Committee requested that the moderator and stated clerk be authorized to borrow up to $100,000 for that purpose.

The synod would struggle to clear this debt for the next nineteen years. At a called meeting in December 1930, the liquidating committee reported that it was unable to borrow money to pay the debts of Chicora and that the inability to pay interest due on the $250,000 worth of bonds had placed that loan in default. Further, the synod's own financial integrity was at stake if it was unable to make good its guarantee when the college failed to pay. In order to protect the interests of the synod in what was deemed to be the valuable property of Chicora, the synod reduced gifts to all other causes and provided 20 percent of its total funds to the Chicora Liquidating Committee. Yet economic conditions did not permit the sale of the property, much of it lying idle and producing no income. More and more money had to be pumped into the liquidating committee.

At least one South Carolina congregation had questions about this whole process. The session of Purity Church in Chester doubted the synod's authority to assume responsibility for Chicora's unsecured debts and did not feel that regular benevolence funds should be used to pay them. Purity's session was willing to solicit specific gifts from the congregation for Chicora; these gifts, rather than the regular benevolence budget, were used toward Chicora's debt. Other benevolent funds were given directly to the various benevolent causes rather than to the synod's general benevolence fund.

Between 1931 and 1935, the synod paid $65,000 to the Chicora Liquidating Committee, considerably less than the $200,000 it requested from the churches, but still 30 percent of the total benevolent funds it received for all of its causes. The Liquidating Committee finally managed to lease the old campus on Blanding Street in Columbia to a Christian Academy (which ultimately became the Columbia Bible College), but the income was small.

By 1935 the liabilities of the Chicora College Liquidating Committee (and therefore of the synod) were $423,000. The bonded indebtedness alone had increased from $233,000 to $273,000 with an additional $8,000 due in interest, and the synod had entered into further debt to meet earlier payments due on the bonds. In the meantime, the estimated value of Chicora's other assets (primarily real estate) declined from $446,000 to $277,000 between 1930 and 1935.

The college itself flourished in Charlotte. The synod was pleased with the work at Queens-Chicora, but it could not see a way to supply the promised funds for campus improvements or endowment. Although reaffirming its commitment to provide a fair share of its annual benevolence budget to the college, the synod allocated just 2 percent of its budget to the college in 1931 (as compared with 16 percent for PC and 5 percent for Columbia Seminary). Starting in 1932, Queens-Chicora's share was cut to 1.6 percent. In 1933 Queens-Chicora's president W.H. Frazer noted that the synod had promised the college $10,000 and only contributed a little less than $3,000, resulting in a 20 percent salary cut "from President to Janitor."[48]

The struggle with Chicora's debt continued for more than ten years. Finally, in 1945 the Liquidating Committee reported to the synod that there remained only one final payment of $25,000 on the bonded indebtedness. Queens reported a balanced budget and capacity enrollment.

By 1948 Queens College was free of debt, and enrollment stood at 652, the largest in its history. Limitations on dormitory space allowed only 240 spaces for boarders, 25 percent of whom were from South Carolina. President Hunter P. Blakely resigned in 1950 after eleven years. He was eventually succeeded by Dr. Edwin Ruthven Walker. Despite the repayment of the various Chicora debts, Queens continued to receive only a small share of the synod's benevolence budget. In 1958 only 7 percent of the Queens budget came from the Synod of South Carolina, even though it was the synod's only college for women. In the early 1960s, enrollments increased steadily as the baby boomers reached college age, and Queens began making plans for future expansion.

In response to increasing calls for the synod's institutions to integrate, in December 1962, Queens trustees voted to admit African American students the following September. President Walker recommended this step to

---

48. McEwen, *Queens College Yesterday and Today*, 117.

the board because of his "'ethical and religious beliefs' and on a conviction that the move was 'in the best interests of the college.'" The president of the student council declared that the decision was "fine," and that she "couldn't be more pleased."[49]

At this time, with PC's move toward coeducation, some synod members wanted to reconsider their relationship with Queens. In 1963 Bethel Presbytery asked the synod to remove Queens from the budget and, beginning on January 1, 1965, to use the money to increase support of Presbyterian College. The overture was referred to the Committee on Educational Institutions for study, with recommendations to be made to the synod in 1964.

Although the synod ultimately failed to adopt the resolution, relative funding for Queens dropped significantly after PC went coed. Indeed in subsequent years, Queens was to receive only about 10 percent of the funds granted PC. In a letter written by Queens president John E. Smylie to synod exec Arthur M. Martin in 1968, Smylie acknowledged that the synod was unable to increase its annual allocation for Queens but thanked Martin for managing to hold it at $15,000. He concluded that everyone at Queens would do their best "to develop the interest of South Carolina in Queens during the coming year. We are planning to create several alumnae chapters in the area, and have taken steps to include alumnae of Chicora in our plans."[50]

After the synods were restructured, the educational institutions came under the Synod of the Southeast's Institutional Coordinating Committee, part of the synod's Coordinating Council. Under the reorganization, Queens, which had been affiliated with the synods of North and South Carolina, also came under the sponsorship of Georgia Presbyterians. It continued its ties with the new Synod of the Southeast and reiterated its desire to have the synod support the South Carolina scholarship fund. At this time, the college was spending $39,000 annually on aid to South Carolina students and receiving only $13,000 per year from the synod's budget. At the same time, aid from the State of South Carolina for students attending in-state colleges began cutting into enrollment at Queens.

In 1974 the Coordinating Committee recommended that the synod increase its gifts to all of its institutions. Queens, which had received $18,000 in 1974, was to receive $25,000 in 1975. This plan, however, turned out to be unrealistic, and in 1975, percentages were suggested for each institution. Queens was to receive 2 percent of the synod's total budget for institutions, a mere pittance compared with PC's 18.22 percent and Columbia's 15.89 percent.

49. "Queens to Accept Negro Applications," *Sumter Daily Item*, 5.
50. Arthur Martin Papers. Letter from John E. Smylie to Arthur M. Martin, April 26, 1968.

Enrollments at Queens continued to drop, producing more budget shortfalls. In 1976, after eight years of deficit operation, the college reduced staff, eliminated raises, and increased tuition by 8 percent. In 1977, while Queens was providing almost $88,000 in grants to students from the Synod of the Southeast, contributions from the synod fell almost $4,000 short of the $18,000 budgeted.

In 1979 the report of the Task Force on Ultimate Goals of the Synod of the Southeast for its Institutions in the Next Ten Years noted that Queens had been carrying a deficit for twelve consecutive years and had a short-term debt of $1.6 million. The synod's Coordinating Council designated the first six months as a "special season of appeal" for Queens College, intended not to raise funds, but to raise its visibility within the synod and identify prospective students, contributors, or friends.

In 1981 President Wireman formed a "President's Church Cabinet," an advisory group of seventeen ministers and lay persons from the synods of North Carolina and the Southeast to "develop strategies for the most creative and effective use of the resources of the college in the ongoing ministry of the Presbyterian Church." While he noted that financial support from the Synod of the Southeast was "relatively modest," the ties remained strong. Seven of Queens's thirty-three trustees were elected from the Synod of the Southeast, another six were Presbyterians from the synod, and students from South Carolina and Georgia made up 20 percent of the traditional undergraduate enrollment and 32 percent of the resident population. In addition, 33 percent of living Queens alumni were residing in South Carolina and Georgia.[51] The Synod of the Southeast, however, continued to reexamine funding levels for Queens. In May 1983, the synod's Coordinating Council appointed a task force to recommend a "process and rationale" for reducing contributions to several institutions, including Queens, with the aim of phasing them out by 1986. The women's college which faced such a bright future in 1925, although still supported by the Synod of the Southeast, had been increasingly marginalized after it moved from Columbia to Charlotte.

Campus Ministry

Presbyterians were vitally interested in ministering to students at public colleges and universities. The PCUS's concern for the spiritual development of students at non-denominational institutions first evidenced itself late in the nineteenth century, when southern Presbyterians began to worry about insuring that the "true faith" was reflected in curricula at tax-supported institutions. During this period, universities were becoming increasingly

---

51. Synod of the Southeast, 1981, 61.

secularized. According to theologian D. Keith Naylor, addressing the new modernity of the university directly was both a bold and sobering undertaking. "Liberal Protestants 'took on' modernity, decided to wrestle with it, to probe it to learn its benefits and its dangers. The campus ministry encountered modernity on its own turf. If the campus ministry was among the first to show enthusiasm for modernity, it was also among the first to sense that the challenge of modernity was massive, persistent, and not altogether benign for liberal Protestantism."[52]

As the work progressed, different types of campus ministry were established. Some larger churches had full-time ministers assigned to work with students at nearby universities. Another model involved actual Presbyterian chaplains or workers placed on public college and university campuses. The earliest attempts at campus ministry took the form of glorified youth fellowship programs but planned within the context of the new modernity: "What one learned in the laboratory, the classroom, on field trips, through contact with peers of different religious and cultural backgrounds, the questions, the doubts, the wonder, the shock, the restlessness . . . was brought to the campus ministry. However awkward, tentative, or amateurish, the campus ministry responded within the arena of the university, seeking, to be sure, to bring a word of God but recognizing the university as a representation of the secularization of the whole society."[53]

South Carolina Presbyterians shared the denomination's concern about secularization on campus. In 1894 members of the Synod of South Carolina expressed concern about the situation at the University of South Carolina despite reassurances from both the president and the chaplain that the institution's constitution required the president to be a Christian, that scripture was an integral part of student life and governance, and that the same was true at South Carolina's other public institutions. By 1905, having the same fears for students at Clemson, the synod had decided to act and voted to provide funds to Fort Hill Church to support a pastor to work with students there.

In 1924 the Synod of South Carolina provided Fort Hill Church $900 from its home missions budget to be used for work with Clemson students. It was hoped that Fort Hill would be able to build a hut on its grounds to house college activities. In 1925 the synod's Committee on Christian Education and Ministerial Relief announced plans to raise $25,000 for work with college and university students, declaring, "In the not too distant future they will be the leaders in the church and in every other branch of human

---

52. Naylor, "Campus Ministry," 118.
53. Ibid., 119.

activity. To neglect them would be nothing short of a crime."[54] The synod budgeted $600 for the work at Clemson and an additional $1,200 toward the construction of the hut.

Unfortunately, the work progressed much more slowly than expected. Although members of the Committee on Christian Education and Ministerial Relief saw a clear duty to follow the students "with the influence of the church" because "should the church fail to follow them ... during these formative years, they will likely care little for the church or the kingdom of God after leaving college," they were able to budget only $450 for college work in 1927.[55] By 1929 the only campus workers were "student secretaries" who were visiting the various campuses. Even when local churches were involved with nearby colleges, this ministry remained on the fringes. Congregational ministry remained the central focus, and there was also the need to support denominational colleges.

Although the Depression had already started, the picture looked brighter in 1930 when the synod was able to give $400 to support Rock Hill's Oakland Avenue Presbyterian Church in its work with Winthrop students and $1,100 to Fort Hill for work at Clemson. In 1932, however, the Depression caused the synod to discontinue any contributions for such work, and they asked the home mission committees of the presbyteries to try to do what they could in this area.

In 1936 the synod, once again concerned, conducted a survey of the work throughout the state. They found no organized work at Clemson, Winthrop, or the University of South Carolina, and complained that "these young men and women have been largely forgotten by the denomination in which they grew up."[56] They also looked at how other denominations were handling this problem and found that Presbyterians were far behind. The Baptists and the Methodists each had strong organizations on every campus. As a result, the synod organized a Committee on Student Work which in 1937 was able to appropriate $500 to the University of South Carolina, $900 to Winthrop, and $1,750 to Clemson. Even this amount, however, was too little to address the needs of the estimated 1,027 Presbyterian students at these three colleges and the Citadel, students who would someday provide the majority of church officers.

Less than half of the money promised in 1937 actually materialized, and the Religious Education Committee was forced to provide funds to make up the budget shortfall. The church's women, however, raised money

54. Synod of South Carolina, 1925, 56.
55. Naylor, "Campus Ministry," 121.
56. Synod of South Carolina, 1936, 10.

to support a worker at Winthrop, and First Presbyterian Church in Columbia hired an assistant pastor to spend part of his time at USC. There was some improvement by 1939. Mrs. John C. Hayes Jr. was working part-time at Winthrop and organized a Presbyterian Student Organization which included 175 students from eleven colleges across the state. Total funding for the effort, however, still stood at less than $3,000.

By 1940, with progress in the economy, things began to improve. The synod hired a full-time worker at Winthrop where there were weeknight and Sunday meetings of the Presbyterian Student Association. In addition, the Women of the Church and various Rock Hill congregations were working to get students more involved with their congregations. Reverend T. F. Wallace was working part time at USC, holding both a morning worship service and a Wednesday night supper and fellowship. The Citadel had its own full-time chaplain, so it was not practical to have a Presbyterian worker there. Area ministers were being used for chapel and communion services, however. The new president of Clemson, R. F. Poole, had set up a faculty committee on religion and ethics which also included the ministers of local churches and the YMCA secretary. Dr. Sidney Crouch, then at Fort Hill Church, was chosen to chair the committee. He would minister to Clemson students for many years.

The work remained basically the same at all three institutions for the following two years. The report to the synod in 1942, however, lamented, "We are barely scratching the surface. Our program is far behind that of other synods. The percentage of appropriation for student work in South Carolina is next to the lowest in the Assembly."[57] Dr. Crouch was sorely pressed trying to minister to almost 400 Clemson students while running the Fort Hill church single-handedly, and improvements were needed at the Citadel.

In 1943 the draft of college-age students and the presence of various military training programs on the campuses greatly impacted the synod's work. At some of the schools, civilians made up only one quarter to one third of the student body. The work had at the same time become more important and more difficult. There was limited time available for activities due to the new schedule of accelerated coursework, and there were frequent changes in the student body. At USC, Reverend T. F. Wallace and Reverend J. W. Jackson were attempting to reach 1,000 men in the Navy V-5 and V-12 programs in addition to 400 civilian students. Dr. Crouch was still at work at Clemson, aided by other ministers; they were serving between 1,500 and 1,800 trainees.

57. Ibid., 1942, 14.

At the Citadel, only about one third of the students were regular cadets; the others were in the service. Reverend G. A. Nickles, Reverend Frank P. Anderson, Reverend Edward G. Lilly, and J. Morrison Leland were working with them. The work at Winthrop was being done by a recent Queens College graduate, Sarah Hunter, with the help of Reverend Julian Lake. In addition, there were Presbyterian workers, many of them pastors, serving students at other colleges: Reverend James Appleby (Anderson College), Reverend A. W. Dick and Rachel Wylie (Converse and Wofford colleges), Reverend C. H. Nabers and Mary Wilds (Furman University), Reverend Roswell C. Long (Lander College), Reverend Hugh C. Hamilton (Limestone College), and Reverend C. A. Calcote (Newberry College).

In 1949 Reverend Thomas Hoover was hired as the minister to all Presbyterian students in Columbia; he was to remain for several years. Jane Chamblee was working with Citadel students as well as coordinating the work of the Westminster Fellowship on campuses across the state. Dr. Crouch continued to work both at Fort Hill and at Clemson. By 1951, however, it was becoming more difficult to hire full-time people to work with students in public colleges. During the war, the Defense Service Council had contributed toward these efforts. By 1951 that money, which had been held in reserve, had all been spent. The synod attempted to fill the gap with church educators and Presbyterian students, sometimes supervised by local pastors and supported by local churches. By this time, Tom Hoover had left the synod, but Jane Chamblee and Dr. Crouch were continuing their work, and Margaret Simrell was working at Winthrop in association with the Oakland Avenue church.

At this time, campus ministers were confronting a number of new issues—an increasing lack of financial support from the churches, college curriculums which were increasingly secular in nature, and a move away from evangelism and toward social justice and ecumenism:

> The disarray of campus ministry proved to be particularly damaging because it had traditionally been for Presbyterians and mainstream Protestants an important means of evangelism to young adults. Campus ministers often comprised a significant network of people who influenced students to enter the ministry or who encouraged the development of lay leaders. College students who confronted challenges to their childhood faith found in Presbyterian and other mainstream Protestant campus pastors a recognition that the intellect is God's creation and

received assistance in deepening their quest for knowledge of God and themselves."[58]

In addition, new non-denominational religious groups were appearing on campus, including Intervarsity Christian Fellowship (founded in 1941), Campus Crusade for Christ (founded in 1951), and the Fellowship of Christian Athletes (founded in 1954).

In 1954 Dr. Crouch left the Fort Hill Church to devote all of his time to the students at Clemson. The church called Reverend Charles E. Raynal as its first full-time pastor, where he served until 1974. The other colleges were still relying on part-time workers assisted by local congregations. Dr. Crouch retired in 1957 and received high praise from Clemson president R. F. Poole who called him a man with a "worthy mission" who "has achieved his goal in an admirable manner" and "deserves God's richest rewards for the splendid work he has accomplished."[59]

In 1957 the synod appointed a committee to determine whether college work could be done better by local churches with the assistance of the synod. While they determined that the synod itself should retain responsibility for the effort, they made the Campus Christian Life Committee into a sub-committee of the Christian Education Committee. They purchased a house across the street from the Winthrop campus to serve as a student center under the direction of Mrs. John Rauch who was working as the Director of Campus Christian Life there.

In 1960 the synod estimated that 12.5 percent of the white college students in South Carolina were Presbyterian and that about two thirds of these students attended state institutions. There were 642 Presbyterian students in Columbia, and Robert Haywood of Austin Seminary, who was funded by the General Assembly, was supervising Mrs. Libby Ledeen in her work with them. The Presbyterian Student Center facility near the USC campus had been condemned, but another building had been acquired for student use. Reverend Harry F. Petersen III was hired as University pastor.

Reverend S. Wylie Hogue Jr. was working as the university pastor at Clemson, serving as the student chaplain and associate minister at Fort Hill Presbyterian Church. Mrs. Rauch was still working with the two hundred Presbyterian women on the Winthrop campus. There was one Presbyterian worker in Charleston whose job it was to keep in touch with students at the Citadel, the College of Charleston, and the Medical College of South Carolina. In addition there were Westminster Fellowships at all the white colleges in the state; these groups joined together in an annual conference each year. It was necessary for the Campus Christian Life Committee to

---

58. Coalter et al, *The Re-Forming Tradition*, 159.
59. Poole, "Tribute," *South Carolina Presbyterian*, 6.

borrow money to complete its work for the year, but the General Assembly had contributed $3,000 for salaries and the budget had been trimmed. Plans for 1961 were to allocate $12,541 for the work in Columbia, $10,748 for Clemson, $5,653 for Winthrop, and $2,176 for the Charleston area.

Work continued in this same fashion for several years. In 1965 the Campus Christian Life Committee reported that there were 2,500 Presbyterian students at the four largest state universities, with almost 1,000 of these at USC. Three full-time workers were provided for the largest groups: Reverend S. Wylie Hogue at Clemson, Reverend C. Jerry Hammett at USC and Columbia College, and Miss Susan Smyth at Winthrop. Reverend Raymond G. Wickersham was working part-time to serve the students in Charleston. At smaller colleges where there was no staff worker, local churches and volunteers were trying to connect with college students. The following year, the committee asked the synod to raise $350,000 to improve facilities at the various institutions. By 1968 only $314,000 had been pledged, and a number of churches had contributed nothing toward the effort.

At the same time, with the turbulence of the late 1960s, the church saw an increased need for campus ministry. According to a report presented to the synod in 1969,

> In the midst of such deep-seated change, the voice of Christ is urgently needed by all involved: students, faculty, administration, trustees, alumni. The causes of peace, of justice, of patience, of righteousness, and of right relationships between individuals are being tried on campuses everywhere . . . The campus today is a battleground for the minds and hearts of those who, by all indications, will be the leaders of church and society tomorrow . . . There are many voices calling out to today's student; siren voices of nihilism, of anarchy, of experimentation in sex and drug addiction, of rejection of society and its values, of the low road rather than the high road. If ever the modern student needed an anchor to hold against the gale, it is now . . . It is extremely important that we see through these incidents on campuses as only symptoms, not as the root cause; it is extremely important that we minister not to these incidents, but to the root cause itself . . . the issues of morality and ethics and right . . . [60]

The committee asked Dr. Robert Bluford, head of campus ministry for the General Assembly, to study the synod's work at Clemson, USC, and Charleston. Committee members also held a conference with several other denominations to explore ecumenical approaches to serving college

60. Synod of South Carolina, 1969, 32–6.

students. In addition they were considering the idea of more participation by the individual presbyteries.

By the early 1970s, the move toward increased involvement by the presbyteries was well underway. In 1973 the house which had been used by USC students was once again condemned, and the potential property for a new student center was transferred to the trustees of Congaree Presbytery to hold in reserve for future work. The work of Reverend Robert M. Matthews at Clemson was being supported by a new Campus Christian Life Committee organized by all of the local Presbyterian churches. Charleston Presbytery was helping to support Reverend Albert H. Keller's work as a visiting professor of ethics at the Medical University. Money already collected to support campus ministry at Clemson and in Charleston was transferred to Piedmont and Charleston Presbyteries. This was also the period when the synods were being restructured, and the Synod of South Carolina was beginning to work with the Synod of Georgia in preparation for work within the new combined synod.

At the same time, however, campus ministers were becoming more estranged from the churches that ordained them. They were becoming more liberal, their theology more independent. They were more critical of their denominations and more supportive than the church as a whole of such organizations as the World Council of Churches and the National Council of Churches. According to theologian D. Keith Naylor, "This marginalization signaled a religious crisis. As campus ministers lost touch with the deep wellsprings of their religious and spiritual communities, they were increasingly at the mercy of the secular university."[61] Since campus ministry was increasingly cut off from individual churches, it was weakened and often ignored.

In 1974 the Campus Ministries Coordinating Committee of the new Synod of the Southeast reported that the synod was supporting ministries at seven institutions. Those in South Carolina were at Clemson, the Charleston cluster, USC, and Winthrop. The work in both states in 1974 would cost a little over $150,000, with most of this amount going toward fixed expenses like salaries and benefits. The committee's request for a budget of $178,000 in 1975 was cut to $162,000. According to the committee, the lack of discretionary money for programming coupled with rampant inflation had forced them to engage the problems of campus ministry, recognizing that the synod could no longer give it a high priority: "Synod cannot carry virtually all the load . . . It is being recommended that presbyteries and local

---

61. Naylor, "Campus Ministry," 123.

constituencies must be drawn into new partnerships with the Synod to support even the present program."[62]

This tension between lack of funding and the perceived need to increase programming continued for a number of years. The committee continued to ask for increased participation by local churches and presbyteries and encouraged local pastors to start campus ministry programs in their churches. In 1975 the committee asked that the coordinating council sell the synod's property in Columbia (three lots and a tenant house) and use the proceeds to establish an endowment to support campus ministry in that area. "As we go through some shaking of our present foundations, we pray that we shall find bedrock underneath us . . . bedrock that will preserve the valuable work being done now . . . bedrock that will be a base upon which we can build a still more effective ministry in the future."[63]

By 1977 the synod had negotiated five-year plans of transfer with Charleston Presbytery which would supervise the work in the Charleston area and Congaree Presbytery which would take over the effort in Columbia. In a similar fashion, Clemson would become the responsibility of Piedmont Presbytery and Winthrop of Bethel Presbytery. Apparently, though, this was slow to happen, as the synod was still supporting work at Winthrop, USC, and in Charleston in 1978, and was planning "to take a comprehensive look at the total work of Campus Ministry as it is now functioning" in 1979.[64] In 1981, even while expecting PCUS and UPCUSA reunion, the synod was still supporting the work at USC, Winthrop, and Charleston for a combined total budget of over $20,000. It was also supporting ministries at the Medical College of Georgia and the University of Georgia. By 1983, however, only the work at the University of Georgia and in the Charleston area was directly supported by the synod.

By the time reunion had been completed, all of the campus ministry work in South Carolina had been transferred to presbyteries or local churches. In 1985, the last year that the Synod of the Southeast existed, the only campus ministry being directly supported was at the University of Georgia. The synod was still involved in negotiations to transfer support of this effort to the presbyteries.

---

62. Synod of the Southeast, 1974, 31–2.
63. Ibid., 1975, 37.
64. Ibid., 1978, 55.

Conclusion

While much had changed for the church's higher education program since 1925, much had also remained the same. Through changes in governing bodies, financial difficulties, and social change, all of the synod's institutions maintained strong ties with the church. All of them were integrated and all were coeducational.

While Columbia Seminary was no longer located in South Carolina, it continued to receive solid support from the state's Presbyterians. The larger constituency it gained by moving to Decatur enabled it to solve its financial problems, and innovative programs attracted more students.

Presbyterian College was a much more vital college, all the while retaining its strong ties to the church. This was in stark contrast to the situation at many church-related colleges which had distanced themselves from the PCUS. At PC, faculty members were still expected to be members of a Christian church as well as ethical persons dedicated to service. The curriculum was firmly rooted in the Judeo-Christian tradition.

Chicora College, the Synod of South Carolina's college for women, had merged with Queens College and moved to Charlotte. While the Synod of South Carolina and later the Synod of the Southeast were officially among the college's sponsoring synods, Queens College became marginalized after its move and received very little funding from South Carolina's Presbyterians.

After more than eighty years of inadequate funding and varied structures, the crucial campus ministry effort envisioned by both the General Assembly and the synod had largely been abandoned, turned over to local churches and presbyteries.

While all of the synod's efforts in education had suffered from drastic decreases in synod funding and were forced to rely more and more on individual fundraising campaigns, South Carolina Presbyterians had continued their commitment to institutions that would educate people as leaders for the church.

7

Institutions of Care and Nurture

IN 1925, IN ADDITION to Chicora and Presbyterian colleges and Columbia Theological Seminary, the Synod of South Carolina was supporting one other institution, the Thornwell Orphanage. This children's home was conceived by the Clinton Presbyterian Church under the leadership of Reverend William Plumer Jacobs.

Reverend William Plumer Jacobs
(Courtesy of Presbyterian College)

His vision for the home was that "the physical needs of the children would be met, they would learn to work, they would be intellectually challenged, they would be spiritually led, they would be loved, and they would become Christian."[1]

By the time Thornwell opened in 1875 with one building and eight orphans, it was under the aegis of the Synod of South Carolina. Reverend Jacobs disapproved of the dormitory style orphanages that were prevalent at the time, so the plan was for Thornwell to house children in smaller cottages which would provide more of a family environment. The orphanage provided a home for whole and half orphans, and had its own school. The onsite farm and printing shop also provided the children with vocational skills. At various times during its early history, the orphanage offered college courses and had a Mission Training School. By 1909 the orphanage boasted its own church, the Thornwell Memorial Church. By 1915 there were twenty-eight buildings on the campus which could accommodate two hundred children.[2] Along with neighboring Presbyterian College, Thornwell provided a Christian education which included study of the Bible and training for lives of service, and produced many pastors, missionaries, and church leaders for the PCUS.

During the late 1940s, the Synod of South Carolina began to consider a new ministry. With families being more widely separated than before, it became clear that there was a need for residential and end of life care for aging members of the church. In 1958, under the leadership of Reverend W. McLeod Frampton, the synod opened the first Presbyterian Home in Summerville. In later years additional homes were opened in Clinton, Florence, Easley, and Columbia, providing care for people across the state.

Thornwell Orphanage

Beginning with its establishment in 1872, Thornwell Orphanage was led by Reverend William Plumer Jacobs who served as the orphanage's president in addition to his duties as pastor of the Clinton Presbyterian Church. When Dr. Jacobs died in 1917, Dr. L. Ross Lynn, a Florida pastor who had served on the orphanage's board for eight years, took charge.

---

1. Sivewright, *God's People Serving God's Purpose*, 11.
2. Ibid.

Dr. L. Ross Lynn (Courtesy of Presbyterian College)

He continued to appeal for the benevolent dollars of South Carolina Presbyterians. Churches collected special Thanksgiving and Christmas offerings for Thornwell, and Sunday school offerings were committed to the orphanage once each month. Young People's Societies and the Women of the Church also undertook special collections for the orphanage. In some years these offerings totaled more than the gifts of the synod's churches to Presbyterian College, Chicora, and Columbia Seminary combined.

When Dr. Lynn took over as president, he felt a need to revise Thornwell's charter, particularly as it pertained to admissions. In 1920 the board approved a charter whereby legitimate white children of both sexes, either totally orphaned or deprived of a father could enter the home. They could be from any religious denomination, but they had to be endorsed by the Presbyterian church in their community.[3]

During the 1920s, the women of the synod made one very significant contribution to the physical plant at Thornwell, the Louise F. Mayes Baby

3. Ibid., 16.

Cottage. Up until 1923, Thornwell had housed only children over five years old. In 1923 Louise Mayes, the President of the South Carolina Synodical, urged the church's women to raise funds to support a cottage for younger children. Although she died in 1923, the project continued. The cottage, built with funds from the synodicals of South Carolina, Georgia, and Florida, opened in 1925.

Although originally under the auspices of the Synod of South Carolina, by 1920 Thornwell was owned and controlled by the synods of South Carolina, Georgia, and Florida, and all of its trustees were elected from those synods. Due to a multitude of generous donors, the orphanage's endowment had reached a healthy $314,000 by 1924. That year the campus consisted of 29 buildings and housed 375 children.[4]

Home of Peace and Library, Thornwell Orphanage
(Courtesy of Presbyterian College)

In 1925, in the face of the looming depression, Thornwell seemed to be doing well financially, receiving strong support from the synod and from individual churches. Between 1925 and 1935, Thornwell garnered 40 percent of the total gifts to the synod's four institutions. In 1927, of the institution's $130,000 budget, only $30,000 came from the endowment, leaving the churches and others to provide the rest.[5] In fact the 1928 treasurer's report indicated that the orphanage had "not suffered financially during the past year"; indeed, "we would say that the Orphanage still holds a big place

4. Lynn, *The Story of Thornwell Orphanage*, 82, 160.
5. Sivewright, *God's People Serving God's Purpose*, 17.

in the interests of the Church at large."⁶ The home's residents continued to be from a number of denominations. In 1928 the 138 Presbyterian residents made up only 39 percent of the enrollment. Other denominations heavily represented were the Baptists (87) and the Methodists (57).⁷

The Depression, which began to affect the synod's other institutions during the 1920s, did not really impact Thornwell until the beginning of the 1930s. In 1931 churches without the means to send money began collecting farm produce for the orphanage's kitchens. The orphanage truck would start its rounds filled with fruit jars to be left with the ladies of the churches for the next year's canning. It would return to Thornwell loaded with produce. The Women of the Church collected clothing which was then altered to fit the children by girls in the home's sewing classes. The amount of materials contributed was sometimes quite large. In 1936 the churches of Cherokee Presbytery in North Georgia loaded a 16,000 pound train car with provisions.⁸

The nation's faltering economy also affected operations on the campus itself. Funds had to be diverted from operations, construction, and maintenance merely to cover the cost of food and clothing for the children. Salaries were cut across the board by 30 to 50 percent. Meal costs at the orphanage were pared to the paltry sum of 30 cents a day per child.⁹ The daily per capita cost per child in 1934 was 81 cents; by 1935 it was down to 77 cents.¹⁰ In 1934 the synod approved another special offering for Thornwell to be collected on Mother's Day. The situation seemed to be improving, and by the following year there were almost three hundred children in residence, and the school had an endowment of $394,000 and was debt free.¹¹

Unfortunately, Thornwell was unable to maintain a balanced budget. From November 26, 1935, to January 1, 1936, gifts from the three supporting synods (South Carolina, Georgia, and Florida) fell more than $4,000 below the amount needed. In an open letter published in April of that year, Dr. Lynn noted that the funds provided by the synods were "totally inadequate, if paid, to support the Orphanage. But this has been by deliberate choice of the Synods and Presbyteries—that the Orphanage might have a more direct relationship to the Church and Church Organizations than is permitted through the budget."¹² Nevertheless, he urged that the level of

6. "Treasurer's Report," *Our Monthly*, 306.
7. Sivewright, *God's People Serving God's Purpose*, 17.
8. "This is the Way Cherokee Presbytery Does It!" *Our Monthly* 73, 340.
9. Wickham, *Thornwell—A Profile of Love*.
10. "An Open Letter," *Our Monthly*, 114.
11. "Annual Report Number," 277–8.
12. "An Open Letter," 114.

support be raised, that Sunday schools give one offering per month to the orphanage, and that the Thanksgiving offering be better organized to produce better results.

The slogan for the Thanksgiving offering in 1936 was "Help get Thornwell out of the Depression." The Synod of South Carolina asked its churches and Sunday schools to provide $25,000 toward this annual offering, and the children at the home were asked to think of ways they could further economize. Some of these suggestions were quite amusing, like letting children sleep through breakfast, using less soap, and tearing up fewer sheets by having fewer kicking fights.

That same year, Thornwell hired Louis C. Lamotte to fill a new position, that of Executive Secretary. In his first nine months on the job, he visited 404 churches or church groups to promote Thornwell and assembled a mailing list of 15,000 names. In 1939 the synod also instructed Thornwell's trustees to balance the budget—by reducing the number of children if necessary.[13]

The early 1940s was a time of transition at the orphanage. Dr. L. Ross Lynn resigned as president in 1943. After the year-long interim presidency of longtime board member W. W. Harris of Clinton, he was replaced by Reverend Malcolm A. Macdonald, then pastor of the First Presbyterian Church of Moultrie, Georgia.

Dr. Malcolm A. Macdonald, right (Courtesy of Presbyterian College

---

13. Synod of South Carolina, 1939, 27.

Macdonald took over an orphanage in dire need of repair and modernization. In 1945 the enrollment was only 220. The plant was valued at $905,000, and the endowment had reached $426,000.[14] To help with fundraising, coin cards with little slots for nickels and dimes so well remembered by the Sunday school children of that generation, were put into use.

The 1950s were years of expansion and building. While the sponsoring synods were providing 77 percent of the home's operating expenses, Thornwell continued to rely mostly on contributions from interested donors for building and expansion. By 1962 Thornwell had fifteen new buildings, all funded by private donations. Many of these, including the Hartness Gymnasium (1950), Sara Jo Hartness Hall (1954), T. P. Hartness Hall (1956), and Sarah's Home (1960) were provided by Mr. and Mrs. T. P. Hartness of Spartanburg.[15] Mr. and Mrs. Hartness, prominent Spartanburg Presbyterians, contributed over $500,000 to fund these buildings, and at the time of Mr. Hartness' death, Malcolm Mcdonald said that he had "done more good for humanity than any person in my knowledge."[16] Indeed, the PCUS provided only a fraction of the funding needed by the home. In 1953, 235 of the 330 students at Thornwell were from the Synod of South Carolina, and almost $300,000 was spent for their care, although only $96,283 was supplied by the synod. By 1954 the enrollment stood at 402.

The 1960s also proved to be a decade of change for Thornwell whose administration voiced increasing concern about the synod's support. Even though building continued on the campus and the endowment had risen, this had all been done without the help of an organized fundraising campaign. Thornwell, among all the institutions, had never had a fundraising campaign organized by the synod, and President Macdonald expressed his hope that the sponsoring synods would authorize such a campaign in the future. Mr. and Mrs. Hartness continued their generosity, providing the Hartness-Thornwell Memorial Church (1966), the Hartness Museum (1972), and the Tom and Jo Infirmary (1973). According to the Committee on Thornwell's report in 1963, while the Synod of South Carolina allotted $115,000 a year for Thornwell, the orphanage actually served 253 South Carolina children at a cost of $339,829. In addition to the institutional expenses of all the children, the budget had to be stretched to take care of all of their personal expenses including clothing, shoes, travel, recreation, and spending money. To further complicate matters, due to the adoption of the Unified Budget by the synod, some churches had ceased to collect a Thanksgiving Offering for Thornwell.

14. Ibid., 1945, 21.
15. Wickham, *Thornwell—A Profile of Love*, 97, 101, 104.
16. "T. P. Hartness Dies at 72," *Spartanburg Herald-Journal*, 18.

President Macdonald's report to the Synod that year said, "Because we get a new building occasionally and make a little progress in different departments of activity, some people arrive at an erroneous conclusion that Thornwell is rich and has plenty of money. Every building on our campus was given by some estate or individual. It is never taken from our regular budget. That is from gifts and monies received from Churches, Sunday Schools, etc." He also reminded the synod that Thornwell was the only synod institution that was not permitted to charge tuition.[17]

In 1963 the Synod of Georgia did a study of its relationship with the orphanage and concluded that relying on one offering a year for support was highly risky, as the amount collected might vary greatly from year to year. In their reply to the Georgia study, Thornwell trustees noted that the Synod of Georgia budgeted only $17,500 annually for the institution (a mere $100 per church), while the Thanksgiving Offering might average $56,000. Consequently, the consultants recommended "that this problem be brought to the attention of the authorities of the several Synods, pointing out also the number of children from each state, requesting a guarantee over and above the Thanksgiving Offering, in proportion to that population."[18]

That same year President Macdonald asked the Synod of South Carolina to allot $115,000 for the coming year. Although he repeated this request in 1964, it was not to be honored. The synods of South Carolina, Georgia, and Florida were to fund only 45 percent of Thornwell's budget. Were it not for increased endowment and funds from the memorial program, the orphanage would have been in debt. By 1968 this figure had decreased further, and the synods were providing only 27 percent of Thornwell's operating expenses.[19]

Changes were also occurring in Thornwell's clientele. For the past several years, the orphanage had been called on to serve an increasing number of children from broken homes and fewer whole or half orphans. This was part of a trend that had begun in the US after World War II. Large orphanages were gradually being replaced by smaller institutions that could provide a group home or private school experience. There were also more children with behavioral problems, and homes increasingly began to provide mental health services.[20]

Beginning in 1964, Thornwell's three sponsoring synods began to study the institution's racially discriminatory admissions policies. This

17. Synod of South Carolina, 1963, 27.
18. Isaac and Spencer, "A Study," 28.
19. Sivewright, *God's People Serving God's Purpose*, 24.
20. "Testimony of Nan Dale."

scrutiny was begun by the Synod of Georgia, and Florida and South Carolina followed. In 1966 the Synod of South Carolina appointed a Thornwell Orphanage Committee to study the institution and report to the next meeting. The committee made a number of recommendations. The first was that the word *illegitimate* be deleted from Thornwell's charter so that children born out of wedlock could be admitted. They also suggested that the children be enrolled in public school rather than attending the private school operated on the Thornwell campus. The orphanage responded by noting that "the commonly accepted opinion of experts in the field of child care is that illegitimate children, per se, should be legally adopted by parents in an established home." They also noted that Thornwell's original charter, as well as the one adopted by the three sponsoring synods in 1920, limited orphanage residents to white children. "It is quite obvious that this one institution, serving three large states, could not possibly take care of the complete needs of all types of children of all races in this territory."[21] As for public schooling, they noted that there was not space available in the public schools of Clinton to admit Thornwell students if the private school were closed. They also noted that the Thornwell school had smaller classes than the public schools and was highly rated. In a final comment, they observed that the continuing investigations of Thornwell were hard on the institution, making it difficult to recruit staff and potential donors and taking up valuable staff time.

Thornwell began to receive pressure to integrate from the federal government and some Presbyterian churches and church bodies. FBI agents actually appeared on campus to notify the institution that it was in violation of the Housing Title of the Civil Rights Act of 1968, and the justice department threatened to sue unless the charter was changed.[22] Feeling that many of the criticisms of the home were the result of a lack of communication, the institution embarked on a community outreach program. Board members were encouraged to attend synod meetings to talk about the home and to answer any questions. Pastors were invited to the campus to see for themselves what was going on.

Thornwell did have support from some South Carolina Presbyterians, however. In January 1966, Congaree Presbytery proposed a resolution which did not pass, affirming the Synod's support of and confidence in the Administration and Board of Trustees of Thornwell Orphanage in regard to procedures for admitting children to its care. In February 1967, the Presbytery of South Carolina resolved that the orphanage's board should be allowed to continue to operate Thornwell under the present charter and policies.

21. Synod of South Carolina, 1967, 46–8.
22. Sivewright, *God's People Serving God's Purpose*, 26.

The synod's committee on institutions noted in 1968, however, that none of the synod's other institutions had racially discriminatory policies, while Thornwell's charter provided for the "support, maintenance, and education of white children of respectable parentage, deprived of the father by death."[23] Opposition to the existing by-laws came from both within and outside the campus, but Dr. Macdonald himself was vocal in resisting integration. In February 1970, the board voted to keep the "whites only" policy. The chairman of the board, Richard de Montmollin, was confronted with a divided board, pressure from the church, and the prospect of a long court battle. Thornwell's lawyers were called in and concluded that the Justice Department would likely win any lawsuit under the "dwelling" provision of the housing title of the 1968 Civil Rights Act. Two months later the board voted again, this time choosing to remove the restrictions on race and the admission of illegitimate children. Thornwell's new mission became "to maintain a home and school for the support, maintenance, and education of children of Presbyterian background."[24] Since the home was clearly not operating as an orphanage anymore, its name was changed to the "Thornwell Home and School for Children."

As chairman de Montmollin said in 1970, "The Board felt that this was a matter which should be settled within the Church, rather than to allow suit to be brought by the Department of Justice. It was felt that the time had come when this matter should be resolved, with the solution coming from within the Church courts, thereby promoting conditions under which Thornwell could perform her great work without undue interference from federal authorities . . . this was, under the present circumstances, in the best interest of Thornwell."[25]

The institution's admission policy was also further defined during this period. Under the new guidelines, residents must have a proven Presbyterian background and the application must come through the pastor of a Presbyterian church. Children with juvenile court records or those with severe physical, emotional, or learning handicaps would not be eligible.[26] These new guidelines resulted in the rejection of 63 students the following year.

In October of 1970, the executive committee of the board met and asked Dr. Macdonald to move out of the president's home by January 1971, at which time his duties as President would be at an end. This action was approved by the board as a whole in December. In a document written by Dr. Macdonald entitled simply "My Resignation," he expressed regret that he was unable to retire "officially and gracefully" in September 1972, which

23. Synod of South Carolina, 1969, 43.
24. Sivewright, *God's People Serving God's Purpose*, 24–7.
25. Wickham, *Thornwell—A Profile of Love*, 141–2.
26. Sivewright, *God's People Serving God's Purpose*, 31.

had been his plan.[27] When news of the resignation was published in the *Southern Presbyterian*, at least one reader wrote to Arthur Martin protesting the use of the word "resignation" when Macdonald had actually been fired and asked to have his name removed from the synod's mailing list.[28] Even though the policy had officially been changed, progress came slowly. The first African American student would not be admitted for fourteen more years; the first black housemother would follow two years later.[29]

After the restructuring of the synods and the creation of the new Synod of the Southeast (encompassing Georgia and South Carolina) in 1973, South Carolina's institutions came under the supervision of the Institutional Coordinating Committee of Synod's Coordinating Council. In 1974 the Coordinating Committee recommended that the synod increase its gifts to all of its institutions. Under this plan, the amount given to Thornwell would increase from $180,000 to $185,000. This turned out, however, to be unrealistic, and in 1976 percentages were suggested for each institution. Thornwell was to receive 15.1 percent of synod's funds compared to 18.22 percent for PC, 15.89 percent for Columbia Seminary, and 2 percent for Queens College.[30]

Changes continued at Thornwell. When Dr. Macdonald left in 1970, he was replaced by Reverend Robert J. Blumer. Blumer was left to heal the bitter divisions that had developed during the fight over integration. During his first year, in an attempt to reconnect with churches and governing bodies, he spoke at one hundred churches, thirteen presbytery meetings, and three synod meetings. He also faced a precarious financial situation due to uncertainty in the US economy, rising energy prices, and divisions caused by the church's restructuring. A significant part of Thornwell's support came from churches opposed to restructuring. Indeed, in his report to the synod in 1974, Dr. Blumer noted that "some of our strongest supporters belong to the continuing church group and their status is questionable."[31]

Dr. Blumer returned to the pastoral ministry in 1978 and was succeeded by Reverend John B. Pridgen, pastor of the First Presbyterian Church of Anderson. During this time, Thornwell continued to ask the synod to increase its support. In 1978, much affected by high inflation, the board asked for the Synod of the Southeast for $175,000 toward a total operating budget of around $1.4 million. In 1979 the three synods provided 11.3 percent of Thornwell's operating budget. By 1980 contributions from the Synod

27. Arthur Martin Papers.
28. Arthur Martin Papers. Letter from B. G. Shaw to Arthur M. Martin, February 28, 1971.
29. Sivewright, *God's People Serving God's Purpose*, 27.
30. Synod of the Southeast, 1975, 39.
31. Ibid., 1974, 86.

of the Southeast covered 9 per cent of the institution's operating expenses and came mostly from the annual Thanksgiving Offering. The orphanage was still relying heavily on private donations and income from endowment.

By this time, the orphanage was much smaller. In 1979 there were fifteen residences equipped to care for 150 students. In 1979 there were 143 residents on campus, 28 of whom were living at Thornwell but attending nearby Presbyterian College. By 1981 this number had dropped to 131 residents, twenty of whom were in college.[32]

Thornwell continued to undergo changes in leadership and scrutiny by various church bodies. Reverend Pridgen resigned as president and was replaced by Zane Moore in 1986. In 1985 the Division of Institutional Ministries recommended yet another Special Committee to study Thornwell's mission, organizational structure, and investment program. They hoped that this study would help the new president and the board of trustees to formulate a long-range plan for Thornwell.

The special committee recommended a redefinition of Thornwell's mission to recognize the shift from the old fashioned orphanage model to provision of "a short term experience for displaced, abused, disturbed children through an encounter of Christian love and professional care."[33] This change in focus would require changes in staffing, including the addition of professionals in clinical psychology and counseling.

The committee also reflected on the relationship between the synod and Thornwell. While officials at Thornwell made regular reports to the synod about activities, some felt that information was lacking and that synod members were unaware of the changing nature of the school's mission. In addition, while Thornwell's trustees were appointed by the various synods, the committee felt that the synods had failed to consider the unique expertise which might be required of an effective trustee. It was left to Zane Moore to address these concerns. He was to lead the home for fourteen years until his retirement in 2000.

One hundred and twenty-five years after a small country church and an inspired pastor collaborated to open the Thornwell Orphanage, it was estimated that 40,000 children had passed through its halls receiving love, nurture, an academic as well as a Christian education and instruction in various trades.[34]

---

32. Sivewright, *God's People Serving God's Purpose*, 37.
33. Isaac and Spencer, "A Study of Thornwell Home and School," 4.
34. Sivewright, *God's People Serving God's Purpose*, 55.

Presbyterian Homes

During the late 1940s, the Synod of South Carolina began considering an entirely new mission—the care of the elderly. Medical advances were allowing people to live longer, but as families became more mobile, older people were often living far from their children. At the same time, a new kind of retirement facility was becoming increasingly popular—the Continuing Care Retirement Community, or CCRC. These communities charged a one time, non refundable entry fee in return for providing a continuum of services from independent living to assisted living to skilled nursing care.

Some members of the Synod of South Carolina began to see the need for such a facility for the state's Presbyterians. In 1948 the synod appointed Reverend W. McLeod Frampton as chair of a committee to study the issue.

Reverend W. McLeod Frampton
(Courtesy of Presbyterian College)

The committee reported in 1949 that very few of the ministers surveyed felt that the church should embark upon this type of ministry.[35] At the synod meeting in 1950, Frampton asked that the committee be expanded by the addition of six laymen including doctors and lawyers who were experienced in the field.[36] In 1951, while the committee declined to make specific recommendations, they urged the synod to approve the concept, to establish a fund for the construction or purchase of a facility, and to form a committee of representatives from each presbytery. The synod also recommended that Thornwell's trustees be consulted about the establishment of a home in connection with that institution.

In 1953 the synod accepted Dr. and Mrs. Jack W. Rhodes's offer of twenty-six acres of land in Summerville as a site for a home for the elderly. At the same time, they suggested that a permanent Executive Committee be appointed to handle all matters relating to the home. They designated the 1954 Mother's Day offering to support the effort. This annual offering continues and over the years has been extremely important to South Carolina's Presbyterian homes.

The Presbyterian Home of South Carolina, with headquarters in Summerville, was incorporated on May 18, 1954. The synod authorized the home's trustees to raise $238,300 to build a facility for twenty residents with an additional facility for twenty more residents to follow as soon as possible. By 1956 the trustees had almost $150,000 cash in hand and approximately $100,000 in additional pledges. The cornerstone was laid in 1957, and the trustees decided to add the second bedroom wing as part of the initial construction. The home opened with eleven residents in January of 1958. As Reverend Arthur Martin said at the time, "This is like a new baby. It came complete, but we expect it to grow."[37] By the end of its first complete year of operation, there were thirty-eight residents. Reverend Charles Robert Tapp was installed as superintendent; he was to remain head of the homes for over twenty-eight years.

---

35. Synod of South Carolina, 1949, 54.
36. Ibid., 1950, 55.
37. Roberts, *Presbyterian Home of South Carolina*, 7.

Charles Robert Tapp

During the 1960s, the Summerville home continued to expand. By 1961 plans were afoot to provide a health care facility. The fourteen-bed infirmary licensed by the state opened in 1962, and the synod borrowed further funds for an addition to the infirmary and the construction of a new bedroom wing. This thirty-one bedroom addition was completed in 1964, and air-conditioning was provided for the entire facility.

South Carolina Presbyterians were beginning to want similar facilities in other parts of the state. In 1967 the synod asked the home's board of trustees "to study and investigate the needs and possibilities of establishing a second unit."[38] The following year the trustees were authorized to acquire land in the upper part of South Carolina as the site for a future home. By 1969 the Board of Trustees had acquired forty acres from Mrs. Nelson Dow of Clinton as the site of a new home and preliminary surveys were underway. Growth at the Summerville home also continued, and the trustees were authorized to borrow funds for a new residential wing.

38. Synod of South Carolina, 1967, 41.

Rendering of the Clinton Presbyterian Home

During the 1970s, the program for the elderly continued to grow. The Summerville facility dedicated a new fifty bed residential wing in 1971. In 1973 the synod authorized a capital funds campaign for $2.5 million to be held the following year. Of that amount 20 percent was to be used for a permanent endowment and 80 percent for expansion at the home in Summerville and construction at the Clinton site. As a result of synod restructuring, arrangements had to be made for the governance of the homes. On June 6, 1972, the Synod of South Carolina released the Presbyterian Homes to the control of the presbyteries of South Carolina, effective upon synod restructure in 1973.[39]

In November 1973, the trustees approved plans for the Clinton Home and the fundraising campaign began. Ground was broken in April 1974. By July of that year, the campaign was oversubscribed, with $2.8 million in cash and pledges. The next year the Mary Musgrove Hotel in downtown Clinton went on the auction block, and with the help of local Presbyterians Collie Anderson, G. Edward Campbell, and W. C. Baldwin, the home's trustees were able to purchase it for $75,000. After renovation this building, later named Frampton Hall in honor of W. McLeod Frampton, provided single rooms for 42 residents.[40] The first residents moved into the Clinton home in October 1975, and it was formally dedicated on December 2 of that

---

39. Roberts, *Presbyterian Home of South Carolina*, 12.
40. Hollis, *As Best We Remember*, 12.

year, with Thomas Francis Hollis as its first administrator. In 1976 a third resident wing was opened in Clinton, followed the next year by a forty-four bed infirmary. The two Clinton facilities operated under the same administrative staff until 1980, when a full-time administrator was hired to run Frampton Hall.

In 1978 Shandon and Eastminster Presbyterian churches in Columbia asked Congaree Presbytery to petition the Board to establish a home in Columbia.[41] That same year, Pee Dee Presbytery petitioned the trustees for a home in the Pee Dee area. Since other fund raising activities were going on at the time, it was impossible to carry on a statewide campaign for funds. Eventually the board of trustees of the McLeod Hospital in Florence agreed to sell the hospital annex and one hundred acres to the Presbyterian Home for $668,000. Some of the land was sold to raise money, leaving forty acres and the old hospital building. Funds for remodeling were raised through the purchase of Presbyterian Home bonds. The first group of residents moved into the new Presbyterian Home of Florence in September 1981. An infirmary was added in 1983, and a chapel and townhouses were added in 1984 and 1985.

In 1983, anticipating the effect of Presbyterian merger, the Presbyterian Homes faced a dilemma about their admission policy. Churches had been leaving the PCUS for ten years over various issues, and this trend was expected to be exacerbated by church reunion. The question was what to do with elderly members of churches that had left the denomination. On February 25 of that year, the Board decided, after some controversy and by a split vote, to allow a fifteen-year grace period during which members of churches that had pulled out would be admitted on an equal footing with members whose churches had remained in the PCUS (and were thus members of its successor, the PCUSA). On June 17, the Board met with the various presbytery executives to discuss its decision. Although most of the execs disagreed with the new policy, they provided no new information to cause the Board to change its decision.

Thus, in a little less than forty years, South Carolina Presbyterians had established four homes to provide care for their aging members, and the program continued to expand. The W. T. Cassells family donated twenty-seven acres of land in Columbia, and fundraising for a new home there began in 1983. Ground was broken in December of 1984, and the new home opened in 1986. Today there are five such Presbyterian Communities in South Carolina located in Clinton, Columbia, Florence, Summerville, and Easley, housing almost 1000 residents.

---

41. Roberts, *Presbyterian Home of South Carolina*, 15.

Conclusion

THE MAIN PURPOSE OF this book has been to consider the work of South Carolina Presbyterians from 1925 until just after the vote to form the Presbyterian Church (USA) in 1983. In particular this history has examined aspects of the ministries of mission at home and in other lands, church and society, women's programs, African American ministries, and Presbyterian institutions of education and care in South Carolina.

Although the Synod of South Carolina of the Presbyterian Church in the United States (PCUS) first commissioned this history, the account includes important parts of the history and work of the Synod of the Atlantic, formerly of the United Presbyterian Church in the United States of America (UPCUSA). The home mission work of northern Presbyterians in the Carolinas after the Civil War established in Catawba and Atlantic synods gave rise to one of the largest regional concentrations of African American Presbyterians in the United States. South Carolina Presbyterianism includes strains of both of these national denominations.

Even though the members and pastors of congregations share the primary stewardship of the work of the church, in Presbyterian polity the synods and presbyteries develop those programs and institutions that require broad support by the denomination. Between General Assembly meetings, the synods and presbyteries collect and disburse financial gifts, report on the statistics of members, ordain and install ministers and officers, and assist congregations in their involvement in mission at home and throughout the world. Synods mediate between the local congregations and the cooperative national and global mission of the denomination. While these activities remained constant, societal changes at home and abroad dictated that the denomination's polity and much of its work change radically between 1925 and 1985.

Before 1925 the decline of the predominant rural and textile businesses caused widespread poverty in South Carolina, years before the Great Depression caused distress to the whole country. The support of Presbyterians for home missionary work fell. New church starts diminished, and support for Appalachian and mill village work languished.

Financial losses undermined the Synod of South Carolina's treasured commitment to higher education. In 1925 the Synod of South Carolina was supporting three institutions of higher learning. Presbyterian College was in Clinton, and Chicora College and Columbia Theological Seminary were in Columbia. By 1930, largely because of financial problems, two of these institutions had moved outside the bounds of the state, Columbia Seminary to Decatur, Georgia, and Chicora to Charlotte, North Carolina, to merge with Queens College. In addition, enrollment dropped, and budgets were tightened at Presbyterian College, which lost its accreditation for a number of years. The schools and colleges established by the PCUSA among African Americans were also affected by the economic situation, and by the late 1930s, many of them had closed.

The New Deal and World War II military preparations finally brought economic relief to the state with positive effect for various educational programs. Presbyterian College's enrollment soared due to an accelerated program intended to train military personnel. The other campuses where Presbyterians had programs also saw not only the influx of the military but also a greater concern for their religious needs. Columbia Seminary, on the other hand, experienced a sharp drop in enrollment as young men were drafted into the armed forces.

Global changes after World War II had great impact on Presbyterian missions. Following the war many countries, especially in Africa, were determined to shake off colonialism. Missionaries raised awareness of diverse Christian contexts in the mission fields and the need for indigenous leadership in churches abroad. They were among the first PCUS voices to call the church to faithfulness in race relations with African Americans in the 1950s. The character of missionary efforts necessarily and sometimes controversially shifted over time from a paternalistic approach to the nurture and eventual establishment of vibrant, independent local churches. There were frequent conflicts about the perceived secularization and politicization of mission work, reacting particularly to the public voices of the ecumenical National and World Councils of Churches.

There were also cultural changes closer to home. Having begun in the nineteenth century, calls for the equality of women were heard across the nation, culminating in 1920 with the passage of the Nineteenth Amendment granting women the right to vote. Women had always been active participants in the life of the Presbyterian Church, but they had no voice in its governance. Before women attained the right to speak in the Synod of South Carolina meetings and while they were excluded from ordained office, many served willingly as home and foreign missionaries. They were gradually added to the church's various committees, and the denomination increasingly called women with strong gifts and training to be Christian educators. Presbyterian women were authorized for ordination to all offices of the church including pastoral ministry in the PCUSA in 1956 and in the PCUS in 1965. In the restructuring of church organization in the 1970s and soon after the merger of the PCUS and UPCUSA in 1983, women led the denominations in espousing broader representation in leadership positions. Since the 1970s, the growing number of women in ordained church ministry has become a lasting and important change in the Presbyterian Church.

Increasing calls to end segregation began in the middle of the century. Most African American Presbyterians in South Carolina were not members of the Southern church (PCUS) but were part of the Synod of the Atlantic of the PCUSA (after 1958, UPCUSA). Those who were members of the PCUS were part of the all black Snedecor Memorial Synod. After the Civil War, the northern Presbyterians established many churches with parochial schools and academies in the Carolinas, and their efforts gave rise to one of the largest regional concentrations of African American Presbyterians in the United States. The all black governing bodies had a sense of solidarity and independence from the white majority. They developed strong traditions in worship and in leadership in the churches and their communities. They provided gathering points for civil rights advocacy and supported candidates for political office while schools were desegregating and voting rights legislation opened the polls to African Americans. There were about 6,400 African Americans in nearly fifty churches in South Carolina when the Presbyterian Church (USA) was formed in 1983.

There was also hopeful change in African American ministries in the PCUS. In 1947 the southern denomination established a Division of Negro Work and appointed Reverend Alex R. Batchelor to lead a program to attract new members and strengthen congregations. Women also had a pivotal role. Long before the US Supreme Court declared segregation unconstitutional, the statewide Synodical held annual conferences at Benedict College in Columbia, bringing together African American women from Presbyterian and other denominations. In 1953 the PCUS General Assembly moved to disband the racially segregated Snedecor Memorial Synod. Many white South Carolina Presbyterians opposed this integration of their governing bodies. This dissension, along with backlash following *Brown v. Board of Education* (US Supreme Court, 1954), played a part in the defeat of the vote on the reunion of the PCUS and the PCUSA in1955. African American churches were not welcomed into the Synod of South Carolina until 1968. At the vote in 1983, some African American members were reluctant to give up their independence and their regional majority status; however, their UPCUSA presbyteries unanimously supported the merger. In contrast, five out of the seven predominantly white PCUS presbyteries in the state voted against the reunion. Charleston and Piedmont Presbyteries joined the majority in the PCUS that affirmed the formation of the Presbyterian Church (USA) in 1983.

Like the public schools, the synod's institutions faced pressure to integrate. Columbia Seminary and Queens College accomplished it smoothly and apparently with little controversy. After extended campus discussion, Presbyterian College accepted African American students in 1965. During the 1960s and early 1970s, controversy over integration caused divisions on the Board of Thornwell Orphanage. Its board ultmately acted to follow the US court order.

In 1948 the Synod of South Carolina, led by Rev. W. McLeod Frampton, pastor in Orangeburg, began to plan for a ministry to older people. Ten years later, the Presbyterian Home of South Carolina, a retirement and continuing healthcare residence, opened in Summerville. It was later joined by Presbyterian homes in Clinton (1975), Florence (1981), and Columbia (1986), and Easley (1998). These retirement communities serve people from across South Carolina.

Christians ask and answer questions of public and personal morality from the perspective of faith and theological commitments. In the 1920s, many southern Presbyterians accepted the idea of "the spirituality of the church." This teaching limited the mission to the spiritual conversion and edification of individuals instead of speaking to matters of civil government and public policy. Before Prohibition the churches largely confined their social comments to personal morality, concentrating on consumption of beverage alcohol, gambling, dancing, and Sabbath observance. However, with the emergence of nationwide interest in such issues as temperance legislation, it became impossible to keep this sharp distinction between church and society. After the repeal of the Prohibition Amendment in 1933, the church's social agenda broadened to include support for alcohol education, improved race relations, public education, and family laws. By the 1970s and 1980s, the focus had become even broader, embracing issues of civil rights, war and peace, poverty, and corporate responsibility. By the end of the period, abortion began to provoke widely differing views among church members. Still later, controversy about homosexuality troubled Presbyterians. Church people reflected society's differing and contested convictions about private and public morality. The cultural challenges to the Presbyterians in South Carolina during the middle decades of the twentieth century required them to reassess their understanding of the relation of Christ and culture.

CONCLUSION

During the 1950s and 1960s, the Presbyterian Church in South Carolina was experiencing unprecedented growth. In 1968 Arthur M. Martin, Executive Secretary of the Synod of South Carolina, was enthusiastic in reporting growth in numbers, financial resources, and inclusion of African American congregations.[1] In fifteen years, thirty-nine new churches were organized, fifteen small ones closed, and seven African American congregations came in from the previously all black Snedecor Synod. From 53,465 members, 306 churches, and 213 ministers in 1953, the numbers had risen to 71,436 members, 337 churches, and 337 ministers. Contributions had increased from $3,500,000 to $9,186,018, with 67 percent going to denominational benevolences. Nine financial campaigns had raised $6,000,000 for institutions, and five of them, including the new Presbyterian Home of South Carolina in Summerville, had assets of $38,000,000. Martin described his office as "cheerleader, watchman, and communications center." Martin's report did not envision that within five years membership and contributions in South Carolina would begin to decline, joining the widespread mainline denominational losses in the United States that continue today.

South Carolina PCUS

Year	Members	Ministers	Churches
1900	20,128	134	271
1925	37,840	172	291
1930	36,228	184	284
1940	41,465	177	277
1950	52,097	198	298
1960	63,893	274	328
1970	72,889	338	329
1980	70,329		

As South Carolina joined in the growth of the Sunbelt, the arrival of immigrants and people from other states brought unprecedented ethnic diversity and new religious commitments. Many newcomers to South Carolina preferred evangelical Protestantism, and Adventist and Pentecostal traditions attracted greater numbers. Many new residents joined the Roman Catholic Church. The great demographic shifts and pluralism diminished the population of those who had traditionally become Presbyterians.

1. *South Carolina Presbyterian,* Newsletter, June 1968, 2

In 1973 a new denomination, the National Presbyterian Church in America, was formed in Birmingham, Alabama. It soon took the name "Presbyterian Church in America" (PCA). Its founding leaders contended that the mainline Presbyterian denominations had abandoned the Bible and the Westminster Confession of Faith, their historic confessional standard. Some Presbyterians who were socially and theologically conservative began to withdraw from the PCUS. In 1973 and 1974, thirty congregations left the Synod of South Carolina for other denominations.

The effort to unite the PCUS and UPCUSA had been on the horizon for decades. Following the failed attempt in 1955, new plans led the PCUS General Assembly in 1972 to undertake restructuring its organization and offices. In 1982 reunion of the two denominations was proposed, and in 1983 three fourths of the presbyteries in the PCUS approved. In South Carolina, organized efforts against the formation of the united denomination proved divisive. The majority of PCUS South Carolina presbyteries voted against the plan. Dissent continued, and by 1985 fifty-one former South Carolina PCUS congregations had joined the Presbyterian Church in America. Six others, led by First Presbyterian Church, Columbia, had joined the Associate Reformed Presbyterian Church.

Denominational merger did not by itself bring unity to the membership of the new PC(USA). The cooperative work of white and black ministers and lay members in setting the policy and program of the Presbyterian Church (USA) was particularly urgent in South Carolina and the other southern states where the division between the denominations had fallen along racial lines. Reverend John Evans, General Presbyter of New Harmony Presbytery encompassing central South Carolina counties, remarked that living together through the storm of Hurricane Hugo (1989) brought neighboring black and white Presbyterians in South Carolina together in rebuilding and gave real meaning to what had seemed previously to be only a matter of combining offices and redrawing boundary lines on a map.[2] Out of many trials and through terrible storms, Presbyterians were beginning to work together on a way forward.

Long before Presbyterian reunion in 1983, members in most churches were feeling the pain of diminished membership and the struggle to maintain healthy congregations. After reunion South Carolina presbyteries began to gather in periodic convocations corresponding to the boundaries of the former Synod of South Carolina and including the former United Presbyterian congregations that were in Atlantic Synod. These meetings, convened every several years, provide a platform for shared worship, contact with the

---

2. John Evans, Interview, May 2007.

state's various Presbyterian institutions, continuing education, and above all shared fellowship. Without the pressures of official business, these voluntary assemblies serve as an innovative way to develop the bonds and friendships that encourage the gathering, nurture, and witness of congregations.

To understand the causes of visible Presbyterian decline, in 1987 Milton J. Coalter, John M. Mulder, and Louis B. Weeks launched *The Presbyterian Presence*, a seven-volume study based at Louisville Presbyterian Theological Seminary and funded by the Lilly Endowment.[3] First, they found that the great numbers of the baby boomers born after World War II in a culture of middle class suburbanization and popular openness to religion made possible the growth during the 1950s. However, the baby boomers gave birth to fewer children and did not continue the increase in membership. Secondly, the loss of members beginning in the middle of the 1960s was part of a cultural shift bringing new values, lifestyles, more social mobility, and cultural pluralism that challenged the accustomed leadership, especially of the middle and upper middle class from which many Presbyterians came. Thirdly, the Presbyterian denomination devised a bureaucratic, hierarchical style of organization contributing to distance between denominational leaders and the membership, and the new structure was very expensive, taking away funding from the previous development of new churches and foreign mission.

In 2013 the PC(USA) reported 1,760,200 members, a loss of 59 percent from the high in 1965 of 4,254,460 members. Presbyterians today are asking questions like "Where can we find renewal? How can we reverse membership declines? What courage shall we claim for the mission of Christ in the world?"

In *A Sustainable Presbyterian Future: What's Working and Why*, Louis Weeks took up the themes uncovered twenty-five years before in *The Presbyterian Presence* books and urged leaders in the General Assembly, synods, and presbyteries to look for clues to a renewed Presbyterian and Reformed identity in congregations that are thriving today. From interviews and case studies of congregations, he recommended recasting the structure of the PC(USA) to reduce its regulatory role and to concentrate on bottoms-up leadership by ministers, ruling elders, and deacons along with active members in "God's mission in the world." He concluded that local congregations large and small were where Presbyterians were nourishing the church's identity and culture. Successful congregational leaders were using technology and social media to supplement the printed word. They were enjoying dignified worship and music with lively, biblical preaching. Weeks notes

---

3. Coalter, Mulder, and Weeks, *Vital Signs*, xi.

that vital Presbyterian congregations are ecumenical in approaching mission and work and show hospitality and welcome in both worship and in service. They share an inclusive understanding of family life, where faith must first find nourishment.

In this day of diminishing membership and declining mainline organization, the claim for strong congregations is certainly a realistic and welcome one. In Reformed history, churches have lived with a variety of organizational patterns including Calvin's consistory, various Presbyterian patterns, episcopal forms, and congregationalism.[4] Today it seems the time is right to emphasize renewal in the congregation. This is not mainly a recommendation about Presbyterian polity. Rather it recognizes that the weekly gathering of Christians in local congregations for the sake of proclamation, praise, prayer, Bible study, and service is the nourishing resource for the renewal and growth of the people of God.

This mission goal is part of the contemporary relevance of John Calvin's assurance to his refugee congregations in Geneva during the Reformation: "Wherever we see the Word of God purely preached and heard, and the sacraments administered according to Christ's institution, there it is not to be doubted, a church of God exists."[5] The "wherever" is everywhere on the globe. The preaching is the declaration, the explanation, and the application of the gospel to individual lives and the communities where they live.[6] The right administration of the sacraments is really "the stewardship of the mysteries of God," which includes the commandment of Jesus to "go out into the roads and lanes, and compel people to come in, so that my house may be filled" (I Corinthians 4:1; Luke 14:23). The fundamental energy in the people of God for worship and work in the kingdom will be welcomed as the gift of the Holy Spirit and nurtured in local communities where members and officers "pray for and seek to serve the people with energy, intelligence, imagination, and love."[7] On this missional foundation, we can together seek the right understanding and form of Presbyterian polity and organized denominational life. Appropriate new organizational patterns within Presbyterianism follow renewal by the Holy Spirit.

In addition to providing a story of the past, the study of the history of the Presbyterian Church can be a part of a commitment to renew the nurture of Christian faith in our new cultural setting. Past experiences can

---

4. Leith, *Introduction to the Reformed Tradition*, 137–47.

5. Calvin, *Institutes of the Christian Religion*, IV, 1, 9.

6. Barth, Church Dogmatics, IV, 3, 2, 843–54.

7. *The Constitution of the Presbyterian Church (USA)*, Presbyterian Church (USA), W4.003h.

suggest new engagements with the Bible and ways of faithful appeal for people to confess faith in Jesus Christ. It can help to develop new worshipping congregations, to renew present ones, to nurture children, youth, and young adults, to offer care for the vulnerable in and outside the churches, and to offer loving service and witness to the poor and those wounded by warfare and natural disasters. It would be good if this book could contribute to such a renewal.

Bibliography

Adair, Joseph H. *Goodwill Larger Parish of Sumpter, Clarendon and Lee Counties, South Carolina*. Thesis, School of Theology, Johnson C. Smith University, 1951.

Advertisement, *Presbyterian of the South* 94 (May 19, 1920) 22.

Akey, John Aaron. "Can We be Saved? Edward Owings Guerrant and the Mission Movement on the Cumberland Plateau, 1861–1916." MA thesis, Appalachian State University, 2012. http://libres.uncg.edu/ir/asu/f/Akey,%20John_2012_Thesis.pdf

Alexander, W. A. and George Frederick Nicolassen. *A Digest of the Acts and Proceedings of the General Assembly of the Presbyterian Church in the United States*. Richmond: Presbyterian Committee of Publication, 1911.

Alvis, Joel L. Jr. *Religion and Race: Southern Presbyterians 1946–1983*. Tuscaloosa: University of Alabama Press, 1994.

Andrews, Mildred Gwin. *The Men and the Mills*. Macon: Mercer University Press, 1987.

"Annual Report Number." *Our Monthly* 72 (1935) 277–78.

Annual Report of the Executive Committee of Foreign Missions of the Presbyterian Church in the United States. Nashville: The Committee, 1936.

Annual Report of the General Assembly's Committee on Freedmen of the Presbyterian Church in the United States of America. Pittsburgh: The Committee, 1872.

Arnold, Frank L. "From Sending Church to Partner Church: The Brazil Experience." *Journal of Presbyterian History* 81 (2003) 178–92.

"Awakening African-American History." *Columbia Star*, February 29, 2008. http://www.thecolumbiastar.com/news/2008-02-29/education/026.html.

B. "The Other Reform." *The Blue Stocking* (Presbyterian College), September 20, 1963, 2.

Barth, Karl. *Church Dogmatics, Volume IV,3,2*. Translated by G. W. Bromiley. Edinburgh: T. & T. Clark, 1962.

Batchelor, Alex R. *Jacob's Ladder: Negro Work of the Presbyterian Church in the United States*. Atlanta: Board of Church Extension, 1953.

"Beer on Every Side, Georgia Still Dry." *New York Times*, April 9, 1933, E7.

Blackwell, Johanna DuBose. *A People and their Faith: The History of Mount Tabor and First Presbyterian Church, Greer, South Carolina, 1841–1991*. Greer: First Presbyterian Church, 1991.

Blue Book Reports to the Synod of South Carolina. Presbyterian Church in the United States.

"'Blue Law' Foes Fail in Carolina." *New York Times*, May 24, 1966, 40.

"Blue Laws Are Revived." *New York Times*, February 21, 1927, 19.

Book of Church Order, Presbyterian Church (USA), W-4.003h.

Boyd, Lois A. and R. Douglas Brackenridge. *Presbyterian Women in America: Two Centuries of a Quest for Status*. Westport: Greenwood, 1996.

———. "Study of the Current Status of Women Pastors." In *The Pluralistic Vision: Presbyterians and Mainstream Protestant Education and Leadership*, edited by Milton A. Coulter et al, 289–307. Louisville: Westminster/John Knox, 1992.

Brown, Benjamin Warren. *Report of the Survey of the Educational Work and Responsibility of the Presbyterian Church in the United States*. Louisville: Presbyterian Education Association of the South, 1928.

Brown, G. Thompson and T. Donald Black. *Presbyterians in World Mission*. Decatur: Columbia Theological Seminary Press, 1995.

———. "Structures for a Changing Church." In *A History of Presbyterian Missions*, edited by Scott W. Sunquist and Caroline N. Becker, 58–84. Louisville: Geneva, 2008.

Calhoun, David B. *The Glory of the Lord Risen Upon It: First Presbyterian Church Columbia, South Carolina, 1795-1995*. Columbia: R. L. Bryan, 1994.

Calvin, John. *Institutes of the Christian Religion*. Edited by John T. McNeill. Translated by Ford Lewis Battles. Philadelphia: Westminster 1960.

Cann, Katherine D. "John G. Richards and the Moral Majority." *Proceedings of the South Carolina Historical Association, 1983*. Aiken: South Carolina Historical Association, 1983.

Carlton, David L. *Mill and Town in South Carolina 1880-1920*. Baton Rouge: Louisiana State University Press, 1982.

Carroll, Jackson W. et al. *Women of the Cloth*. San Francisco: Harper & Row, 1983.

Cash, W.J. *The Mind of the South*. New York: Vintage, 1991.

Cathcart, Ellenor Lee, et al. *Yesteryears: The Heritage and History of the First Presbyterian Church of Anderson, South Carolina*. Anderson, South Carolina: First Presbyterian Church, 1967.

"Church Faces World Mission." *South Carolina Presbyterian* 15 (December, 1963) 1.

"Churchmen Join in Morals Move." *Clinton Chronicle*, September 8, 1931, 3.

Clarke, Erskine, *Our Southern Zion: a History of Calvinism in the South Carolina Low Country, 1690-1990*. Tuscaloosa: The University of Alabama Press, 1996.

"Closing of Schools in Korea Approved by Presbyterians." *Atlanta Constitution*, May 26, 1937, 2.

Coalter, Milton J. et al, eds. *The Re-forming Tradition: Presbyterians and Mainstream Protestantism*. Louisville: John Knox, 1992.

———. *Vital Signs: the Promise of Mainstream Protestantism*. Grand Rapids: Eerdmans, 1996.

Coker, Joe L. "The Sinnott Case of 1910: The Changing Views of Southern Presbyterians on Temperance, Prohibition, and the Spirituality of the Church." *Journal of Presbyterian History* 77 (Winter 1999) 247–62.

"College Earns Accreditation at Texas Meet." *Clinton Chronicle*, December 8, 1949.

The Constitution of the Presbyterian Church (U.S.A.) Part II, Book of Order. Louisville: The Office of the General Assembly Presbyterian Church (USA), 2013; 2015–17.

Dawson, David. "Counting the Cost: Statistics and What They May Tell Us." In *A History of Presbyterian Missions*, edited by Scott W. Sunquist and Caroline N. Becker, 36–57. Louisville: Geneva, 2008.

Dawson, Edward Hood. *Purity and Its People*. Greenville: A Press, 1997.

Dendy, H.B. "How the Journal Began." *Southern Presbyterian Journal* 16 (May 3, 1967) 10–11.

Department of the Interior, Bureau of Education. Bulletin, 1916, no. 39. *Negro Education as and for Colored People in the United States*, edited by Thomas Jesse Jones. Washington: Government Printing Office, 1916.

"The Diversities of Discipleship: Mission, Racial Ethnic Ministries, Ecumenism, and Social Justice." In *The Re-Forming Tradition: Presbyterians and Mainstream Protestantism*, edited by Milton J. Coalter et al, 165–91. Louisville: Westminster/John Knox, 1992.

Douglas, Davison McDowell. Report of the President to the Board of Trustees of the Presbyterian College of South Carolina, May 30, 1925. RG 2/2, Archives and Special Collections, Thomason Library, Presbyterian College, Clinton, S.C.

———. Report of the President to the Board of Trustees of the Presbyterian College ofSouth Carolina, May 30, 1926. RG 2/2, Archives and Special Collections, Thomason Library, Presbyterian College, Clinton, S.C.

"Dum Vivimus XX." *Presbyterian College Report* 38 (December 1985) 4–5.

"The Duties of the Secretaries of S.P.C. Home Missions." *The Presbyterian of the South* 94 (July 13, 1921) 6.

Edgar, Walter B. *South Carolina, a History*. Columbia: University of South Carolina Press, 1998.

———. *South Carolina Encyclopedia*. Columbia: University of South Carolina Press, 2013.

———. *South Carolina in the Modern Age*. Columbia: University of South Carolina Press, 1992.

Evans, John B. , interview by Charles E. Raynal, May 2007.

Fairfield McClelland Presbyterial. "A Historical Overview of Fairfield-McClelland Presbytery and the Presbyterial Women's Involvement." Unpublished manuscript, 1984.

Farrior, Louise H. *Journey toward the Future: A History of the Women of the Church, Presbyterian Church, U.S., for a Quarter of a Century, 1958-1983*. Published by the Author, 1987.

———. "Status of the Women of the Church." *Southeast Presbyterian Life* 4 (November 1976) 2–3.

Fitzmeier, John R. and Randall Balmer. "A Poultice for the Bite of the Cobra: The Hocking Report and Presbyterian Missions in the Middle Decades of the Twentieth Century." In *The Diversity of Discipleship: The Presbyterians and Twentieth-Century Christian Witness*, edited by Milton J. Coalter et al, 105–25. Louisville: John Knox/Westminster, 1991.

Flynt, J. Wayne. "'Feeding the Hungry and Ministering to the Broken Hearted': The Presbyterian Church in the United States and the Social Gospel, 1900–1920." In *Religion in the South*, edited by Charles Reagan Wilson, 83–137. Jackson: University Press of Mississippi, 1985.

Fulton, C. Darby et al. "The North American Council of the Churches of Christ." *The Southern Presbyterian Journal* 2 (May 1943) 8–11.

Fulton, C. Darby. "Centennial Address, Synod of South Carolina." Minutes of the Meeting of the Synod of South Carolina, 1961, 84–90.

———. "Contemporary Problems in Missions." *Southern Presbyterian Journal* 17 (July 20, 1959) 5–17.

———. "Evangelism: The Heart of Missions." *Christianity Today* 10 (April 29, 1966) 9–12.

———. "The Evangelistic Task." *Columbia Theological Seminary Bulletin* 53:3 (1965) 15–17.

———. *Now is the Time*. Richmond: John Knox, 1946.

———. *Star in the East*. Richmond: Presbyterian Committee of Publication, 1938.

Gibbins, Rosa. "Christian Conferences for Negro Women." *The Presbyterian Survey* (1935) 666–67.

Gill, Theodore A. "Historical Context for Mission, 1944–2007." In *A History of Presbyterian Missions*, edited by Scott W. Sunquist and Caroline N. Becker, 13–35. Louisville: Geneva, 2008.

Gist, Margaret A., ed. *Presbyterian Women of South Carolina*. History Committee of the Woman's Auxiliary of the Synod of South Carolina, 1929.

Goldin, Claudia and Lawrence F. Katz. "Putting the 'Co' in Education: Timing, Reasons, and Consequences of College Coeducation from 1835 to the Present." *Journal of Human Capital* 5 (2011) 402–13.

"The Great Migration." In *The South Carolina Encyclopedia*, edited by Walter B. Edgar. Columbia: University of South Carolina Press, 2006, 393–94.

Green, Evelyn. "A Goodly Heritage: Women of the Church." *Concern* (February, 1977) 24–33.

Griffith, Nancy Snell. *All Beautiful the March of Days: First Presbyterian Church Clinton, South Carolina, 1855–2005*. Columbia: Professional Printing, 2005.

Hammet, Ben Hay. *The Spirit of PC: A Centennial History of Presbyterian College*. Clinton: Jacobs, 1982.

Handbook, Synod of the Southeast. Presbyterian Church in the United States.

Herring, Harriet L. *Passing of the Mill Village*. Chapel Hill: University of North Carolina, 1949.

Hollis, Tommy et al. "As Best We Remember." Clinton: Presbyterian Home, Clinton and Frampton Hall, 2004. Unpublished manuscript.

"Horse Whipping." *The Blue Stocking*, February 22, 1963, 2.

"Integration: Open Stand Now?" *The Blue Stocking*, October 2, 1964, 2.

Isaac, F. Reid and Sue W. Spencer. "A Study of Thornwell Home and School for the Synod of Georgia, The Presbyterian Church in the United States, July 1, 1963." Unpublished report.

Jacobs, Thornwell, ed. *Diary of William Plumer Jacobs*. Atlanta: Oglethorpe University Press, 1937.

Jacobs, William P. II. To the Board of Trustees of Presbyterian College, February 25, 1936. RG 2/2, Archives and Special Collections, Thomason Library, Presbyterian College Clinton, South Carolina.

Jamieson, Claire E. "Change in the Textile Mill Villages of South Carolina's Upstate During the Modern South Era." MA Thesis, University of Tennessee, 2010. http://trace.tennessee.edu/cgi/viewcontent.cgi?article=1298&context=utkgradthes

Johnson, Benton. "From Old to New Agendas: Presbyterians and Social Issues in the Twentieth Century." In *The Confessional Mosaic*, edited by Milton Coalter, et al, 208–35. Louisville: Westminster/John Knox, 1990.

Jones, F. D. and W. H. Mills. *History of the Presbyterian Church in South Carolina Since 1850*. Columbia: R. L. Bryan, 1926.

Kohn, August. *The Cotton Mills of South Carolina*. Columbia: South Carolina Department of Agriculture, Commerce and Immigration, 1907.
Kraemer, Charles S. "A Pastoral Letter from the Moderator to the Church." *Presbyterian Survey* 63 (October 1973) 3–4.
Lancaster, Eliza N. "Memories of Life Together with Lewis H. Lancaster." Unpublished manuscript.
Lander, Ernest McPherson Jr. *A History of South Carolina, 1865–1960*. Chapel Hill: University of North Carolina Press, 1960.
Leith, John H. *An Introduction to the Reformed Tradition*. Richmond: John Knox, 1977.
Longfield, Bradley J. and George M. Marsden. "Presbyterian Colleges in Twentieth-Century America." In *The Pluralistic Vision: Presbyterians and Mainstream Protestant Education and Leadership*, edited by Milton J. Coalter, et al, 99–125. Louisville: Westminster/John Knox, 1992.
Lynn, L. Ross. *The Story of Thornwell Orphanage, Clinton, South Carolina, 1875–1925*. Richmond: Presbyterian Committee of Publication, 1924.
MacCauley, Deborah Vansau. *Appalachian Mountain Religion: A History*. Urbana and Chicago: University of Illinois Press, 1995.
Maddex, Jack P. "From Theocracy to Spirituality: The Southern Presbyterian Reversal on Church and State." *Journal of Presbyterian History* 54 (1976), 438–57.
Martin, Arthur M. "Brainwashing." *South Carolina Presbyterian* 11 (May 1959) 2.
———. Papers. Griffith/Raynal Collection, PC0020, Box 1. Archives and Special Collections, Thomason Library, Presbyterian College, Clinton, South Carolina.
Martin, Joseph B. III. "Guide to Presbyterian Ecclesiastical Names and Places in South Carolina 1685–1985." *South Carolina Historical Magazine* 90 (January–April 1989) 4–212.
McClurg, Patricia. "Twenty Years of the Ordination of Women—A Progress Report." *Austin Theological Seminary Bulletin* 94 (May 1984) 15–19.
McCoy, Henry Bacon. *A History of the First Presbyterian Church in Greenville, South Carolina*. Greenville: First Presbyterian Church, 1962.
McElveen, Billy. "The Collegiate Answer." *The Blue Stocking*, September 22, 1956, 4.
McEwen, Mildred Morse. *Queens College Yesterday and Today*. Charlotte: Queens College Alumni Association, 1980.
McMillan, Homer. *"Unfinished Tasks" of the Southern Presbyterian Church*. Richmond: Presbyterian Committee of Publication, 1922.
Miller, Samuel. "The Earth Filled with the Glory of the Lord." *The American National Preacher* 10 (1835) 289–304.
"Ministers' Conference Offers Fresh Insights for Pastoral Work." *The Presbyterian College Report* 31 (February 1978) 4.
Minutes of the Executive Committee of the Board of Trustees, Presbyterian College, January 27, 1965. RG 1/3, Archives and Special Collections, Thomason Library, Presbyterian College, Clinton, S.C.
Minutes of the General Assembly. Presbyterian Church in the United States 1916–1983.
Minutes of South Carolina Presbyteries (Bethel, Charleston, Congaree, Enoree, Harmony, Pee Dee, Piedmont and South Carolina). Presbyterian Church in the United States.1925–83.
Minutes of the Synod of South Carolina. Presbyterian Church in the United States, 1925–1972.

Minutes of the Synod of the Southeast. Presbyterian Church in the United States, 1972–83.
Minutes of the Women of the Church. Synod of South Carolina. Presbyterian Church in the United States.
Missionary Biographies, Presbyterian History Center, Montreat, North Carolina, http://www.phcmontreat.org/bios
"Missioners Reach Shanghai in Safety." *Atlanta Constitution,* January 2, 1938, 2A.
"Missions Challenge by Dr. Street." *South Carolina Presbyterian* 15 (December 1963) 7.
Moore, John Hammond. *The Baileys of Clinton.* Clinton: The Bailey Foundation, 1998.
Murray, Andrew E. *Presbyterians and the Negro.* Philadelphia: Presbyterian Historical Society, 1966.
Naylor, D. Keith. "Campus Ministry and the Liberal Protestant Dilemma." In *Liberal Protestantism: Realities and Possibilities,* edited by Robert S. Michaelsen and Wade Clark Roof, 115–28. New York: Pilgrim, 1985.
Neace, James Clell. "Dr. Edward O. Guerrant's 'Society of Soul Winners.'" 1997. http://kentuckyexplorer.com/nonmembers/02-04story.html
"New Moderator Stresses Negro Responsibility." *Herald Journal* (Spartanburg, S.C.) July 23, 1964, 6.
"New Problems Today for World Missions." *Southern Presbyterian* 22 (November 1970) 4.
"An Open Letter." *Our Monthly* 73 (1936) 114.
Oral History Interview with David Burgess, September 25, 1974. Interview E-0001. Southern Oral History Program Collection (#4007) in the Southern Oral History Program Collection, Wilson Library, University of North Carolina at Chapel Hill. http://docsouth.unc.edu/sohp/E-1001/excerpts/excerpt3888.html
Oral History Interview with George Perkel, May 27, 1986. Interview H-0281. Southern Oral History Program Collection (#4007) in the Southern Oral History Program Collection, Wilson Library, University of North Carolina at Chapel Hill. http://docsouth.unc.edu/sohp/H0281/excerpts/excerpt5405.html
Palmer, B. M. "Minutes of the General Assembly of the Presbyterian Church in the United States of America . . . 1859." Reprinted in *The Southern Presbyterian Review* 12 (1859), 513–603.
Parker, Inez Moore. *The Rise and Decline of the Program of Education for Black Presbyterians of the United Presbyterian Church U.S.A., 1865–1970.* San Antonio: Trinity University Press, 1977.
Parker, Thomas F. "Some Educational and Legislative Needs of South Carolina Mill Villages: An Address." *Bulletin of the University of South Carolina* 24:3 (1911) 3–15.
"PC Tries Campus Program of International Missions." *The Presbyterian College Report,* 32 (August 1979) 10–11.
Penfield, Janet Harbison. "Women in the Presbyterian Church: An Historical Overview. *Journal of Presbyterian History* 55 (Summer 1977) 107–124.
"The Plan of Campaign for the Local Church." Clinton: Presbyterian College Endowment Fund Campaign Headquarters, c1945. Unpublished pamphlet.
Poole, R. F. "Tribute to Dr. Crouch." *South Carolina Presbyterian,* 9 (September 1957) 6.
Pope, Liston. *Millhands and Preachers: a Study of Gastonia.* New Haven: Yale University Press, 1942.
"Polls Indicate Changing Attitudes of Students." *The Blue Stocking,* April 10, 1964, 2.

"Presbyterian Campaign Ends With $600,000 Total Fund Insuring Big Seminary Here." *Atlanta Constitution*, December 18, 1925, 7.
"Presbyterian Churchmen United Hold Rally in Atlanta." *The Presbyterian Guardian* 38 (1969) 125.
Presbyterian College Questionnaire, March 31, 1928. Unpublished.
"Presbyterian College Seeks to Serve the Church." Undated mimeographed document.
"Presbyterian News." Atlanta: The General Council, Presbyterian Church in the United States. Undated press release.
"Presbyterian Youth Day." *Keeping Posted on Presbyterian College* 12 (October, 1963) 3.
"Presbyterians and the Council." *The State*, July 28, 1964. Clipping.
"Presbyterians in Appalachia" http://www.phcmontreat.org/Exhibit-ReligionAppalachia.htm
"Presbyterians May Establish Seminary Here." *Atlanta Constitution,* October 18, 1923, 1.
"Queens to Accept Negro Applications." *Sumter Daily Item,* December 8, 1962, 5.
Rabun Gap-Nacoochee School. "History and Presbyterian Heritage." http://www.rabungap.org/page.cfm?p=988
Raynal, Charles E. *Johns Island Presbyterian Church*. Charleston, South Carolina: The History Press, 2010.
Reimers, David M. *White Protestantism and the Negro*. New York: Oxford University Press, 1965.
"Report of the Executive Committee of the Southern Board of Foreign Missions." December 19, 1840. http://www.pcahistory.org/documents/boarddebates/sbfm1840.pdf
"Report of the Executive Secretary." *Our Monthly* 74 (1937) 264.
"Report on Early Steps." *Time Magazine*, July 1, 1974.
"Results Thanksgiving Offerings for Thornwell." *Our Monthly* 73 (1936) 1.
Richards, J. McDowell. *As I Remember It: Columbia Theological Seminary, 1932-1971*. Decatur: Columbia Seminary Press, 1985.
Roberts, Daniel M. "Presbyterian Home of South Carolina, 1952-1984, the Tapp Years." Undated monograph.
"School Rejects Beer Aid." *New York Times*, August 6, 1933, E6.
"Seek Dry Law Referendum." *New York Times*, May 22, 1930, 3.
Settle, Paul G. "Why PCUS Evangelism is Sterile." *Contact* 10 (December 1972) 3.
"Shall We Sacrifice our Education?" *The Blue Stocking*, January 13, 1961, 1.
Shriver, Donald. *The Unsilent South: Prohetic Preaching in Racial Crisis*. Richmond, Virginia: John Knox, 1955.
Simpson, William Hayes. *Life in Mill Communities*. Clinton: Presbyterian, 1943.
Sivewright, Alexander M. *God's People Serving God's Purpose: 125 Years of Ministry at Thornwell Home for Children 1875-2000*. Clinton: Thornwell Orphanage, 2000.
Smith, Clarence McKittrick. *Waymarks: a History of Aveleigh Presbyterian Church, Newberry South Carolina, 1835-1985*. Newberry: Sun Printing, 1985.
Smith, John Coventry. *From Colonialism to World Community*. Philadelphia: Geneva, 1982.
Smith, R. P. *Experiences in Mountain Mission Work*. Richmond: Presbyterian Committee of Publication, 1931.
Snavely, Guy E. *The Church and the Four-Year College*. New York: Harper Brothers, 1955.

Southern Mountain Schools Maintained by Denominational and Independent Agencies. New York: Russell Sage Foundation, 1929.

"South Carolina." *Presbyterian of the South* 98 (August 13, 1924) 9.

"South Carolina Vote Gives Drys a Big Lead." *New York Times*, August 29, 1940, 14.

"South's Private Schools Relax Bias." *Jet* 1 (November 8, 1951) 56.

Spears, Robert Wright. *Journey Toward Unity: The Christian Action Council in South Carolina.* Columbia: Christian Action Council, 1983.

———. *The South Carolina Christian Action Council, 1933–1983.* The South Carolina Christian Action Council: Crowson-Stone, 1983, 6–7.

Sprinkle, Patricia Houck. *The Church and young Women: a Case of Mutual Neglect.* Presbyterian Board of Women's Work, 1968.

Stansell, Christine. "A Forgotten Fight for Suffrage." *New York Times*, August 24, 2010, A21.

Street, T. Watson. "Missionary Strategy and our African Work." *Presbyterian Outlook*, 134 (August 11, 1952) 5–7.

Sunquist, Scott W. and Caroline N. Becker. "Introduction." *A History of Presbyterian Missions.* Louisville: Geneva, 2008.

"Survey of Presbyterian College." Clinton, S.C., 1957. Unpublished survey.

Swann, Darius L. *African-American Congregational Histories.* Notebook compiled by The Committee for the Reunion of Congregations, 2002.

———. *All-Black Governing Bodies: The History and Contributions of All-Black Governing Bodies in the Predecessor Denominations of the Presbyterian Church (USA).* Louisville, Kentucky: The Office of the General Assembly, 1996.

"Synod Annuls Harmony Action." *Presbyterian of the South.* 94 (July 13, 1921), 6.

"T. P. Hartness Dies at 72 of Wreck Injuries." *Spartanburg Herald-Journal*, January 19, 1962, 1, 18.

Telford, G.M. *Our Home Task: A Home Mission Study Book for the Synod of South Carolina.* Synod of South Carolina: Home Mission Committee, [1927].

"Testimony of Nan Dale" before the House Ways and Means Subcommittee on Human Resources . . . ," July 20, 1999. https://www.cwla.org/advocacy/childprotnandale.htm

"Thanksgiving Time is Thornwell Time." *Our Monthly*, 73 (October 1936) 1–3.

"Thirty-Fifth Annual Report of the Woman's Department of the Board of Missions for Freedmen in the Presbyterian Church, U.S.A., March 31st, 1918–March 31st, 1919." Published in *Reports of the Missionary and Benevolent Boards and Committees to the General Assembly of the Presbyterian Church in the United States of America.* Philadelphia: Presbyterian Board of Publication, 1919. http://archive.org/stream/reportsofmission1919pres#page/n1129/mode/2up/search/freedmen

"This is the Way Cherokee Presbytery Does It!" *Our Monthly* 73 (December, 1936) 340.

Thompson, Ernest Trice. *Presbyterian Missions in the Southern United States.* Richmond: Presbyterian Committee of Publication, 1934.

———. *Presbyterians in the South, Volumes One–Three: 1890–1972.* Richmond: John Knox, 1973.

———. *The Spirituality of the Church.* Richmond: John Knox, 1961.

Thornwell, James Henley. "The Church a Spiritual Power." *Southern Presbyterian Review* 12 (1859) 476–90.

Tollison, Courtney Louise. "Moral Imperative and Financial Practicality: Desegregation of South Carolina's denominationally-Affiliated Colleges and Universities." PhD dissertation, University of South Carolina, 2003.

"Treasurer's Report." *Our Monthly* 65 (1928) 306.

"Two New Student Centers in Synod of S.C." *South Carolina Presbyterian* 9 (September 1957) 5.

Verdesi, Elizabeth H. and Lillian M. Taylor. *Our Rightful Place: The Story of Presbyterian Women 1970–1983*. Council on Women and the Church, PCUSA, 1985.

"A Vital Part of the Total Process." *Presbyterian College Report* 40 (August 1987) 9.

"Votes for Repeal Represent 110,685,000." *New York Times*, November 9, 1933, 2.

Weatherford, Willis D. and Earl D. C. Brewer. *Life and Religion in Southern Appalachia*. New York: Friendship, 1962.

Weeks, Louis B. "Faith and Political Action in American Presbyterianism, 1776–1918." In *Reformed Faith and Politics*, edited by Ronald H. Stone, 101–19. Washington: University Press of America, 1983.

———. "The Scriptures and Sabbath Observance in the South." *Journal of Presbyterian History* 59 (1981) 267–83.

———. *A Sustainable Presbyterian Future: What's Working and Why*. Louisville: Westminster/John Knox, 2012.

White, Ronald C. Jr. "Presbyterian Campus Ministries: Competing Loyalties and Changing Visions." In *The Pluralistic Vision: Presbyterians and Mainstream Protestant Education and Leadership*, edited by Milton J. Coalter et al, 126–47. Louisville: Westminster/John Knox, 1992.

White, William Boyce Jr. *History of the First Presbyterian Church of Rock Hill, South Carolina, 1869–1969*. Rock Hill: Session of the First Presbyterian Church, 1969.

Wickham, Maxine S. *Thornwell—A Profile of Love*. Newberry: Sun Printing, 1980.

Wilhelm, Christopher J. "Cultural Modernization in Southern Cotton Mills." MA thesis Florida State University, 2004. http://etd.lib.fsu.edu/theses/available/etd-11142004-164943/unrestricted/ThesisWilhelm.pdf

"Will Vote Dry Today." *New York Times*, Dec. 4, 1933, 3.

Wilson, Frank T., ed. "Living Witnesses: Black Presbyterians in Ministry." *Journal of Presbyterian History* 51 (1973) 347–91.

Winsborough, Hallie Paxson. *Yesteryears*. Atlanta: Assembly's Committee on Woman's Work, 1937.

"Women Brighten Campaign." *Keeping Posted on Presbyterian College* 8 (March, 1962) 2.

"Women's Ordinations Practically Approved." *South Carolina Presbyterian* 16 (February 1964) 1.

Works, George A. *Report of a Survey of the Colleges and Theological Seminaries of the Presbyterian Church in the United States*. Louisville: Presbyterian Church US, 1942.

"World Missions Gifts Reach New High." *Southern Presbyterian* 1 (February, 1958) 1.

"Would Make Georgia New 'Reno' of Nation." *New York Times*, January 18, 1937, 19.

Wright, Kathleen Wood. "Some Fruits of Faith among Women of the Presbyterian Church U.S. in South Carolina." Unpublished manuscript, 1973.

www.ingramcontent.com/pod-product-compliance
Lightning Source LLC
Chambersburg PA
CBHW050437240426
43661CB00055B/2416